THE CAVENDISH Q

C000023921

LAW OF TORTS

Dr David Green
Barrister

Cavendish
Publishing
Limited

First published in Great Britain 1993 by Cavendish Publishing Limited, 23A Countess Road, London NW5 2XH.

Telephone: 071-485 0303   Facsimile: 071-485 0304

British Library Cataloguing in Publication Data

Green, David
Tort - (Q & A Series)
I Title II Series
344.2063

ISBN 1-874241-26-0

Printed and bound in Great Britain

Contents

Introduction

The law of tort is a fundamental area of English law, and in addition to being a 'core' subject for the legal profession, a clear understanding of its principles is required for other areas as diverse as employment law and company law. It illustrates, moreover, another characteristic of English law in that it is primarily a common law area, ie that its rules have been developed through the decisions of the courts rather than being laid down by statute. As a result of this the student of the law of Tort is faced with a bewildering array of cases and rules, and often finds difficulty in deciding what information is relevant to a problem.

This book attempts to help students of Tort. It is not intended as a substitute for lectures or for reading standard textbooks or law reports or articles It is rather aimed at students whose problem is not that they feel that the legal input they have received is insufficient, but rather that it is too great and that they have difficulty in ascertaining what material is essential and what is of lesser importance. A careful study of the answers to the questions contained in this book should revel those essential areas, and the student will see how basic concepts reappear not only in questions designed to test that topic in depth, but in other questions which at first sight appear to be testing unrelated areas.

Another function of this book is to illustrate how to answer questions in the law of Tort. These answers are not intended to be perfect solutions, if such a thing exists. Rather they are intended to illustrate the sort of well-structured answer that would attract high marks using the knowledge that a well-prepared student should possess. All the cases and principles cited should be familiar to the student - the author is attempting to show how with the knowledge that the student has he or she can present it in such a way as to gain the best possible grades. In particular, emphasis has been placed on the way in which the fundamental legal principles relevant to a question should be stated; it is a habit of both authors of suggested solutions and students to hunt through law reports or their minds to find a long-forgotten case which is an all fours with the facts of a question and triumphantly present it as the 'right' answer. As any examination question should be designed to test the students' grasp of legal principles and ability to apply those principles to a factual situation, a moment's reflection will show that although such an approach may point to the correct answer as regards (say) liability it will not attract the best possible grades.

Thus, the author has tried at all times to cite cases with which the student should be familiar. An ideal reaction by the reader to the suggested solutions in this book should be 'I can do that' not 'Gosh, how clever the author is; I could never write an answer like that'.

The questions used in this book at typical LLB examination questions, both as regards style and complexity.

This book is not intended to replace lectures or standard textbooks. It is, however, intended to fill a need which during decades of teaching law the author has found does exist, namely to enable the student to gain the best possible examination grades from whatever knowledge he or she possesses. The more reading a student does of lecture notes and standard textbooks the more he or she should benefit from a study of this book.

The author has attempted to state the law as of 1 December 1992.

David Green
London
December 1992

Table of Cases

Table of Statutes

Vicarious Liability

Introduction

Vicarious liability is a topic which is regularly tested by examiners, either as a question in its own right or as part of a question on (say) negligence or employers' liability. Course of employment and express prohibitions are areas that are especially popular with examiners, but in all vicarious liability questions it is vital to remember that a primary liability between the tortfeasor and the victim must be established before any liability can be transferred.

Checklist

Students must be familiar with the following areas:
- Definition of employer and employee
- Course of employment
- Frolics and detours
- Courts' differing attitudes to careless and deliberate acts

Question 1

Alpha Manufacturing plc are having their premises decorated by Beta Decorators Ltd. Brian is employed by Beta and needs to collect some additional decoration materials from Beta's premises. He meets Alan, who is employed by Alpha as a driver, and asks Alan if he can given him (Brian) a lift to Beta's premises. Alan agrees and gives Brian a lift in one of Alpha's vans which displays the following notice on the dashboard: – 'Only employees of Alpha Manufacturing plc are allowed to travel in this vehicle. Alpha Manufacturing plc accepts no liability whatsoever to any other persons who travel in this vehicle'.

Whilst travelling to Beta's premises the van hits a lamp post because Alan is adjusting the car radio and not looking where he is going. Brian is thrown out of the van and is severely injured. He was not wearing a seat belt and if he had been his injuries would have been much reduced.

Advise Brian.

Answer plan

This is a traditional vicarious liability question that raises various other points of contributory negligence, *volenti*, *res ipsa loquitur*.

The following points need to be discussed:

- liability of Alan to Brian
- vicarious liability of Alpha for Alan's actions
- effect of prohibition
- contributory negligence on Brian's part

Answer

It must first be decided whether Brian can sue Alan and if so, whether Alpha are vicariously liable to Brian. Brian must first show that Alan owed him a duty of care. This poses no problem as it has been held in a number of cases that a driver owes a duty of care to his passengers, eg *Nettleship v Weston* (1971). Where a duty of care has been found to exist previously there is no need to apply the modern formulation preferred by the House of Lords in *Caparo v Dickman* (1990) or *Murphy v Brentwood DC* (1990). One could also note the statement of Potts J at first instance in *B v Islington Health Authority* (1991) where he stated that in personal injury cases the duty of care remains as it was pre-*Caparo*, namely the foresight of a reasonable man as in *Doughue*, a finding that does not appear to have been disturbed on appeal (1992).

Secondly, Brian must show that it was in breach of this duty, ie that a reasonable person would not have acted in this way, *Blyth v Birmingham Waterworks* (1856) and this is clear from the facts of the problem. *Res ipsa loquitur* is not applicable here as the reason for the crash is known, *Barkway v South Wales Transport Co Ltd* (1950). Brian will have to show that the breach caused him injuries, and the 'but for' test in *Cork v Kirby MacLean* (1952) proves the required causal connection. Finally, Brian will have to prove that the damage that he has suffered was not too remote, ie that it was reasonably foreseeable: *The Wagon Mound* (1961). This should cause no difficulty to Brian because all that he will have to show is that some personal injury was reasonably foreseeable, he will not have to show that the extent was foreseeable: *Smith v Leech, Brain* (1962).

Brian could, therefore, successfully sue Alan so now the question arises as to whether Alpha are vicariously liable for Alan's negligence. We are told that the employer/employee relationship exists, so it is now necessary to see whether Alan was acting in the course of his employment at the relevant time. The question is whether Alan's act is some wrongful and unauthorised mode of doing an authorised act or whether it is so unconnected with the authorised act as not to be a mode of doing it, but rather an independent act.

It is clear that at the time of the act in question, ie the negligent driving of Alan, the express prohibition will not automatically take the act outside the course of employment. What the restriction can do is to restrict those acts which lie within the course of employment, but it cannot restrict the mode of doing an act that does lie within the course of employment - see, for example *Limpus v London General Omnibus* (1862). Thus, we need to decide whether Alan's act in driving in contravention of the prohibition is an authorised act or whether he is merely carrying out an authorised act in an unauthorised manner.

In Limpus a driver, contrary to an express prohibition obstructed a bus from a rival company and caused an accident; it was held that the employers were vicariously liable, because the driver's act was merely a wrongful mode of carrying out an authorised act in the driving of a bus. However, in *Twine v Beans Express* (1946) where a hitch hiker was given a lift it was held that the driver, by giving a lift to an unauthorised person, was acting outside the course of his employment: *Conway v Wimpey* (1951) is a similar decision involving unauthorised passengers. However, in the more recent case of *Rose v Plenty* (1978) the Court of Appeal disapproved of the decision in Twine which was based on, inter alia, the ground that the unauthorised passenger was a trespasser and, thus, was owed no duty of care. While this was true in 1946 it no longer represents the law since the House of Lords' decision in *BRB v Herrington* (1972) and the Occupier's Liability Act 1984. Another ground for the decision was based on the duty of care that the employer owed to the passenger, an approach which is not longer correct, see *ICI v Shatwell* (1965). As a result the Court of Appeal found it possible to depart from Twine and took a broad view of course of employment.

It is submitted that a court would follow Rose (1); it is certainly irrelevant that Brian is a trespasser and in Brian's favour it could be arguable that his presence in the van is furthering Alpha's interests since he is decorating their premises. Thus, provided that Alan is still within the course of his employment, Alpha plc will be vicariously liable for Alan's negligence. One way in which Alan could have moved out of the course of his employment is if he has departed from his authorised route and is on a frolic of his own. The whole area of frolics was considered in *Whatman v Pearson* (1868), *Storey v Ashton* (1869) and more recently by the House of Lords in *Williams v Hemphill* (1966), where it was held that to constitute a frolic of his own the journey in question had to be entirely unconnected with the employer's business. Hence the fact that Alan is giving a lift to Brian in order that Alan may collect further decorating supplies to use in decorating Alpha's premises means that it cannot be said that the journey was undertaken entirely for Alan's selfish purposes, so that he remains within the course of his employment and Alpha will be vicariously liable for his negligence. While this seems likely it is by no means certain. The courts have in recent years distinguished between careless acts and deliberate acts and have taken a very narrow view of course of employment where deliberate acts are concerned - see *Heasmans v Clarity Cleaning Co Ltd* (1987) and *Irving v Post Office* (1987). Perhaps the most dramatic example of this approach is to be found in *General Engineering Services v Kingston and St Andrews Corp* (1989) where firemen who drove very slowly to a fire were held not to be within their course of employment in so doing on the grounds that they were employed to travel to the scene of the fire as quickly as reasonably possible and in travelling as slowly as possible they were not doing an authorised act in an unauthorised manner, rather they were doing an unauthorised act. In view of the fact that Alan's giving of a lift to Brian was a deliberate act a court might feel inclined to follow *Conway* or *Twine*.

In addition Alpha plc's notice will be subject to s 2 UCTA 1977 so that to the extent that it purports to exclude liability for death or personal injury it is void.

Alan and, thus, Alpha plc could invoke the defence of contributory negligence against Brian. Brian's failing to wear a seat belt has contributed to the extent of his injuries and, therefore, his damages would be reduced by 15%: *Froom v Butcher* (1975).

The defence of *volenti* may also be raised against Brian for accepting a lift despite the notice in the van. For this to succeed Brian must have submitted voluntarily to the risk of damage. This seems most unlikely, especially as Brian was unaware of any danger when he accepted the lift from Alan and by s 2(3) UCTA 1977 the awareness of the notice is not of itself to be taken as indicating voluntary acceptance of any risk, and in any case s 149(3) Road Traffic Act 1988 precludes reliance on *volenti* - see for example *Pitts v Hunt* (1990).

Notes

1 In *Rose v Plenty* Lord Denning distinguished between two groups of cases, namely those where the prohibited act was done for the employer's business, when it will usually be held to be within the course of the employment, eg *Limpus*, and those done for some other purpose, eg giving a lift to a hitchhiker which if prohibited may lie outside the course of the employment, eg *Twine, Conway*. On this analysis Alan would still be within the course of his employment.

Question 2

Gamma plc employs David as a driver and Elaine as a salesperson. One day Elaine has to call on a customer but as her car is being serviced she asks David if he can drive her to the customer's premises. David agrees but when they are in the car he tells Elaine that he must first call at his private house to collect a suit to take to the dry cleaners. Whilst on the way to David's house David sees a patch of oil that has been spilt on the road and says to Elaine 'see that oil - I'll show you how to control a skid'. David then drives onto the patch of oil but fails to control the subsequent skid and hits a wall, injuring Elaine and damaging beyond repair a valuable painting that Elaine was carrying in her brief case.

Advise Elaine.

Answer plan

This question involves the area of frolics and detours and the recent attitude of the courts when considering the course of employment in situations involving deliberate acts by the employee rather than negligent acts. As is typical of exam questions, however, an additional area is also tested, namely, the principle that a tortfeasor takes his victim as he finds him as that principle applies to property damage.

The following points need to be discussed:

- liability of David to Elaine
- vicarious liability of Gamma plc for David's victim
- consideration of course of employment as regards deliberate acts of the employee
- possibility of *volenti*
- David takes Elaine as he finds her

Answer

We must first decide whether Elaine can sue David and if so whether Gamma plc is vicariously liable for David's actions. Elaine must first show that David owes her a duty of care. In those situations where a duty of care has previously been found to exist, there is no need to apply the modern formulation preferred by the House of Lords in *Caparo v Dickman* (1990) or *Murphy v Brentwood District Council* (1990). We could note here the statement of Potts J at first instance in *B v Islington Health Authority* (1991) where he stated that in personal injury cases the duty of care remains as it was pre-*Caparo*, namely the foresight of a reasonable man as in *Donoghue v Stevenson* (1932), a finding that does not appear to have been disturbed on appeal (1992). In fact, a duty of care has been found to exist in number of cases involving drivers and their passengers: eg *Nettleship v Weston* (1971), but even without knowledge of such cases we could deduce the existence of a duty of care as it is reasonably foreseeable that by driving carelessly a passenger may suffer injury.

Next Elaine must show that David was in breach of his duty, ie that a reasonable person, or rather a reasonably competent driver, in David's position would not have acted in this way:

Blyth v Birmingham Waterworks (1856); *Nettleship v Weston*. It seems clear that a reasonable driver would not drive deliberately onto a patch of oil, and so David is in breach of his duty. Elaine will also have to show that this breach caused her injuries, and the 'but for' test in *Cork v Kirby MacLean* (1952) proves the required causal connection. Finally, Elaine will have to prove that the damage that she has suffered was not too remote, ie that it was reasonably foreseeable: *The Wagon Mound* (1961). This should give rise to no problems as all that Elaine will have to show is that some personal injury was foreseeable, she will not have to show that the extent was foreseeable, nor the exact manner in which the injury was caused: *Smith v Leech, Brain* (1962); *Hughes v Lord Advocate* (1963).

Elaine could, therefore, sue David and now we must consider whether Gamma plc are liable for David's actions. We are told that the employer/employee relationship exists and its seems clear that at the start of the journey David is acting within the course of his employment. We need to consider, however, whether by calling at his house David has moved outside the course of his employment, ie whether the detour consists of a 'frolic of his own'. In *Whatman v Pearson* (1868) a driver who went home for lunch contrary to his employer's instructions was held to still be within the course of his employment, whereas in *Storey v Ashton* (1869) employers were held not liable when the employee, after completing his work, embarked on a detour. It was held that this detour constituted a new and independent journey which had nothing to do with his employment and was, therefore, outside the course of his employment. This problem of detours was considered by the House of Lords in *Williams v Hemphill Ltd* (1966) where a driver carrying some children undertook a considerable detour and it was held by the House that the driver was still within the course of his employment. Lord Pearce stated it was a question of fact in each case whether the deviation was so unconnected with the employers business that the employee was on a 'frolic of his own', and in *Williams* the presence of the boys on the bus showed that it was not a frolic of the driver's own. Lord Pearce stated that had the driver in *Storey*, for instance, been carrying some property of his employers then he might have remained in the course of his employment. Having considered *Joel* and *Storey*, Lord Pearce stated that to constitute a frolic of his own the journey had to be entirely unconnected with the employers business as opposed to a mere detour for the employee's selfish purposes. However, on the facts of *Williams* Lord Pearce held that the presence of passengers who the employee has to take to their destination made it impossible to say that the detour was entirely for the employee's purposes. Applying this criterion to our case the presence of Elaine will make it impossible to say that the detour was undertaken entirely for David's selfish purposes and, thus, David remains in the course of his employment.

The next question we must consider is whether David remains in the course of his employment when he drives onto the patch of oil. The court has taken a much more restrictive approach to course of employment where wrongful acts have occurred, as can be seen by the Court of Appeal decision in *Heasmans v Clarity Cleaning* (1987) and *Irving v The Post Office* (1987). In *Heasmans* an employer was held not to be vicariously liable for the actions of an employee who was employed to clean telephones, but who made unauthorised telephone calls costing some £1,400. The court noted that the employee was employed to clean the telephones and that in using them he had not cleaned them in an unauthorised manner, but had done an unauthorised act which had taken him outside the course of his employment. In *Irving* the employee, who worked for the Post Office and was employed to sort mail, wrote some racial abuse concerning the plaintiff upon a letter addressed to the plaintiff. The employee was authorised to write upon letters, but only for the purposes of ensuring that the mail was properly dealt with. It was held that the employers were not vicariously liable for the actions of the employee, as in writing a racial abuse he was doing an unauthorised act, and not an authorised act in an unauthorised manner. The court stated, per Fox LJ, that limits had to be set to the doctrine of vicarious liability, particularly where it was sought to make employers liable for the 'wilful wrongdoing' of an employee. Thus, in *General Engineering Services v Kingston and St Andrews Corp* (1989) the firemen who drove very slowly to a fire were held not to be in the course of their employment in so doing as they were employed to travel to the scene of fires as quickly as reasonably possible, and in travelling as slowly as possibly they were not doing an authorised act in an unauthorised manner, but were doing an unauthorised act. Given the attitude of the courts to deliberate acts, it is submitted that in carrying out this deliberate act David has moved outside the course of his employment and that Gamma plc will not be liable for his action. The fact that in driving onto the oil David was not acting for the benefit of his employer is not necessarily relevant to taking the act outside the course of his employment: *Lloyd v Grace, Smith & Co* (1912); *Century Insurance v Northern Ireland Road Transport Board* (1942).

David may seek to raise the *volenti* defence against Elaine. To do this successfully David will have to show that Elaine voluntarily assented to the risk of damage, which seems unlikely: *Dann v Hamilton* (1939). Although the defence of *volenti* succeeded in *Morris v Murray* (1991) this was a case where the risk was glaringly obvious from the outset. In any event s 149(3) of the Road Traffic Act 1988 precludes reliance on *volenti* in road traffic situations - see *Pitts v Hunt* (1990).

As regards the damage to the valuable painting, David (and Gamma plc if he is still within the course of his employment) will be liable. David may not be able to foresee that Elaine will be carrying such valuable property, but he can foresee that Elaine will be carrying some property and this will be sufficient: *Vacwell Engineering v BDH Chemicals* (1971). When considering damage to property, a narrower attitude to foreseeability is taken than with damage to the person: *The Wagon Mound* (1961), and the egg-shell skull rule in *Dulieu v White* (1901) cannot be applied without great caution. However, Elaine should be able to recover for the damage to her paintings on the authority of *Vacwell*.

Question 3

Delta plc owns a small office. They ask Frank to undertake various work at their premises and tell Frank that his work will take about one week.

While Frank is working in Delta's offices he carelessly rewires a switch and Gloria, an employee of Delta, is injured when she uses the switch. Henry, who is visiting Delta plc in an attempt to sell them some office equipment, is also injured when he trips over a length of electrical cable that Frank has left in a corridor.

Advise Gloria and Henry.

Answer plan

This question involves a consideration of the liability of an employer for the acts of an independent contractor. As such it is less run of the mill than the standard vicarious liability questions and is much shorter providing the student is aware of the relevant legal principles.

The following areas need to be considered:

- differentiation between employees and independent contractors
- liability of employer for each of independent contractors
- non delegable duties of employer
- liability of employer for acts of collateral negligence

Answer

We must decide whether Gloria and Henry could sue Frank and if so whether Gamma plc are liable for Frank's actions. Gloria must first show that Frank owes her a duty of care. In those situations where a duty of care has previously been found to exist, there is no need to apply the modern formulation preferred by the House of Lords in *Caparo v Dickman* (1990) or *Murphy v Brentwood District Council* (1990). We could note here the statement of Potts J at first instance in *B v Islington Health Authority* (1991) where he stated that in personal injury cases the duty of care remains as it was pre-*Caparo*, namely the foresight of a reasonable man as in *Donoghue v Stevenson* (1932), a finding that does not appear to have been disturbed on appeal (1992). In fact, a duty of care has been found to exist in a similar situation in *Green v Fibreglass Ltd* (1958), but even without knowledge of this case we could deduce the existence of a duty of care as it is reasonably foreseeable that by carelessly rewiring the switch a person who subsequently uses it may suffer injury.

Next Gloria must show that Frank was in breach of this duty, ie that a reasonable person, or rather a reasonably competent electrician, in Frank's position would not have acted in this way: *Blyth v Birmingham Waterworks* (1856); *Bolam v Friern Hospital Management Committee* (1957). It seems clear that a reasonable electrician would not rewire a switch carelessly, and so Frank is in breach of his duty. Gloria will also have to show that this breach caused her injuries, and the 'but for' test in *Cork v Kirby MacLean* (1952) proves the required causal connection. Finally, Gloria will have to prove that the damage that she has suffered was not too remote, ie that it was reasonably foreseeable: *The Wagon Mound* (1961). This should give rise to no problems as all that Elaine will have to show is that some personal injury was foreseeable, she will not have to show that the extent was foreseeable, nor the exact manner in which the injury was caused: *Smith v Leech, Brain* (1962); *Hughes v Lord Advocate* (1963).

Given then that Frank is negligent, can Delta plc be held liable for his negligence? It seems clear that Frank was acting within the course of his employment. The fact that he has acted carelessly will not take him outside the course of his employment; provided that the relevant act, ie the rewiring of the switch was an authorised act, the fact that Frank has carried it out in a wrongful and unauthorised manner will not take the act outside the course of his employment: *Century Insurance v Northern Ireland Road Transport Board* (1942). We need to decide, next, therefore, whether Frank is an employee of Delta plc or whether he is an independent contractor. It is extremely difficult to formulate a universal test for an employee. The original test, laid down in *Yewens v Noakes* (1880) was the control test in that the employer had the right of control as to the way in which the employee carried out his work. This test has obvious problems when the person concerned has a particular skill, especially if the employer himself does not possess that skill and Denning LJ (as he then was) proposed the 'business integration' test in *Stevenson, Jordan & Harrison Ltd v MacDonald* (1952) posing the question does the person do his work as an 'integral part of the business' when he will be an employee or is he merely 'accessory' to it when he will be an independent contractor. The test is just as difficult to apply as the control test and in *Market Investigations v Minister of Social Security* (1969) it was held that a person was not an employee because she was not in business on her own account. This test also seems vague, although *Andrews v King* (1991), it was described by Browne-Wilkinson VC as the 'fundamental test'. The modern approach of the courts is to eschew any single test and examine all the facts of the case. Looking at the facts of Frank and Delta plc it would seem that Delta have the right to tell Frank what work is to be done but not how to do it, so that Frank is an independent contractor. In *Ready Mixed Concrete v Minister of Pensions* (1968) MacKenna J laid down several conditions for a contract of employment, one of which was that the worker agrees to be directed as to the mode of carrying out the work. MacKenna held that this right of control was a necessary (though not sufficient) condition of an employment contract and it seems to be lacking in Frank's case, leaving him as an independent contractor. Thus, *prima facie* Delta plc are not liable for Frank's actions.

However, as regards Gloria, Delta plc as Gloria's employers are under a non-delegable duty to take reasonable care for the safety of their employees: Wilsons and *Clyde Coal v English* (1938). By the phrase 'non-delegable' one does not mean that the employer cannot delegate performance to an independent contractor, but that the employer cannot delegate responsibility for performance. Thus, although the standard rule is that an employer is not liable for the actions of an independent contractor: *Morgan v Girls Friendly Society* (1936); *D & F Estates v Church Commissioners* (1989), Delta plc will be liable to Gloria for failing to take reasonable care for her safety.

As regards Henry, as he is not an employee of Delta plc he cannot claim the benefit of this exception.

However, there are some situations where an employer is liable for the torts of an independent contractor. The employer is so liable if he has authorised the independent contractor to commit the tort: *Ellis v Sheffield Gas Consumers Co* (1853); if he is negligent in choosing an independent contractor who is not competent: *Pinn v Rew* (1916); and if a non-delegable duty is imposed upon him by common law, ie a duty the performance of which can be delegated but not the responsibility. Neither of the first two situations is relevant here, but one of the situations that may be relevant as regards common law non-delegable duties is where the independent contractor is employed to carry out work that is extra hazardous: *Honeywell & Stein v Larkin Bros* (1934); *Alcock v Wraith* (1991). In *Alcock* the Court of Appeal held that a crucial question was 'did the work involve some special risk or was it from its very nature likely to cause damage'. It is submitted that the work in question was not extra hazardous, and so Delta plc will not be liable: *Salsbury v Woodland* (1969) (1).

If Henry were to sue Delta plc under the Occupiers' Liability Act 1957 he would be met with the defence in s 2(4)(b) that Delta acted reasonably in entrusting the work to an independent contractor and took such steps as were reasonable to satisfy himself that the contractor was competent and that the work had been properly done. In *Haseldine v Dew* (1941) it was held there was not need to check the work of contractors employed to repair a lift as the work was technical; in *Woodward v Mayor of Hastings* (1945) it was held that as the work was non-technical there was a need to check that it had been properly done.

Notes

1   If it were to be decided that Frank's work was extra hazardous, Delta plc might be able to claim that Frank's negligence was merely collateral to the performance of his work and that as employers they were not liable for this collateral negligence: *Padbury v Holliday & Greenwood* (1912). Whether the negligence was in fact collateral would depend on the particular facts of the case, and we are not given sufficient details to come to any firm conclusion.

Negligence - Duty of Care Generally and Restricted Situations

Introduction

Questions on the imposition of a duty of care usually take the form of an essay, typically on the development of a test for imposing a duty of care. It is vital to also be thoroughly familiar with situations in which limits are placed on the duty of care, ie in particular with the areas of negligent mis-statement, nervous shock and economic loss. These topics, especially the first two, have been the subject of important decisions recently, and are popular with examiners, either as problems or essay questions. It is vital to be aware of the recent leading cases in these areas.

Checklist

Students must be familiar with the following aspects:
- Development of a test for ascertaining the existence of duty of care
- Negligent mis-statement
  Statements made to a known recipient and the special relationship
  Statements put into general circulation
- Nervous shock
  Criteria for recovery
  Restrictions on recovery
  Possible extensions of persons owed a duty of care
- Economic loss: Decision in Junior Books - Judicial retreat from *Junior Books* - Current position regarding economic loss

Question 4

Since the decision of the House of Lords in *Anns v Merton London Borough Council* (1978) the courts have gradually come to realise that the imposition of a duty of care involves considerations that are considerably more complex than merely applying two simple tests.

Discuss.

Answer plan

This is a typical essay question on the development of a test for imposing a duty of care since *Anns*.

The following areas should be considered:

- brief background to *Anns*
- test in *Anns* and its application to nervous shock, economic loss
- retreat from *Anns*
- current approach of the courts

Answer

Although an attempt to formulate a general test or principle to decide whether in any particular circumstances a duty of care arose was made in *Heaven v Pender* (1883) it was not until 1932 and the judgment of Lord Atkin in *Donoghue v Stevenson* (1932) that a general principle was finally established. There were, of course, many situations in which the courts had recognised the existence of a duty of care but no principle existed to decide in any new situations whether a duty existed. The courts were, for some time, a little hesitant in applying the neighbour test as a general principle but in *Home Office v Dorset Yacht* (1970) Lord Reid stated that the neighbour test was a statement of principle and should be applied unless there was some reason for excluding it. Proceeding from this, Lord Wilberforce in *Anns v Merton LBC* (1978) stated that in order to establish whether a duty of care exists the question is to be approached in two stages; firstly, between the wrongdoer and the person who has suffered damage, is there a sufficient relationship of proximity of neighbourhood such that in the reasonable contemplation of the former, carelessness on his part may cause damage to the latter, in which case a *prima facie* duty of care arises. Secondly, are there any considerations which ought to negative or reduce or limit the scope of the duty of the class of person to whom it is owed or the damage to which a breach of it may give rise.

It is true to state that the courts have gradually come to realise that imposition of a duty of care involves more complex considerations as *Anns* was used by the courts to expand the area of the duty of care. Thus, in *Junior Books v Veitchi* (1983) the House of

Lords held that liability could arise in respect of economic loss: in *McLoughlin v O'Brian* (1983) the House considered the scope of nervous shock and in *Emeh v Kensington & Chelsea and Westminster AHA* (1985) the courts were prepared to extend the range of persons to whom a duty of care was owed. However, from 1985 onwards, the courts have retreated from the broad general principle of *Anns*. The starting point of this approach was *Peabody Donation Fund v Sir Lindsay Parkinson* (1985) AC 210 where Lord Keith stated that the *Anns* test was not of 'a definitive character' and stated that although a relationship of proximity must exist before a duty of care can arise the duty must depend on all the circumstances of the case and that it must be considered whether it is just and reasonable to impose a duty. Further criticism of the two tier test is to be found in *Leigh and Sillivan v Aliakmon Shipping* in both the Court of Appeal (1985) and the House of Lords (1988). Oliver LJ in the Court of Appeal stated that *Anns* did not establish a new test of duty of care that was applicable in all cases, nor did it enable the court to determine policy in each case. The fear is that the first tier is so easily satisfied that it leaves too much to the second tier, namely policy. In the House of Lords, Lord Brandon adopted a similar approach and claimed that *Anns* had been decided in a novel fact situation and not in a factual situation where no duty had previously been held to exist, and in the latter case *Anns* was not applicable and no duty of care was owed, which seems to be a pre-*Donoghue* approach let alone pre *Anns*. This attack was continued in *Curran v Northern Ireland Co-Ownership Housing Association* (1987) by Lord Bridge who stated that *Anns* obscured both the distinction between misfeasance and non-feasance and between contract and tort. Lord Bridge also approved the judgment of Brennan J in the High Court of Australia in *Sutherland Shire Council v Heyman* (1985) where the judge analysed the two tier test and rejected it, holding that the test for the existence of a duty of care was more complex and said that it was preferable to develop novel categories of negligence incrementally and by analogy with established categories rather than by a massive extension of a *prima facie* duty of care restrained only by indefinable considerations which ought to negative, to reduce or limit the scope of the duty or the class of persons to whom it is owed.

The two tier test was again criticised in *Yuen Kun-Yeu v A-G of Hong Kong* (1988) by the Privy Council and by the House of Lords again in *Hill v Chief Constable of W Yorks* (1989), and in *Caparo Industries v Dickman* (1990) and *Murphy v Brentwood DC* (1990) the House of Lords again expressed its preference for the incremental approach of Brennan J. Indeed in *Ravenscroft v Rederiaktiebolage Transatlantic* (1991) Ward J held at first instance that the two tier test in *Anns* had been overruled by *Murphy*. In strict legal terms this appears incorrect but as the House of Lords has twice expressed its preference for the incremental approach over the two tier test in *Anns* it seems highly unlikely that the *Anns* test will be applied in future.

As an example of the considerations other than those expressed in *Anns* that the courts have recently taken into account, one could note the following factors which the courts have considered, often to come to the conclusion that no duty of care should exist:

a) The difference between misfeasance and non-feasance. It has been argued, both judicially and extra-judicially that the *Anns* test is defective in that it ignores the distinction between misfeasance and non-feasance. Thus, Lord Bridge in *Curran* referred to the 'cogent criticisms' that had been raised by Professors Smith and Burns in an article in 1983 to the effect that the Donoghue principle applies to misfeasance rather than to non-feasance, ie that a duty to prevent harm arising is normally created by contract, where one person promises to improve the other persons position, and arises in tort only in exceptional circumstances. Although the actual decision in *Curran* turned on a point of statutory interpretation as regards breach of statutory duty, the courts have refused to find the existence of a duty of care in non-feasance situations in *Hill*; *Yuen Kun-Yeu*; *Davis v Radcliffe* (1990). This does not mean that a duty of care will never arise in non-feasance situations, rather that this is the general rule that applies to pure omissions, subject only to a number of exceptions that were described by Lord Goff in *Smith v Littlewoods Organisation* (1987).

b) The availability of an alternative remedy to the plaintiff. Thus, in *Simaan General Contracting v Pilkington Glass* (1988) the court refused to impose a duty of care, leaving the plaintiff instead to a chain of contractual claims. In *Jones v Department of Employment* (1988) the availability of judicial review mitigated against finding the existence of a duty of care, and in *Mills v Winchester Diocesan Board of Finance* (1989) the existence of a statutory remedy did likewise.

c) If Parliament has regulated an activity and the imposition of a duty of care would go further than Parliament has proceeded, then the courts will be loath to find a duty of care. So in *D & F Estates v Church Commissioners* (1989), the House of Lords refused to find a duty of care because it would have gone further than Parliament did in the Defective Premises Act 1972. *Reid v Rush and Tomkins Group* (1989) is another example of the court refusing to go further than Parliament, and in *McNerny v London Borough of Lambeth* (1988) the court stated that the rule in *Cavalier v Pope*, which had stood since 1906 should be changed by Parliament and not by the courts.

d) The courts are reluctant to impose a duty of care in situations where they have refused to impose a duty of care in the past, eg *Leigh & Sillivan v Aliakmon Shipping* (1986); *Stephens v Anglian Water Authority* (1987). The courts are also unwilling to impose a duty of care in situations where the only foreseeable loss is economic loss: *Calveley v Chief Constable of Merseyside* (1989).

In describing the retreat from the wide test in *Anns* and the number of occasions recently where the courts have denied the existence of a duty of care or reduced its scope or potential plaintiffs, it should not be thought that in appropriate situations the courts are unwilling to find a duty of care in novel situations, eg in *Kirkham v Chief Constable of Greater Manchester* (1990) the Court of Appeal held police owed a duty of care to a person of unsound mind to pass on to a prison information regarding that person's suicidal tendencies. In *Ephraim v Newham LBC* (1992), the High Court held that a local housing authority owed a duty of care to a homeless person to ensure that premises to which it was sending her were reasonably safe for use as a bed and breakfast establishment.

Perhaps the clearest example of the approach of the courts is *Ancell v McDermott* (1992), where Garland J held that whether or not police officers who came upon a potential hazard in the highway during their duties owed a duty of care to individual members of the police who might suffer injuries caused by the hazard depended on the precise circumstances. The court refused to be bound by either *Hill* or *Clough v Bussan* (1990) and held whether a duty of care existed depended on the precise circumstances.

Question 5

Martin was on a train reading a copy of the Financial Times. Norman, who was sitting next to him, asked Martin what his job was and Martin replied that he was a stockbroker. Norman then asked Martin for some advice on investment and Martin jokingly replied that publishing seemed to be a good area. As a result of this discussion Norman invested his life savings in publishing shares and a few months later the value of these shares fell dramatically and Norman lost all his money. Depressed at being penniless Norman then committed suicide.

Advise Norman's widow, Olive, of any remedy she might have against Martin.

Answer plan

This is a typical 'one to one' negligent mis-statement question that requires a discussion of *Hedley Byrne* and later relevant decisions.

The following points need to be covered:
- duty of care between Martin and Norman
- social occasions and *Chaudry v Prabhakar*
- Martin's liability for loss of money and Norman's death

Answer

In order to advise Olive we must first decide whether or not Martin owed Norman a duty of care. The traditional approach to this question is to see whether a special relationship exists between Martin and Norman, as laid down in *Hedley Byrne v Heller* (1964). In *Hedley Byrne* there were held to be three elements to special relationships.

Firstly, that the representor must possess a special skill. In *Mutual Life & Citizens Assurance v Evatt* (1971) the Privy Council held that liability would only arise when the statement was made in the course of a business. However, as Evatt is a decision of the Privy Council it is only of persuasive authority, and the dissenting minority held that *prima facie* a duty was owed by anyone who took it upon himself to make representations knowing that another person will reasonably rely on those representations. This view has been followed by the

Court of Appeal in *Esso Petroleum v Mardon* (1976) and *Howard Marine v Ogden* (1976) and recently in *Gran Gelato v Richcliffe* (1992) it was held as unarguable that a vendor of premises did not owe a duty of care to a purchaser to take reasonable care when answering enquiries regarding the property. It is suggested that future courts would follow the approach of the Court of Appeal above and, thus, Martin would satisfy this element of the test.

Secondly, that the representee must reasonably rely on the representations. In *Smith v Eric Bush* (1990) it was held to be reasonable for the purchaser of a modest house to rely on the survey carried out by the lender's surveyor and in *Edwards v Lee* (1991) it was held that it was reasonable for the recipient of a reference provided by a solicitor concerning a client to rely on that reference. In *Royal Bank Trust (Trinidad) v Pampellonne* (1987) the Privy Council held that there was a difference between the giving of advice and the passing on of information and that it may be more reasonable to rely on the former than the latter. Thus, the question here is whether it was reasonable for Norman to rely on Martin's statement - it does not seem reasonable for Norman to rely on such a reply to his question so as to invest his life savings. In *Chaudry v Prabhakar* (1989), LJ stated that one would not impose a duty of care regarding statements made on social occasions and it seems that the meeting between Martin and Norman could so be described. Overall, therefore, it seems that Martin does not satisfy this requirement.

Thirdly, the representor must have some knowledge of the type of transaction envisaged by the representee and this does seem to be so from the facts of the problem. Thus, Martin owes no duty of care to Norman on this overall analysis as the essential ingredient of reasonable reliance is absent.

In *Caparo Industries v Dickman* (1990) Lord Oliver analysed *Hedley Byrne* and held that the required relationship between the representor and the representee may typically be held to exist where:

a) the advice is required for a purpose, whether particularly specified or generally described, which is made known, either actually or inferentially, to the representor when the advice is given;

b) the representor knows, either actually or inferentially, that his advice will be communicated to the representee, either specifically or as a member of an ascertainable class, in order that it should be used by the representee for that purpose;

c) it is known, either actually or inferentially, that the advice so communicated is likely to be acted upon by the representee for that purpose without independent inquiry; and

d) it is so acted upon by the representee to his detriment.

Lord Oliver emphasised that these conditions were neither conclusive nor exclusive, but merely that the decision in *Hedley Byrne* did not warrant any broader proportions. Considering these conditions it seems that Martin satisfies a), b) and d), but that condition c) is not satisfied and so again we conclude that Martin owes Norman no duty of care as regards the statement concerning shares (1). Thus, Olive cannot sue Martin in respect of the loss in value of the shares purchased by Norman nor can she sue in respect of Norman's subsequent suicide. Even if Martin owed Norman a duty of care as regards the statement and was in breach of that duty, he would not be liable to Norman's subsequent suicide as this is not a reasonable foreseeable consequence of the breach as required by *The Wagon Mound* (No 1) (1961).

Norman's suicide could also be regarded as a *novus actus interveniens* which broke the chain of causation between the earlier negligence (if any) of Martin and the damage suffered by Norman. The criterion used by the courts seems to be whether the later conduct by the plaintiff is reasonable is reasonable or not. Thus, in *McKew v Holland & Hannen & Cubitts* (1969) the plaintiff was injured due to the negligence of the defendants, and as a result suffered a residual intermittent loss of control of one leg. Despite this the plaintiff went down a flight of steep stairs that had no handrail and while doing so his leg gave way and he was injured. It was held by the House of Lords that his action in going down a steep flight of stairs without a handrail was so unreasonable that it broke the chain of causation. Lord Reid stated that 'if the injured man acts unreasonably he cannot hold the defendant liable for injury caused by his own unreasonable conduct'. In contrast, in *Wieland v Cyril Lord Carpets* (1969) the plaintiff, due to the original negligence of the defendants, found difficulty in using her bi-focal spectacles properly. She nevertheless continued to use them, but as she could not do so with her customary efficiency she too fell down a flight of stairs. It was held that the defendants were also liable for this injury as the plaintiff had not been unreasonable in continuing to wear bi-focals. As by its nature suicide is unreasonable conduct, it is submitted that even if Martin were to owe a duty of care in respect of his advice and to be in breach of that duty, that he would not be liable for Norman's suicide, as that act would have broken the chain of causation. This is fortunate for Martin because Norman's suicide would not allow the defence of *ex turpi causa non oritur actio*: *Kirkham v Chief Constable Greater Manchester* (1990), nor would it allow the *volenti* defence as presumably Norman was of unsound mind when he committed suicide: *Kirkham*.

Note

1   In *Hedley Byrne* it was suggested that a duty of care will arise, where the representor voluntarily assumed a responsibility to the representee, and it seems from the facts that Norman has not done this as we are told he jokingly recommended publishing shares. However, the House of Lords in *Caparo and Smith v Eric Bush* have criticised this concept and, thus, Martin could not be advised to rely on this defence.

Question 6

Neil, who is an accountant, writes a book entitled 'How to make a fortune on the Stock Market'. Karen buys a copy from a bookshop and Peter is given a copy as a birthday present. Neil gives a copy to Rachel, his girl friend, saying 'Have a look at this and see how clever I am' and a copy to Terence, his brother, saying 'Follow these tips and you will become a millionaire'. Karen, Peter, Rachel and Terence have followed the advice in the book and have lost a large amount of money thereby, as the book is erroneous in several important aspects.

Advise Karen, Peter, Rachel and Terence.

Answer plan

This is a question on negligent mis-statement that involves the 'one to one' situation, the placing of a statement into general circulation and a consideration of what constitutes a social occasion.

The following points need to be considered:
*   *Hedley Byrne* and Rachel and Terence
*   *Caparo* and Karen and Peter
*   reasonable reliance and Rachel and Terence

Answer

In advising the parties we must consider whether Neil owes them a duty of care in respect of the statements that he has made in his book.

As regards Karen and Peter, Neil has put a statement into general circulation. In *Caparo Industries v Dickman* (1990) the House of Lords considered the situation of a person who places a statement into general circulation as opposed to those situations such as *Hedley Byrne v Heller* (1964) and *Smith v Eric Bush* (1990) where the representor communicated and knew that the advice was to be communicated to the representee, knew that it was very likely that the representee would rely on the advice and was fully aware of the nature of the transaction that the representee had in mind (the 'one to one' situation). The House stated that the criteria for imposing a duty of care were foreseeability of damage, proximity of relationship and reasonableness or otherwise of imposing a duty.

In particular where a statement put into more or less general circulation might be relied upon by strangers for one of a variety of different purposes which the maker of the statement had no specific reason to anticipate there was no relationship of proximity to between the maker of the statement and any person relying on it unless it was shown that the maker knew that his statement would be communicated to the person relying on it, either as an individual or as a member of an identifiable class, specifically in connection with a transaction of a particular kind and this person would be very likely to rely on it in deciding whether to enter into that transaction.

Thus, it was held in *Al Saudi Banque v Clarke Pixley* (1989) that the auditors of a company owe no duty of care to a bank who lends money to the company, regardless of whether the bank is an existing creditor making further advances or is only a potential creditor, because in either case even if it is foreseeable that the bank might request a copy of the company's accounts and rely on them there is not a sufficiently close or direct relationship between the auditors and the bank to give rise to a degree of proximity necessary to establish a duty of care. In *Caparo* it was held that the auditor of a public company owes no duty of care to a member of the public who relied on the accounts to buy shares in the company, because the court would not deduce a relationship of proximity between the auditor and a member of the public when to do so would give rise to unlimited liability on the part of the auditor. Furthermore, an auditor owed no duty of care to an individual shareholder who wished to buy more shares in the company, since an individual shareholder was in no better position than a member of the public and the auditors' statutory duty to prepare accounts was owed to the body of shareholders as a whole, the purpose being to enable the shareholders, as a body, to exercise informed control of the company and not to enable individual shareholders to buy shares with a view to profit. Finally, in *Al Nakib Investments v Longcroft* (1990) it was decided that although the directors of a company owe a duty of care to persons who subscribe for shares in reliance of a prospectus (which was directly addressed to such persons in connection with a rights issue), they do not owe a duty of care to a shareholder or anyone else who relies on a prospectus for the purpose of deciding whether to purchase shares through the Stock Market.

In *James McNaughton Paper Group v Hicks Anderson* (1991), Neil LJ analysed the cases and identified a number of guidelines that may be relevant where a statement was acted on to his detriment by a recipient other than the person directly intended by the maker to act on it, in determining whether the maker owed a duty of care to the recipient not to be negligent, viz:

a) The purpose for which the statement was made. If the statement was made by the adviser for the express purpose of being communicated to the advisee, a duty of care may often arise. If the statement was made for a different purpose and for the benefit of someone other than the advisee, the precise purpose for which the statement was communicated must be carefully studied.

b) The purpose for which the statement was communicated, eg was the communication for information only or was it for some action to be taken.

c) The relationship between the adviser, the advisee and any relevant third party. If the statement was made for the benefit of someone other than the advisee the relationship between the parties should be considered, eg is the advisee likely to look to the third party (and through him to the adviser) for guidance.

d) The size of the class to which the advisee belongs. If the advisee is a single person or a member of a small class it will be easier to infer that a duty of care was owed than if he was a member of a large class, especially where the statement was first made to someone outside that class.

e) The state of knowledge of the adviser. This is a most important factor. Did the adviser know the purpose for which the statement was made and the purpose for which it was communicated. Any duty of care will be limited to types of transactions of which the adviser had knowledge and will only advise where the adviser knows or ought to know that the statement will be relied on by a person or class of persons in connection with that transaction: see *Caparo*. One should also consider whether the adviser knew that the advisee would rely on the statement without obtaining independent advice.

f) Reliance by the advisee. Was the advisee entitled to rely on the statement to take the action that he did; did he in fact rely on the statement; should he have used his own judgment; should he have sought independent advice?

The most important guideline as regards Peter and Karen would appear to be d), for although it might be argued that a) - c) and e) - f) are in favour of imposing a duty of care, the size of the class to which Karen and Peter belong is so great that there is insufficient proximity between them and Neil to impose a duty.

In the light of these decisions it would seem that although the criterion of foreseeability of damage can be met there is insufficient proximity between Neil and Karen, see *Saudi Banque* and *Caparo*, and certainly insufficient proximity between Neil and Peter who was not even a purchaser of the book.

As regards Rachel and Terence we have the one to one situation so we need to consider whether the necessary special relationship exists between Neil and Rachel and between Neil and Terence. The usual approach to deciding whether a special relationship exists between Neil and Rachel is to consider the three elements that were held to be required in *Hedley Byrne v Heller* (1964).

Firstly, that the representor must possess a special skill. In *Mutual Life & Citizens Assurance v Evatt* (1971) the Privy Council held that liability would only arise when the statement was made in the course of a business. However, as *Evatt* is a decision of the Privy Council it is only of persuasive authority, and the dissenting minority held that *prima facie* a duty was owed by anyone who took it upon himself to make representations knowing that another person will reasonably rely on those representations. This view has been followed by the Court of Appeal in *Esso Petroleum v Mardon* (1976) and *Howard Marine v Ogden* (1976), and in *Gran Gelato v Richcliff* (1992) it was held to be unarguable that a vendor of premises did not owe a duty of care to a purchaser to take reasonable care when answering enquiries regarding the property.

It is suggested that the future courts would follow the approach of the Court of Appeal and, thus, Neil would satisfy this element of the test.

Secondly, that the representative must reasonably rely on the representations. In *Smith v Eric Bush* (1990) it was held to be reasonable for the purchaser of a modest house to rely on the survey carried out by the lender's surveyor and in *Edwards v Lee* (1991) it was held that it was reasonable for the recipient of a reference provided by a solicitor to a client to rely on that reference. In *Royal Bank Trust (Trinidad) v Pampellonne* (1987) the Privy Council held that there was a difference between the giving of advice and the passing on of information and that it may be more reasonable to rely on the former than the latter. Thus, the question here is whether it was reasonable for Rachel to rely on Neil's statement - it does not seem reasonable for Rachel to rely on the statements in the book. In *Chaudry v Prabhakar* (1989), May LJ stated that one would not impose a duty of care regarding statements made on social occasions, and it seems that the meeting between Neil and Rachel could so be described. Overall, therefore, it seems that Neil does not satisfy this requirement.

Thirdly, the representor must have some knowledge of the type of transaction envisaged by the representee, and this does seem to be so from the facts of the problem.

Thus, on this analysis Neil owes no duty of care to Rachel as although he satisfies the first criterion it is not reasonable for Rachel to rely on the statements in the book. Neil has given Rachel the book for a different purpose, namely to impress her, and has not suggested the she follows the advice contained therein. Additionally Neil can argue that the advice was given on a purely social occasion, its function being to impress Rachel. Thus, it is submitted that in all these circumstances it is not reasonable for Rachel to rely on the contents of the book. Furthermore, as Neil has only given the book to Rachel to impress her he will have no knowledge of the type of transaction undertaken by Rachel as he does not intend her to act on the book in the first place. Hence Neil can argue that he owes no duty of care to Rachel in respect of the advice in the book In *Caparo Industries v Dickman* (1990) Lord Oliver analysed *Hedley Byrne* and held that the required relationship between the representor and the representee may typically be held to exist where:

1) the advise is required for a purpose, whether particularly specified or generally described, which is made known, either actually or inferentially, to the representor when the advice is given;

2) the representor knows, either actually or inferentially, that his advice will be communicated to the representee, either specifically or as a member of an ascertainable class, in order that it should be used by the representee for that purpose;

3) it is known, either actually or inferentially, that the advice so communicated is likely to be acted upon by the representee for that purpose without independent inquiry; and

4) it is so acted upon by the representee to his detriment.

Taking this approach, the required relationship will not arise because Neil is unaware that Rachel intends to rely on the advice in the book for the purposes of investing in the Stock Market.

However, when we come to Terence it seems clear that Neil does owe Terence a duty of care, because he does satisfy the above three criteria in that he takes it upon himself to make representations (*Esso v Marden; Howard Marine v Ogden*), it is reasonable for Terence to rely on these representations as Neil has told him to do so, and Neil must be aware of the transactions envisaged by Terence.

Thus, Neil owes a duty of care to Terence and is liable for the loss Terence has suffered.

Note

1   In *Hedley Byrne* it was suggested that a duty of care will arise
    where the representor voluntarily assumed a responsibility to
    the representee, and it seems from the facts that we were
    given that Neil has not done this. However, the House of
    Lords in *Caparo* and in *Smith v Eric Bush* (1990) have criticised
    this concept, and, thus, Neil could not be advised to rely on
    this defence.

Question 7

Bay Builders plc built a supermarket for Allfoods plc; under the
contract Bay Builders were to complete the foundations, walls,
roof, windows, etc and an air conditioning system was to be
installed by Keepcool plc. The whole of the building operations,
including the installation of ancillary equipment was supervised
by Alamo Architects who were employed by Allfoods plc. The
contract between Allfoods plc and Bay Builders plc required Bay
Builders to exercise due professional skill in the design of the
building and the selection of materials to be used therein. The
building was completed and Allfoods plc took possession and
commenced trading. A few months after opening cracks appeared
in the ceiling of the supermarket due to faults in its construction
and Allfoods plc ceased trading while the ceiling was repaired.
Just before the repair work to the ceiling was completed a fire
broke out which was caused by the negligent installation of the
air conditioning equipment by Keepcool plc, and as a result the
supermarket remained closed for an additional four weeks.

Advise Allfoods plc.

Answer plan

This question turns on the area of economic loss and in particular
the complex area of defective product economic loss.

The following points need to be discussed:

- liability for economic loss caused by Bay Builders plc
- liability for economic loss caused by Alamo Architects
- liability for loss caused by Keepcool plc - is there economic
  loss or consequential economic loss?

Answer

We should first note that no liability will attach to Bay Builders plc via s 1 Defective Premises Act 1972 as that only applies to dwellings. Thus, any liability that Bay Builders have to Allfoods plc will lie in contract or tort. As regards Bay Builders' tortious liability to Allfoods plc in respect of the ceiling, this is a case of defective product economic loss. The general rule is that such loss, which is treated as economic loss, cannot be recovered in tort; if the defective product damages other property of the plaintiff or causes personal injury that is recoverable but damages in tort do not cover the cost of repairing the defective product itself.

However, this general rule must be considered in the light of the decision in *Junior Books v Veitchi* (1983) when a majority of the House of Lords held that nominated sub-contractors were liable to building owners for economic loss caused by the faulty laying of a floor which posed no danger to health and damaged no other property of the plaintiff. The House of Lords based its decision on the grounds that there was such a relationship of proximity between the parties that the defendant owed a duty of care not simply not to cause harm to the plaintiff but to avoid faults being present in their work. Several points were emphasised by the Court in coming to this conclusion; the fact that the plaintiffs had nominated the defendants to carry out the work and were relying on the defendant to do this work properly; that the defendants knew that the plaintiffs were relying on this skill and that the damage was a direct and foreseeable result of the defendants' carelessness. Lord Brandon dissented on the grounds that the decision effectively created contractual obligations between non-contracting parties and as there was no danger to the plaintiffs or their property the case did not come within *Donoghue v Stevenson* (1932).

However, unfortunately for Allfoods plc, Junior Books has been subject to intense judicial criticism and later cases have tended to confine it within its specific facts. Thus, in *Aswan Engineering Establishment v Lupdine* (1987) Lloyd LJ stated that where a defect renders the property less valuable the plaintiff's remedy lies in contract but where it created damage to other property of the plaintiff the remedy lies in tort and that Junior Books was the first case to cross the line.

Following this reiteration of the pre-*Junior Books* situation, in *Simaan General Contracting v Pilkington Glass* (1988) where a nominated sub-contractor's carelessness caused the plaintiff pure economic loss it was held that the plaintiff could not sue the sub-contractor in the absence of a contract. But in *Greater Nottingham Co-Op v Cementation Piling & Foundations* (1989) where there was a contract between the plaintiff and a nominated sub-contractors it was held that the existence of this contract precluded a duty of care in tort. The contract in question related to the supply of materials and not how the work was to be done and the court held that this contract exhaustively defined the relationship between the parties. The relationship between Allfoods plc and Bay Builders plc would appear to be very close to Greater Nottingham Co-Op and following this case Bay Builders would owe no duty of care in respect of the defective ceiling. In support of this conclusion we should note the decision in *D & F Estates v Church Commissioners* (1989) where it was held a that a builder was not liable in tort for remedying defects in a building constructed by him if the defect was discovered before any damage to other property of the plaintiff or personal injury was caused.

Perhaps the view of the courts to *Junior Books* can best be summed up by some judicial statements of high authority. In *D & F Estates* Lord Bridge stated that 'the consensus of judicial opinion seems to be ... that the decision cannot be regarded as laying down any principle of general application in the law of tort', and Lord Oliver stated that it was 'really of no use as an authority on the general duty of care'; in *Simaan General Contracting* Dillon LJ stated that *Junior Books* had been 'the subject of so much analysis and discussion with differing explanations of the basis of the case that the case cannot now be regarded as a useful pointer to any development of law ... indeed I find it difficult to see that future citation from *Junior Books* can ever serve any useful purpose'. In view of our discussion, it should come as no surprise to learn that the High Court recently refused to follow *Junior Books* in *Nitrigin Eireann Teoranta v Inca Alloys* (1992) holing that it was 'unique'. As regards a remedy in contract, then by analogy with *Greater Nottingham Co-Op* the contract between Bay Builders plc and Allfoods plc will be taken to have exhaustively defined the relationship between the parties, and as the contract refers only to the design and materials and not how the work is to be carried out it will give no course of action in respect of the negligent work.

Alamo Architects have also caused economic loss to Allfoods plc by their negligent supervision of the building works but they too will not be liable, see *Portsea Island Mutual Co-Op v Michael Brashier Associates* (1989) (1).

Turning now to Keepcool plc, they would be liable under normal Donoghue principles if the air conditioning could be considered as a separate item from the building. Although the House of Lords in *Murphy v Brentwood DC* (1990) held that the fine distinction that had been employed in *D & F Estates* to explain *Anns*, namely the complex structure theory where the walls of a building were considered as separate to the foundations was unrealistic and could not be sustained, the court expressly held that negligence as regards auxiliary equipment that had been provided by other parties could give rise to liability under normal *Donoghue* principles (4) and on the view that the air conditioning is separate from other property (ie the building) other property has been damaged.

One might consider here the exact extent of Keepcool's liability. Can they take advantage of the fact that they damaged an already damaged product, ie that they are not liable for the four weeks but only for the four weeks less that part of the fourth week it would have taken to complete the repair to the ceiling. Looking at the two leading cases in the House of Lords on successive causes, *Baker v Willoughby* (1970) and *Jobling v Associated Dairies* (1982) it seems that the court reached opposite conclusions, in one case to prevent the plaintiffs from being over compensated (*Jobling*) and in the other to prevent under compensation (*Baker*). Assuming that a future court follows this pragmatic approach, as the loss due to the ceiling is not compensatable Keepcool should be liable for the whole of the four week loss and any overlap with the ceiling repair will be ignored.

Note

1   If Alamo Architects provided Allfoods plc with a written statement stating that the work had been properly carried out then the judgment of Lord Keith in *Murphy v Brentwood*

District Council (1990) suggests that it could be treated as a *Hedley Byrne* case, and then economic loss could be recovered.

Question 8

Alan is burnt to death in a car accident caused by the negligence of Brian. Charles and Daphne witnessed the accident and Daphne unsuccessfully tried to rescue Alan.

Alan's wife, Elaine, was told of the accident and saw Alan's mutilated body at the hospital and Alan's mother, Freda, saw the accident live on television during an outside broadcast concerning redundancies at a nearby factory. Alan's father, George, was told of the accident but could not bring himself to see Alan's body. Henry and James also witnessed the accident; Henry knew that Alan had in the car the only handwritten copy of his PhD thesis which Henry had taken three years to complete and James realised that Alan was wearing James' evening suit which James had lent Alan.

Advise all the parties (other than Alan), who have suffered nervous shock, whether they can sue Brian.

Answer plan

This is a wide ranging question on nervous shock and should only be attempted by candidates who have a good knowledge of the recent developments in this area.

The following points should be considered:
- criteria for liability laid down in Alcock
- factors which may negative liability, eg intervention of third parties
- possible extension of liability to bystanders, TV viewers

Answer

The law on nervous shock, or psychiatric damage as it is sometimes called, has developed considerably since the original refusal to impose liability in *Victorian Railway Commissioners v Coulthas* (1888), and it has progressed from allowing recovery where the plaintiff was reasonably put in fear of her own safety - *Dulieu v White* (1901) - to allowing recovery for a wide range of persons, though with the exception of rescuers, *Chadwick v British Transport Commission* (1967), these persons have usually been close family members - see the speech of Lord Wilberforce in *McLoughlin v O'Brian*.

However, all liability for nervous shock must now be considered in the light of the recent decision of the House of Lords in *Alcock v Chief Constable of South Yorkshire* (1991). In *McLoughlin* the House of Lords considered the area of nervous shock and held that the test to be applied was whether it was reasonably foreseeable that the plaintiff would suffer nervous shock as a result of the defendant's negligence. However, the House adopted two distinct approaches to liability; Lord Wilberforce held that as nervous shock is capable of affecting such a wide range of persons there was a need for the law to place some limitations on claims and he considered that there were three elements inherent in any claim, namely the class of persons who could claim, the proximity of such persons to the accident in time and space and the means by which the shock was caused. Lord Bridges considered that this approach would place arbitrary limits on recovery and preferred the test of reasonable foreseeability simpliciter. In *Alcock* the House of Lords adopted Lord Wilberforce's approach and held that a plaintiff could only recover for nervous shock if he satisfied both the test of reasonable forseeability that he would be so affected because of the close relationship of love and affection with the primary victim, and the test of proximity to the tortfeasor in terms of physical and temporal connection between the plaintiff and the accident.

Hence a plaintiff could only recover if:

i) his relationship to the primary victim was sufficiently close that it was reasonably foreseeable that he might suffer nervous shock;

ii) his proximity to the accident or its immediate aftermath was sufficiently close in both time and space; and

iii) he suffered nervous shock through seeing or hearing the accident or its immediate aftermath.

Thus, a plaintiff who suffered psychiatric illness not caused by sudden nervous shock through seeing or hearing the accident or its immediate aftermath or who suffered nervous shock caused by being informed of the accident by a third party did not satisfy the tests of reasonable forseeability or proximity. Also, given the television broadcasting guidelines, persons who witnessed a disaster live on television had not suffered nervous shock induced by the sight and hearing of the event as they were not in proximity to the event and did not suffer nervous shock in the sense of a sudden assault on the nervous system.

The House of Lords also held that the class of persons who may claim for nervous shock was not limited to particular relationships such as husband and wife or parent and child, and went on to suggest that a bystander who witnessed a particularly horrific catastrophe may be able to recover and that in certain circumstances a plaintiff may recover on witnessing an event on contemporaneous television.

We shall, therefore, apply the criteria in *Alcock* to each potential plaintiff in turn.

Before we apply these criteria to the parties in question it is worth noting that by nervous shock we mean actual mental injury or psychiatric illness, and that mere grief and sorrow is insufficient: *Brice v Brown* (1984), although in *Re The Herald of Free Enterprise* (1989), it was held that post traumatic stress disorder and pathological grief in excess of normal grief are recognised psychiatric illnesses for which compensation can be awarded. Thus, the Court of Appeal recently held in *Nicholls v Rushton* (1992), that a plaintiff who had undergone no physical injury but who suffered a nervous reaction falling short of an identifiable psychological illness could not recover. Hence all the potential plaintiffs in this question would have to show that they had suffered an actual psychological illness before any recovery was possible.

Charles

Charles is apparently a mere bystander and has no close relationship of love and affection with Alan. *Prima facie*, therefore, he cannot recover. However, the absence of the necessary relationship is only a presumption that Charles could rebut by proving that such a relationship did in fact exist. In addition, it was suggested in *Alcock* that a bystander who witnessed a particularly horrific catastrophe could recover and it would be a question of fact for the court to decide whether this particular accident came within that definition.

Daphne

Although Daphne is also apparently a mere bystander with no close relationship of love and affection with Alan, *Alcock* expressly preserved the right of rescuers to recover (as the presence of a rescuer is reasonably foreseeable) as in *Chadwick v British Transport Commission* (1967). Hence Daphne can recover relying on her status as a rescuer, and, of course, could also recover if she could prove the required relationship of love and affection with Alan or that the accident was a 'particularly horrific catastrophe' in the same way that Charles could.

Elaine

Elaine, as Alan's wife, has the required relationship of love and affection with Alan. The law will presume that such a relationship exists between spouses, and it will be up to Brian to adduce evidence to show that in this particular case the required relationship is absent (eg evidence that Alan and Elaine had separated prior to the accident, etc). However, even if Elaine can show the required relationship a problem arises in that Elaine did not directly witness the accident to Alan but was told of the accident and saw Alan's mutilated body at the hospital. It seems clear from *Alcock* that if Elaine's nervous shock was caused by being told of the accident that she cannot recover. If, however, her nervous shock was caused by seeing Alan's mutilated body, ie by seeing the immediate aftermath then *prima facie* she can recover: *McLoughlin*; *Alcock*. Even in this situation, Elaine must show that she was reasonably proximate in time and space to the accident. In *McLoughlin* recovery was allowed where the plaintiff came upon the aftermath of the accident within two hours of the accident, and this was regarded by Lord Wilberforce as being on the borderline of recovery. Thus, Elaine will have to show both that her nervous shock was caused by the sight of Alan"s mutilated body and that she saw the aftermath within a reasonable time.

Note that in *Alcock* Lord Oliver stated that two persons who were at the actual football ground were not sufficiently proximate in time and space. He stated that what they saw was distressing and caused worry and concern but that they did not perceive the actual consequences until later. Similarly, he held that the shock to television viewers arose not from the transmitted images but from the worry and concern about the possible consequences, followed at a later time by confirmation of those consequences, ie that a gradual perception was insufficient and that an assault on the nervous system was required. This approach poses problems for Elaine, making it vital that she can show that her nervous shock was caused by the sight of Alan's mutilated body and that this occurred within a reasonable time of the accident.

Elaine should also be advised that the High Court decision in *Ravenscroft v Rederiaktiebolaget Transatlantic* (1991), in which a mother was allowed to recover in respect of nervous shock caused by her son's death, even though she was not present at the accident or its immediate aftermath, was disapproved of in *Alcock* and has now been overruled by the Court of Appeal (1992). The similar case of *Hevican v Ruane* (1991), in which a father was allowed to recover for nervous shock suffered as a cumulative result of learning some time after an accident that this son was involved, being told later that his son had died in the accident and later seeing his son's body, was also disapproved of in *Alcock*. *Hevican* was not specifically overruled in *Alcock*, but on the basis of *Alcock* and the Court of Appeal decisions in *Ravenscroft* it can clearly no longer be relied upon.

Freda

As with Elaine, Freda has the required relationship from which a presumption of love and affection arises, and Brian must adduce evidence if he wishes to rebut this presumption. In *Alcock* it was specifically suggested that a plaintiff could recover for nervous shock suffered as a result of witnessing an accident live on television (although on the facts of *Alcock* recover was not allowed in the circumstances).

However, although Freda's witnessing of the accident on simultaneous television is not fatal to her case, she must show that nervous shock was reasonably foreseeable. In Freda's case it seems that her nervous shock was not reasonably foreseeable, as the television transmission was not connected with Brian's driving but was rather connected with the redundancies at the nearby factory. In *Alcock*, the viewing of the football match by close relatives of the persons injured was foreseeable, as were the parents in the example given by Nolan LJ in the Court of Appeal and agreed by Lord Ackner and Lord Oliver in the House of Lords. Thus, it seems that Freda will fail at the first hurdle, namely that of reasonable foreseeability (1).

George

Again, as with Elaine and Freda, George has the relationship from which the presumption of the necessary tie of love and affection will arise. George's problem in recovering is that he neither witnessed the accident nor its immediate aftermath, and so by *Alcock* he cannot recover.

Recovery was allowed in similar circumstances in *Ravenscroft* in the HIgh Court, but this was overruled by the Court of Appeal on the grounds that the necessity of the nervous shock being caused by sight or hearing of the accident or its immediate aftermath was part of the ratio decidendi of *Alcock*. The problems of relying on *Hevican* have already been considered when we advised Freda.

Henry

Henry is in a slightly different position to the previous parties in that he has suffered nervous shock as a result of witnessing property damage. In *Attia v British Gas* (1988) recovery was allowed for nervous shock consequent upon property damage, and reasonable foreseeability was used as the criterion. Since *Alcock*, in which property damage was not discussed, it seems unlikely that reasonable foreseeability alone is a sufficient test - presumably there must be some form of proximity between the plaintiff and the property destroyed. In *Attia* Bingham LJ gave as an example of allowable recovery nervous shock suffered by a scholar who saw his life's work destroyed before his eyes by the defendant's negligence. This example is close to Henry's situation, but the nervous shock would still have to be reasonably foreseeable by Brian. Brian would not have to foresee the presence of the thesis in Alan's car, merely that Alan had in his car property belonging to a third party. Once Brian can foresee the presence of a third party's property in Alan's car, the value of that property is immaterial as Brian takes his victim as he finds him. As the presence of a third party's property is foreseeable it is submitted that Brian would be liable for Henry's nervous shock.

James

Again James has suffered nervous shock consequent upon property damage, but it is submitted that nervous shock following the destruction of his evening suit is unforeseeable and, thus, James cannot recover (2).

Notes

1   In *Alcock* it was held that nervous shock to television viewers who possessed the necessary ties of love and affection with the primary victims was not foreseeable, because the defendant was aware of the code of ethics followed by the television authorities that they would not show pictures of suffering any recognisable individuals. Indeed, it was accepted by counsel for the plaintiffs that had these guidelines been breached that would have constituted a *novus actus interveniens* which would have broken the chain of causation between the defendant's negligence and the plaintiffs' nervous shock. This would also mitigate against Brian being found liable for Freda's nervous shock.

2   By analogy one might mention that the Australian decision which denied recovery to a plaintiff who suffered nervous shock as a result of seeing her pet cat killed: *Davies v Bennison* (1927).

Question 9

Although it would seem that the law does not normally allow direct recovery for pure economic loss due to negligent acts, such loss can be recovered by indirect routes.

Discuss.

Answer plan

This question calls for a discussion of the present position as regards recovery for pure economic loss due to negligent acts, together with a consideration of the other legal routes to such recovery, namely by relying on contract or negligent mis-statement.

The following aspects should be discussed:

- pure economic loss before *Junior Books*
- the decision in *Junior Books*
- resiling from *Junior Books*
- possible use of contractual remedies
- possible reliance on negligent mis-statement

Answer

The rule on economic loss was that economic loss could be
recovered where it was consequent upon damage to the property
or person of the plaintiff; if no such damage had occurred then the
loss was pure economic loss and was irrevocable: *Spartan Steels &
Alloys v Martin* (1972). *Spartan Steel* is an excellent example of the
rule in practice as regards both its application and its arbitrary
nature. The defendants carelessly severed a power cable leading to
the plaintiffs' factory, and the electricity supply was cut off for
some 14 hours. The plaintiffs' business was the production of
various alloys using electrically heated furnaces. As a result of the
power cut some molten metal which was in a furnace at the time
was damaged and the plaintiffs lost the profit they would
otherwise have made on the sale of this batch. In addition, because
of the power cut, the plaintiffs could not run some additional
batches through the furnaces as they had intended. It was held by
the Court of Appeal that the plaintiffs could recover for the
damage to the actual batch that was in the furnace at the time of
the power cut, together with the profit that that batch would have
yielded. However, they could not recover for the loss of profits on
the additional batches they would have run but for the power cut.
This latter loss was pure economic loss and was irrecoverable.
Lord Denning justified this conclusion mainly on the grounds of
public policy, citing the 'floodgates' argument, the possibility of
fraudulent claims which would be difficult to check, and the fact
that most people who are inconvenienced by power cuts just put
up with it and work a little harder the next day to make up any
economic loss, an attitude Lord Denning said the law should
encourage. However, Edmund Davies LJ said that he did not think
that these policy consideration were legal principles, and that he
thought that pure economic loss could be recovered provided that
it was reasonably foreseeable and a direct consequence of the
breach of duty. He dismissed the floodgates and fraudulent claims
arguments as far fetched. This was a dissenting judgment, but ten
years later the House of Lords in *Junior Books v Veitchi* (1983)
allowed recovery for pure economic loss, holding that nominated
sub-contractors were liable to building owners for economic loss
caused by the faulty laying of a floor which posed no danger to
health and damaged no other property of the plaintiff. The

decision was based on the grounds that there was such a relationship of proximity between the parties that the defendant owed a duty of care not simply not to cause harm to the plaintiff but to avoid faults being present in their work. Several factors were emphasised by the House in coming to this conclusion: the fact that the plaintiffs had nominated the defendants to carry out the work and were relying on the defendants to do this work properly; that the defendants knew that the plaintiffs were relying on this skill and that the damage was a direct and foreseeable result of the defendants carelessness. Lord Brandon dissented on the ground that the decision effectively contractual obligations between non-contracting parties, and as there was no danger to the plaintiffs or their property the case did not come within *Donoghue v Stevenson* (1932).

Junior Books has been subject to intense judicial criticism, and later cases have tended to confine it within its specific facts. Thus, in *Aswan Engineering Establishment v Lupdine* (1987) Lloyd LJ stated that where a defect renders the property less valuable the plaintiff's remedy lies in tort but where it created damage to other property of the plaintiff the remedy lies in tort and that *Junior Books* was the first case to cross this line. Following this reiteration of the pre-*Junior Books* situation, in *Simaan General Contracting v Pilkington Glass* (1988) where a nominated sub-contractor's carelessness caused the plaintiff pure economic loss it was held that the plaintiff could not sue the sub-contractor in the absence of a contract. But in *Greater Nottingham Co-operative Society v Cementation Piling & Foundation* (1989), where there was a contract between the plaintiff and a nominated sub-contractor, it was held that the existence of this contract precluded a duty of care in tort. The contract in question related to the supply of materials and not to how the work was to be done, and the court held that this contract exhaustively defined the relationship between the parties. In *D & F Estates v Church Commissioners* (1989) the House of Lords held that a builder was not liable for pure economic loss caused by him, and in *Murphy v Brentwood District Council* (1990) the House of Lords again refused to allow recovery for pure economic loss. in *D & F Estates* Lord Bridge stated of *Junior Books* that 'the consensus of judicial opinion seems to be ... that the decision cannot be regarded as laying down any principle of general application in the law of tort' and Lord Oliver stated that it 'was really of no use as an authority on the general duty of care'. In *Simaan General Contracting* Dillon LJ went so far as to say that *Junior Books* had been 'the subject of so much analysis and discussion with differing explanations of the basis of the case that the case cannot now be regarded as a useful pointer to any development of law ... indeed I find it difficult to see that future citation from *Junior Books* can ever serve any useful purpose' (1).

From the above discussion it can be seen that it is most unlikely that a future court would follow *Junior Books*, so that recovery for pure economic loss via this route is most unlikely. However, the decision in *Greater Nottingham Co-operative Society* does point to a possible route, namely by a contract with the builder or sub-contractor in question. Following *Nottingham Co-op* the contract would have to cover all the possible modes in which the work could be performed defectively, as such a contract would exhaustively define the relationship between the parties. Problems could arise relating to privity and consideration, especially where builders and subsequent tenants are concerned. Possibly developers could assign their contractual rights to subsequent purchasers, or purchasers could obtain a collateral warranty from the builders and any sub-contractors, and provide consideration for this warranty, a solution that has been suggested by E McKendrick (1989) NLJ 624.

As an alternative a future purchaser might rely on dicta of Lord Keith in *Murphy* where he stated that he regarded *Junior Books* as failing within the principle of *Hedley Byrne v Heller* (1963). Thus, presumably, an owner could obtain a statement from a sub-contractor (or a subsequent purchaser from a builder) to the effect that the work has been carried out in a workmanlike and professional manner and relying on this statement proceed with the transaction. Such methods of sidestepping the problem of pure economic loss would be fraught with difficulties, and might well meet with hostile judicial interpretation of the contracts or duty of care on which the plaintiff relies, but it does seem certain that it is more likely to be successful than a simple reliance on *Junior Books*.

Note

1   As an example of the differing explanations of the basis of the
     case one might mention that in *Murphy*, Lord Bridge stated
     that he regarded *Junior Books* as being a *Hedley Byrne* case. It
     came as no surprise, therefore, when the High Court recently
     in *Nitrigin Eireann Teoranta v Inca Alloys* (1992) refused to
     follow *Junior Books* holding that it was 'unique'.

Chapter 3

Negligence - Breach Causation and Remoteness of Damage

Introduction

Questions involving breach, causation and remoteness of damage are popular with examiners, either as questions in their own right or as part of a question. Thus, the rule that a tortfeasor takes his victim as he finds him often features as part of a negligence question.

Checklist

Students must be familiar with the following areas:

- Breach:
    Standard and guidelines used to assess whether defendant's actions fall within standard
    Res ipsa loquitur
- Causation:
    The 'but for' test
- Remoteness:
    Reasonable foreseeability and the egg shell skull rule
    Novus actus interveniens

Question 10

One day when walking home William trips and falls, damaging his knee. Several days later while driving to work he sees Victor crossing the road and brakes to avoid running into him. Unfortunately, due to the pain in William's knee, he cannot fully press his brake pedal and as a result runs into Victor. The collision occurs at a fairly slow speed and a normal person would only have suffered bruising as a result, but Victor has brittle bones and suffers two broken legs and a number of broken ribs. He is taken to the local hospital where, due to an administrative mistake, his right arm is amputated.

Advise Victor.

Answer plan

This is a straightforward question on breach and causation together with remoteness of damage, the egg shell skull rule and *novus actus interveniens*. As it is relatively simple care must be taken to discuss the relevant legal principles in depth.

The following issues need to be considered:

- breach of duty by William
- William takes Victor as he finds him
- amputation of arm - *novus actus interveniens* by hospital

Answer

It is well established law that a road user owes a duty of care to other road users,including pedestrians: *Donoghue v Stevenson* (1932); *Roberts v Ramsbottom* (1980). Where a duty of care has been previously found to exist that there is no need to apply the modern formulation preferred by the House of Lords in *Caparo v Dickman* (1990) or *Murphy v Brentwood District Council* (1990). One could also note the statement of Potts J at first instance in *B v Islington Health Authority* (1991) where he stated that in personal injury cases the duty of care remains as it was pre-*Caparo*, namely the foresight of a reasonable person as in *Donoghue*, a finding that does not appear to have been disturbed on appeal (1992). As William owes Victor a duty of care we must next consider whether he is in breach of this duty of care. The standard of care required is the objective one of a reasonable person; thus, in *Blyth v Birmingham Water Works* (1856) Alderson B stated 'Negligence is the omission to do something which a reasonable man, guided upon those conditions which ordinarily regulate the conduct of human affairs, would do, or the doing of something which a prudent and reasonable man would not do'. It is important that the correct question is addressed - the question is not did William act reasonably, but what would a reasonable person, placed in his position, have done, and did William meet that standard. Applying this objective standard to car drivers it can be seen that the correct standard to adopt is that of the reasonable, competent driver. Thus, it is irrelevant that a particular driver is a learner - *Nettleship v Weston* (1971) or through no fault of his own he cannot fully control the car for medical reasons and he is otherwise not at fault: *Roberts v Ramsbottom* (1980).

To hold otherwise, as Megaw LJ pointed out in *Nettleship* would mean adopting a variable standard which could not logically be confined to car drivers and would have to be a universal principle giving great uncertainty and making it impossible to arrive at consistent decisions. Thus, William must be judged by the standard of the reasonable, competent driver, and he clearly does not meet this standard. The fact that this is due to a medical reason which is outside his control is irrelevant: *Roberts v Ramsbottom* (1). Having decided that William is in breach of his duty we must now determine whether his breach caused Victor's injuries. Turning first to Victor's broken legs and ribs it is clear, applying the 'but for' test proposed by Lord Denning in *Cork v Kirby MacLean* (1952) that this damage would not have happened but for his breach of duty. Hence William will be liable for Victor's broken legs provided that the damage is not too remote, and the test for remoteness of damage is that the damage must have been reasonably foreseeable: *The Wagon Mound* (No 1) (1961) AC 388. However, the important question is just what damage has to be foreseeable to render that damage not too remote, and for damage to the person as long as some personal injury is foreseeable it does not matter that the exact consequences were unforeseeable, see eg *Dulieu v White* (1901) and *Smith v Leech, Brain* (1962). Thus, William must take his victim as he finds him with brittle bones.

We must now consider whether William is responsible for Victor's amputated arm. Applying the 'but for' test, and as a matter of pure logic, but for William's negligence Victor would not have been at the hospital and the amputation would not, therefore, have taken place. But we need to consider whether there has been a break in the chain of causation, ie whether the negligence of the hospital constitutes a *novus actus interveniens*. The new act is that of a third party over which William has no control, and to break the chain of causation it must be something unwarrantable, a new cause which disturbs the sequence of events, something which can be described as either unreasonable or extraneous or extrinsic per Lord Wright in *The Oropesa* (1943). Thus, the defendant will remain liable if the act of the third party is not truly independent of the defendant's negligence; it seems in William's case that the act of the hospital does satisfy this criterion. In *Knightley v Johns* (1982) a third party acted negligently and the court held that negligent conduct was more likely to break the chain of causation than non-negligent conduct, and that in *Knightley* there were so many errors and departures from the common sense procedures that the chain of causation had been broken. Looking at the facts of Victor's case it seems that the hospital has been negligent and there must have been some errors and departures from common sense procedures; hence the chain of causation has been broken and, thus, William is not liable for the amputated arm but liability for this damage will rest with the hospital.

As presumably Victor was under anaesthetic when his arm was amputated he may have problems in proving the hospital's lack of care. However, in such a situation he can rely on the maxim *res ipsa loquitur*, ie the thing speaks for itself, and where the maxim applies the court may be prepared to find a breach of duty in the absence of specific evidence of the defendant's actions - see for example *Scott v London and St Katherine's Docks* (1865.

For the maxim to be applicable it must be shown:

a) that the defendant is in control of the thing which caused injury to the plaintiff
b) that the accident would not have occurred in the ordinary course of events without negligence
c) that there is no explanation for the accident

An example of the maxim in action is *Mahon v Osborne* (1939) where a surgeon left a swab in a patient's body, which is similar to Victor's case. The application of the maxim will not shift the burden of proof, which will remain on Victor throughout, *Ng Chun Pui v Lee Chuen Tat* (1988), but it will allow the court to draw on inference of negligence, per Lord Griffiths in *Ng Chun Pui*.

Thus, Victor is advised to sue William in respect of his broken legs and ribs and the hospital in respect of the amputated arm.

Note

1   One might also mention here that William is in breach of duty to all other road users in that he is driving when he knows or ought to know that his ability to control his vehicle is impaired.

Question 11

Dennis works as a labourer for Hopeless plc and needs to use a ladder to carry out some work. He collects a ladder from Eric in the stores but when he is halfway up the ladder Dennis steps on a faulty rung and falls to the ground, cutting his shoulder. He goes to his doctor and is given an anti-tetanus injection to which he is allergic and he suffers such an adverse reaction that he is off work for three months without pay. Hopeless plc deny any liability pointing out that is is a strict company rule that if an employee uses a ladder he must place a restraining block behind it to ensure that it does not slip and that Dennis had neglected to do this.

Advise Dennis.

Answer plan

This question covers a variety of topics including employer liability, causation and remoteness of damage.

The following points must be examined:
- Hopeless' duty to Dennis
- Hopeless in breach of duty
- Hopeless' liability for costs and loss of wages
- liability of Dennis's doctor for loss of wages
- effect of Dennis's non-compliance with ladder rule

Answer

It is trite law that Hopeless as Dennis's employer owe Dennis a duty of care to take reasonable care for Dennis's safety. In particular Hopeless owes Dennis a duty to provide properly maintained plant and equipment: *Smith v Baker* (1891). This is a primary, non delegable duty, that rests with the employer and in addition Hopeless will be vicariously liable for any negligence on the part of Eric while Eric is acting in the course of his employment.

As regards these duties, where a duty of care has been previously found to exist, as in the employer/employee situation (ie Hopeless plc and Dennis) and between fellow employees (ie Eric and Dennis), there is no need to apply the modern test to determine the existence of a duty of care preferred by the House of Lords in *Caparo v Dickman* (1990) and *Murphy v Brentwood District Council* (1990). One could also note the statement of Potts J at first instance in *B v Islington Health Authority* (1991) where he said that in personal injury cases the duty of care remains as it was pre-*Caparo*, namely the foresight of a reasonable person as in *Donoghue v Stevenson*, a finding that does not appear to have been disturbed on appeal (1992).

Taking these two possible causes of action in turn as the ladder with which Dennis has been supplied is defective Hopeless is in breach of its duty to provide properly maintained plant and equipment. It would be no defence to Hopeless to allege that it bought the ladder from a reputable supplier and had no reason to suspect that it was defective as by s 1 Employers' Liability (Defective Equipment) Act 1969 where an employee suffers personal injury in the course of his employment in consequence of a defect in equipment provided by his employer for the purposes of the employer's business and the defect is attributable wholly or partly to the fault of a third party (whether identified or not) the injury shall be deemed to be also attributable to negligence on the part of the employer. In addition Eric owes Dennis a duty of care under straightforward Donoghue principles. It may well be the case that Eric was in breach of his duty by failing to notice that the ladder had a faulty rung and as we have the employer/employee relationship between Hopeless and Eric and Eric is acting in the course of his employment then Hopeless will be vicariously liable for Eric's negligence.

In both situations as we have shown the existence of a duty of care and a breach of that duty we need to consider whether the damage suffered by Dennis was caused by the breach. Applying the 'but for' test described by Lord Denning in *Cork v Kirby MacLean* (1952) it seems clear that the damage to Dennis would not have occurred but for the faulty rung, ie for the breach. The effect of Dennis ignoring the company rule regarding the restraining block is irrelevant to the question of causation for even if Dennis had complied with this rule the damage would still have occurred: see *Barnett v Chelsea & Kensington Hospital Management Committee* (1968). In *Barnett*, a man went to the casualty department of a hospital complaining of vomiting. The doctor on casualty duty refused to examine him and sent him home. Some five hours later the man died from arsenical poisoning. It was held that the doctor was negligent in not examining the man, but that this negligence had not caused the man's death, as even if the doctor had examined and treated him, he would still have died as the poisoning could not have been detected and cured in time. Similarly, even if Dennis had placed a restraining block behind the ladder, the faulty rung would have caused his fall to the ground.

We now need to see whether all or any of the damage suffered by Dennis is too remote, ie whether or not the damage is reasonably foreseeable, *The Wagon Mound* (No 1) (1961). For damage to the person the requirement is that some damage is foreseeable and it is irrelevant that the specific damage suffered cannot be foreseen: *Dulieu v White* (1901); *Smith v Leech, Brain* (1962). It is often said that the tortfeasor takes his victim as he finds him. Clearly, therefore, Hopeless will be liable for the cut to Dennis's shoulder and we must consider whether or not Hopeless is liable for the three months' loss of wages. In *Robinson v Post Office* (1974) the plaintiff was injured at work and suffered an allergic reaction to an anti-tetanus injection; it was held by the court that the defendants were liable for this reaction, because the need for such an injection was reasonably foreseeable and the defendant must take the victim as he finds him. However, it is vital to note that no test for allergic reaction was carried out, and even if it had been done there would have been no indication of allergy (see *Barnett* again). But medical science has advanced from 1974 and if a test is now available that would indicate an allergy in time, then Eric's doctor would be negligent in not carrying out such a test and this negligent act would break the chain of causation.

Where it is alleged that the act of a third party, over whom the plaintiff has no control, has broken the chain of causation, then it must be shown that the act was something unwarrantable, a new cause which disturbs the sequence of events. It must be something which can be described as either unreasonable or extraneous or extrinsic, per Lord Wright in *The Oropesa* (1943). Thus, the defendant will remain liable if the act of the third party is not truly independent of the defendant's negligence. In *Knightley v Johns* (1982) the Court of Appeal held that negligent conduct was more likely to break the chain of causation than non-negligent conduct, and that in *Knightley* there were so many errors and departures from the common sense procedures that the chain of causation had been broken.

If a test for the allergy exists then Eric's doctor is in breach of his duty to Eric in not carrying out such a test. In *Bolam v Friern Hospital Management Committee* (1957), it was held that in cases of alleged medical negligence the standard to be applied in determining whether a breach of duty had occurred was that of a reasonably competent medical practitioner. If such a person would have applied an allergy test (if such a test exists) and Eric's doctor did not, then the doctor is in breach of his duty to Eric, and this would amount to such an error and departure from common sense procedures as to break the chain of causation (1). In this situation Eric should sue his doctor in respect of his three months loss of wages. In the absence of such a test, then following the authority of Robinson, Hopeless plc is liable for all the damage suffered by Eric.

Note

1 One could point out here that if there were two schools of thought regarding the efficiency or wisdom of carrying out such a test, and Eric's doctor chose one school of thought rather than the other, that would not, by itself, amount to negligence: *Maynard v West Midlands Health Authority* (1985). The fact that the decision turned out to be wrong does not prove breach; the question is did the doctor display such lack of clinical judgment that no doctor, using proper care and skill, could have reached the same decision: *Maynard; Hughes v Waltham Forest Health Authority* (1990). If an ordinary skilled doctor could have made the same decision there would be no breach: *Knight v Home Office* (1990).

Question 12

Frank was knocked down by a car carelessly driven by George, and suffered a broken thigh that left him with a limp and the necessity to use a walking stick. One day he was crossing the road when he had to hurry to avoid a motor cyclist who was approaching him at a very high speed. Because of his restricted movements Frank become flustered and fell over, injuring his back on the kerb and as a result of this suffered partial paralysis of his legs. The motor cyclist drove away and cannot be traced.

Advise Frank.

Answer plan

This is an answer involving causation and successive causes which requires a consideration of *novus actus interveniens*. It is not a difficult question but it does require clear thinking and planning.

The following aspects must be analysed:

- George's liability for broken thigh
- George's possible liability for paralysis: effect of Frank's actions - *novus actus interveniens*
- George's liability for Frank's paralysis

Answer

It is well established law that a road user owes a duty of care to other road users, including pedestrians: *Donoghue v Stevenson* (1932); *Roberts v Ramsbottom* (1980). Where a duty of care has been previously found to exist that there is no need to apply the modern formulation preferred by the House of Lords in *Caparo v Dickman* (1990) or *Murphy v Brentwood District Council* (1990). One could also note the statement of Potts J at first instance n *B v Islington Health Authority* (1991) where he stated that in personal injury cases the duty of care remains as it was pre-*Caparo*, namely the foresight of a reasonable person as in *Donoghue*, a finding that does not appear to have been disturbed on appeal (1992). As George owes Frank a duty of care we must next consider whether he is in breach of this duty of care. The standard of care required is the objective one of a reasonable person; thus, in *Blyth v Birmingham Water Works* (1856) Alderson B stated 'negligence is the omission to do something which a reasonable man, guided upon those conditions which ordinarily regulate the conduct of human affairs, would do, or the doing of something which a prudent and reasonable man would not do'. It is important that the correct question is addressed - the question is not did George act reasonably, but what would a reasonable person, placed in his position, have done, and did George meet that standard. Applying this objective standard to car drivers it can be seen that the correct standard to adopt is that of the reasonable, competent driver. Thus, it is irrelevant that a particular driver is a learner - *Nettleship v Weston* (1971), or through no fault of his own he cannot fully control the car for medical reasons and he is otherwise not at fault; as Megaw LJ pointed out in *Nettleship* would mean adopting a variable standard which could not logically be confined to car drivers and would have to be a universal principle giving great uncertainty and making it impossible to arrive at consistent decisions. Thus, George must be judged by the standard of the reasonable, competent driver, and he clearly does not meet this standard. Having decided that George is in breach of his duty we must now determine whether his breach caused Frank's injuries. Turning first to Frank's broken thigh it is clear, applying the 'but for' test proposed by Lord Denning in *Cork v Kirby McLean* (1952) that this damage would not have happened but for his breach of duty. Hence George will be liable for Frank's broken legs provided that the damage is not too remote, and the test for remoteness of damage is that the damage must have been reasonably foreseeable: *The Wagon Mound* (No 1) (1961). However, the important question is just what damage has to be foreseeable to render that damage not too remote, and for damage to the person as long as some personal injury is foreseeable it does not matter that the exact consequences were unforeseeable, see eg *Dulieu v White* (1901) and *Smith v Leech, Brain* (1962).

Hence Frank should sue George in respect of the damage to his thigh but the question arises as to who is responsible for the paralysis to his legs. Normally the motor cyclist would be the proper plaintiff but as he cannot be traced Frank's only effective course of action will be to seek to prove that George was also responsible for the damage arising from the second accident.

The immediate legal problem lying in Frank's path is that George will claim that the incident involving the motor cyclist was a *novus actus interveniens* that broke the chain of causation. If the act of a third party is the true cause of the damage to the plaintiff then the defendant will not be held liable to the plaintiff. To break the chain of causation the third party's act must be 'something unwarrantable, a new cause which disturbs the sequence of events, something which can be described as either unreasonable or extraneous or extrinsic' per Lord Wright in *The Oropesa* (1943). Thus, the defendant will remain liable unless the act of the third party is truly independent of the defendant's negligence, and in George's case it seems that the negligence of the untraceable motor cyclist is truly independent of George's original negligent act. In *Knightley v Johns* (1982) the Court of Appeal held that a negligent act was more likely to break the chain of causation than a non-negligent act, and that in *Knightley* there were so many errors and departures from common sense procedures that the chain of causation had been broken.

As it seems that the motor cyclist's actions in driving at high speed was an error and departure from common sense then it is likely that he will be held liable for the cause of the paralysis and Frank will not be able to sue George in respect of this particular loss.

George could also claim that Frank caused his own paralysis by continuing to use the highways when he was not fully fit to do so. In *Wieland v Cyril Lord Carpets* (1969) the plaintiff suffered injury due to the defendant's negligence. As a result she had to wear a surgical collar which restricted her ability to use bi-focal spectacles and she fell down a flight of stairs. It was held by the House of Lords that the defendants were liable for this injury also, as the plaintiff had not been unreasonable in continuing to wear bi-focals and had been left, as a result of the first injury, in a condition where she was unable to cope with the vicissitudes of life. However, in *McKew v Holland and Hannen and Cubitts* (1969) again the plaintiff was injured by the defendant's negligence and again was left with a residual medical problem in that he occasionally lost control of his leg. Despite this the plaintiff went down a steep flight of stairs without a handrail and was injured when his leg gave way. The House of Lords held that the defendants were not liable as the plaintiff's action in going down a steep flight of stairs without a handrail was so unreasonable that it broke the chain of causation.

In Frank's case it seems that he did not act unreasonably in continuing to use the road and that his case is much closer to *Wieland* than to *McKew.*, although George can still rely on the *novus actus interveniens* defence discussed above.

However, as we are in the area of successive injuries we need to consider Frank's situation in the light of the two House of Lords decisions - *Baker v Willoughby* (1970) and *Jobling v Associated Dairies* (1982). In *Baker* the plaintiff injured a leg in a road accident and later his leg was amputated following a shooting in an armed robbery. The House of Lords held that the defendant was liable for the damage to the plaintiff's leg which was not obliterated by the subsequent amputation. An opposite conclusion was reached in *Jobling*, but in that case although the primary cause of the plaintiff's loss was the negligence of the defendant, the later cause which increased his loss was an inherent disease and the defendants were held not to be liable for any loss which accrued after this event. Frank's case is closer to *Baker* than *Jobling* suggesting that George will be liable for the loss flowing from the broken thigh and that the subsequent act of the motor cyclist will not obliterate this. As another ground to the decision in *Baker* was to prevent the plaintiff from being under-compensated, which is what would happen if the act of the motor cyclist were held to have obliterated George's negligence. This reinforces our conclusion regarding the extent of George's liability (1).

Note

1   If George were held liable for the subsequent damage it would not be open to George to argue that Frank's action in becoming flustered and falling was the true cause of the action as it was itself a *novus actus interveniens*, because George has acted as he did in the agony of the moment his actions do not appear to be unreasonable, *Jones v Boyce* (1816). Nor, on the authority of *Jones*, would Frank's action amount to contributory negligence.

Question 13

'... two causes may both be necessary preconditions of a particular result ... yet the one may, if the facts justify that conclusion, be treated as the real, substantial, direct or effective cause and the other dismissed ... and ignored for the purposes of legal liability ...' per Lord Asquith in *Stapley v Gipsum Mines* (1953).

Does this statement accurately reflect the law, and if so does it allow a judge to choose any previous act as the real cause of the plaintiff's damage?

Answer plan

This question calls for a discussion of the 'but for' test of causation, and some of the situations in which its application is not straightforward.

The following aspects of causation should be discussed:

- the 'but for' test
- pre-existing conditions
- successive causes
- *novus actus interveniens*

Answer

The test that the courts usually use in deciding whether or not a particular act was the cause of the plaintiff's damage is the 'but for' test which was elucidated by Lord Denning in *Cork v Kirby McLean* (1952) where he said 'if the damage would not have happened but for a particular fault, then that fault is the cause of the damage; if it would have happened just the same, fault or no fault, the fault is not the cause of the damage'.

A good example of this test is provided by *Barnett v Chelsea & Kensington Hospital Management Committee* (1969) where a man went to the casualty department of a hospital complaining of vomiting. The doctor refused to examine him and sent him home. Some five hours later he died from arsenical poisoning. It was held that the doctor was negligent in not examining the man, but that his negligence had not caused the man's death, as even if the doctor had examined and treated him, he still would have died as the poisoning could not have been detected and cured in time.

Although the 'but for' test works well in the vast majority of cases it does give rise to problems in some situations, especially where there is more than one possible cause of the plaintiff's loss. Thus, where the plaintiff's loss is due to a pre-existing condition rather than to the defendants actions, then the defendant may only be liable for part of the damage suffered by the plaintiff.

So in *Cutler v Vauxhall Motors* (1971) the plaintiff suffered a graze to his ankle due to the negligence of the defendants; the plaintiff had an existing varicose vein condition and as a result of the graze it was decided to operate immediately to cure this condition. It was held that the plaintiff could recover for the graze, but not for the operation as the varicose vein condition would have required an operation at some time in the future in any event. *Performance cars v Abraham* (1962) is an example of a pre-existing condition working in favour of the plaintiff rather than against him as in *Cutler*. In both *Cutler* and *Performance Cars* the pre-existing condition was treated as the effective cause of part of the plaintiff's loss.

Another area in which the 'but for' test can give rise to problems is where there is more than one cause of the plaintiff's damage, eg where two persons both cause damage to the plaintiff so that he still would have suffered damage but for the negligence of either of the defendants. In such a situation the 'but for' test would mean that neither defendant was liable to the plaintiff, but a court would not reach such a conclusion in practice. The courts tend to be rather proud of the fact that they approach causation as a matter of common sense rather than from any academic or theoretical point of view. As Lord Wright stated in *Yorkshire Dale Steamship v Minister of War Transport* (1942) 'causation is to be understood as the man in the street, and not as either the scientist or the metaphysician, would understand it'.

This common sense approach to causation can be seen in those situations in which another act has occurred after the original negligent act of the defendant, ie the *novus actus interveniens* situation. The *novus actus* may be either an act of the plaintiff or of a third party or of nature. Taking these in turn, the later act of the plaintiff which causes additional damage may be held to have broken the chain of causation between the original negligent act of the defendant and the additional damage suffered by the plaintiff, ie this later act of the plaintiff may be treated as the real or effective cause of the plaintiff's additional loss and the original negligent act of the defendant ignored for the purposes of the additional liability. However, a judge does not have a completely free choice in deciding whether or not this later act is the effective cause of the additional damage; the decided cases lay down a rule that the later act of the plaintiff will only be held to be the true cause if the additional damage where this act is unreasonable. Thus, in *McKew v Holland & Hannen & Cubitts* (1969) the House of Lords held that a plaintiff who, as a result of the defendants negligence, occasionally lost control of his leg but still went down a steep flight of stairs which had no handrail and fell when his leg gave way, could not recover for this damage. The House of Lords held that this act was so unreasonable that the original negligence of the defendants could be ignored for the purposes of legal liability. In contrast, in *Wieland v Cyril Lord Carpets* (1969), where the plaintiff as a result of the defendants negligence was unable to use her bi-focal spectacles in the normal manner, and as a result fell down a flight of stairs, it was held that the defendants were liable for this additional damage to the plaintiff as she had not acted unreasonably in continuing to wear her bi-focals. Thus a judge has a guideline in deciding whether to allow recovery for the later damage suffered by the plaintiff, although as the guideline involves a decision as to the reasonableness or otherwise of the plaintiff's conduct it will often give the judge a certain amount of discretion.

Where the later act is that of a third party, then this later act will be treated as the real cause of the plaintiff's additional damage where it is something 'ultroneous, something unwarrantable, a new cause which disturbs the sequence of events, something which can be described as either unreasonable or extraneous or extrinsic', per Lord Wright in *The Oropesa* (1943). Thus, the later act of the third party will not be treated as the true cause of the additional damage unless it is independent of the defendants original negligence. If the act of the third party is itself negligent then the courts are usually willing to hold that this act is the true cause of the plaintiff's additional damage: *Knightley v Johns* (1982) (1). Again a guideline is available to a judge, though the decision as to whether the actual later act is unreasonable or independent will involve a certain amount of discretion.

Finally, the later act may be an act of nature, and if it is independent of the original negligence of the defendant then the defendant will not be liable for the additional consequences: *Carslogie Steamship v Royal Norwegian Government* (1952). Again a test is available to the judge and again it will involve a certain amount of discretion.

Hence overall it can be seen that in a number of situations one cause may be treated as the real cause and the other cause ignored for the purposes of legal liability. This does not mean, however, that a judge has an unfettered choice as to which cause he decides is the true cause of the plaintiff's damage - there are clear guidelines the judge should follow, although as these will often involve a finding as to whether certain conduct is reasonable or unreasonable the guidelines do give the judge a certain amount of discretion (2).

Note

1   In the recent case of *Wright v Lodge* (1992) the Court of Appeal held that a driver who is involved in a collision, partly due to his own negligence, could be exonerated for responsibility for subsequent events which occurred because another driver drove recklessly if those events would not have occurred if that other driver had merely been negligent.

2   It could be noted here that an additional restriction on a judge's freedom to chose either of any previous actions as the real cause of the plaintiff's damage is the need for the plaintiff to prove causation. A plaintiff who had difficulties in this area traditionally relied on the decision of the House of Lords in *McGhee v National Coal Board* (1973). For many years the case was thought to be authority for the proposition that a plaintiff could recover if he could show that the actions of the defendant materially increased the risk of damage occurring. However, the House of Lords has recently taken a very restrictive approach to *McGhee* in *Kay v Ayrshire and Arran Health Board* (1987), *Hotson v East Berkshire AHA* (1987) and *Wilsher v Essex AHA* (1988); in *Wilsher* Lord Bridge stated that *McGhee* 'laid down no new principle of law whatsoever. On the contrary it affirmed the principle that the onus of proving causation lies on the plaintiff'. Thus, the question of whether the statement allows a judge to chose any previous act as the real cause of the damage is subject to the limitation that the causative nature of the act must be proved before it is even available to the judge as the possible real reason for the plaintiff's damage.

Breach of Statutory Duty

Introduction

Questions on breach of statutory duty often appear in examinations and usually involve a consideration as to whether as breach of statutory duty gives rise to a cause of action in tort. Such questions can also be contain issues such as causation together with employer's liability and contributory negligence.

Checklist

Students must be aware of the following areas:
- Whether breach gives rise to a tort :
  i   Presumption that enforcement provided by statute is exclusive
  ii Exception to presumption where statute enacted for the benefit of a class and where plaintiff has suffered damage in excess of that by the public at large
- If breach does give rise to a tort note the plaintiff must prove that:
  The action caused damage of a type regulated by statute
  Plaintiff is a person the statute was intended to protect
  Damage suffered is of the kind the statute was intended to protect

Question 14

Regulations made under the (fictitious) Oil Products (Protection of Workers) Act 1987 provide, inter alia, that 'Employers shall ensure that all workers engaged in the manufacture of oil products wear the protective clothing prescribed in these regulations when they are at work or likely to come into contact with oil products and shall ensure that such clothing is maintained in a good state of repair'. These regulations apply to the premises of Refiners plc.

One day Alan, who works directly with oil products, puts on a pair of protective overalls, but because he cannot be bothered to take his safety boots off he rips them down the leg. He replaces these torn overalls on a hanger and puts on a fresh pair. Shortly afterwards

Brian, who works in the accounts section, goes into an area where it is necessary to wear overalls. He puts on the torn overalls without noticing the defect and whilst in the oil product area he trips over the torn leg of the overalls and falls, injuring his elbow.

Advise Brian.

Answer plan

This is a typical breach of statutory duty question and requires consideration of the following areas:

- does breach give rise to a tort
- is damage of type intended to be prevented by statute
- employer's liability of Refiners
- Alan's liability and vicarious liability of Refiners

Answer

Brian has three possible causes of action here against Refiners. The first is for breach of statutory duty, the second is for breach of their duty as employers and, thirdly, Refiners may be vicariously liable for Alan's negligence. We shall consider each possible action in turn.

As regards possible liability for breach of statutory duty the regulations provide that the protective clothing worn by Brian 'must be maintained in a good state of repair'. The important question is just what standard of care the regulations impose on Refiners. Typically, statutory obligations are subject to a phrase such as 'so far as is reasonably practicable' when they usually add little to the common law of negligence, or are absolute when the only question to be decided is whether the statutory regulations have been met or not, the reasons for not meeting them being irrelevant to liability, eg the duty to fence dangerous machines imposed by s 14 Factories Act 1961 -see *John Summers v Frost* (1955). In the instant case the requirement is that the employer shall ensure that such clothing is maintained in a good state of repair, and as there is no relaxation of this obligation in the regulations the obligation is absolute and so they are in breach of their statutory duty. The next question to be decided is whether or not this breach gives rise to an action in tort. (The correct test is to see whether the regulations on their true construction confer upon Brian a right of action in tort: *Cutler v Wandsworth Stadium* (1949). If the regulations address this point eg Guard Dogs Act 1975 s 5(1) then that disposes of the matter, but if as is usual the statute (or regulations) is silent on the point then the court must ascertain the intention of Parliament. In the House of Lords in *Lonrho v Shell Petroleum* (1982) Lord Diplock stated that the initial presumption was that where the statute created an obligation together with a means of enforcing that obligation, eg by a criminal penalty then the obligation cannot be enforced in any other way. We are not told of any such means in the regulations but even so the presence of a criminal penalty would not necessarily be fatal to Brian's case: in *Atkinson v Newcastle Waterworks* (1877) the imposition of a fine for breach of a statutory duty was held to be exclusive, whereas in *Groves v Lord Wimborne* (1898) the provision in the regulations of a fine for breach was held not to deny the plaintiff a cause of action. It is worth noting in this respect that in *Groves*, as in the present case, the statute was enacted for the benefit of a class. The absence of any such provision would make it easier for Brian to claim that a right in tort existed: *Thornton v Kirklees Metropolitan Borough Council* (1979). Lord Diplock continued to state that there were two exceptions to this general rule and one is relevant here, namely when the statute is enacted for the benefit of a class of persons and the plaintiff is a member of that class. As employees are regarded as a class of persons for whose benefit industrial safety legislation is enacted, as in *Groves*, it would seem that *prima facie* Brian can sue in respect of Refiners' breach of statutory duty.

However, Brian has only cleared the first hurdle here; the next thing he must prove is the act which caused the damage is regulated by statute; that he was one of the persons the statute were intended to protect and that damage suffered was of a kind that the statute was intended to prevent.

Brian should have no problem with the first two requirements, but he will have a problem with the third. It seems from the regulations that the requirement to provide protective clothing in good condition was to stop oil products from coming into contact with a person's body and not to prevent tripping or falling. In *Gorris v Scott* (1874) a shipowner was required by statute to provide pens on board his ship for cattle. He failed to do this and the plaintiff's cattle were swept overboard. It was held that the shipowner was not liable, because the damage the statute was intended to prevent was the spread of contagious diseases and not to prevent the cattle being swept overboard.

By analogy with *Gorris v Scott* it would seem that Brian cannot bring himself under the ambit of the statute.

We must next consider whether Brian can sue Refiners in negligence. As Brian's employer Refiners owes Brian a duty of care to provide proper plant and equipment, *Smith v Baker* (1891), clothing comes under the definition of equipment (see eg s 1(1) Employers Liability (Defective Equipment) Act 1969). However, this duty is not an absolute one but merely to take reasonable care for the employees' safety. In *Toronto Power v Paskwan* (1915) Sir Arthur Channell stated 'if in the course of working plant becomes defective and the defect is not brought to the master's knowledge and could not by reasonable diligence have been discovered by him the master is not liable'. As we are told that Brian put on the overalls 'shortly afterwards' it would not seem that Refiners plc is in breach of its duty regarding equipment. Brian could perhaps attempt to show that Refiners are in breach of their duty to provide a safe system of work in that they have failed to provide a disposal system for torn overalls and a sufficient quantity of overalls in good condition. Refiners could reply that they do normally meet these two requirements of a safe system of work and that it was the action of Alan in replacing the overalls that was the cause of the damage, but in *McDermid v Nash Dredging & Reclaimation* (1987) the House of Lords held that the duty of the employer was not just to provide a safe system of work but to ensure that a safe system was actually operated. Such a duty is non-delegable and it would be no defence to Refiners to show that they delegated performance to an employee who they reasonably believed to be competent to perform it (per Lord Brandon).

It is clear that Alan himself owes Brian a duty of care under normal *Donoghue v Stevenson* (1932) principles, in that he can reasonably foresee that any lack of care on his part may cause injury to Brian. There is no need to apply the modern formulation preferred by the House of Lords in *Caparo v Dickman* (1990) and *Murphy v Brentwood District Council* (1990). Indeed in *B v Islington Health Authority* at first instance Potts J stated that in personal injury cases the duty of care remained as it was pre-*Caparo*, namely the foresight of a reasonable person as in Donoghue, a finding that does not appear to have been disturbed on appeal (1992). Alan will be in breach of this duty if a reasonable person, placed in his position, would not have acted in this way: *Blyth v Birmingham Waterworks* (1856), and it is submitted that a reasonable person would not have replaced the torn overalls on the hanger but would have disposed of them in a safe manner. This breach must have caused Brian's damage, and the 'but for' test in *Cork v Kirby MacLean* (1952) proves the required causal connection. Additionally, the damage suffered by Brian must not be too remote in that it must be reasonably foreseeable: *The Wagon Mound* (1961). All that Alan need foresee is some personal injury; he need foresee neither the extent: *Smith v Leech, Brain* (1962) nor the exact manner in which the damage occurs: *Hughes v Lord Advocate* (1963). All these criteria are satisfied and so Alan has been negligent as regards his conduct to Brian. As Alan is an employee of Refiners, and was acting in the course of his employment when this negligence took place, it follows that Refiners are vicariously liable for Alan's negligence.

It could be argued that neither Refiners' breach of statutory duty nor Alan's breach of common law duty caused Brian's damage, rather it was Brian's decision to use a damaged overall that caused the damage, ie that this action by Brian constituted a *novus actus interveniens* which broke the chain of causation. A subsequent act of the plaintiff may amount to a *novus actus* where his conduct has been so careless that his damage can no longer be attributed to the negligence of the defendant. An examination of the two leading cases in this area, *McKew v Holland & Hannel & Cubitts* (1969) and *Wieland v Cyril Lord Carpets* (1969), shows that the test the courts apply is whether the plaintiffs conduct was reasonable or not, and if it is unreasonable it will break the chain of causation. It does not seem unreasonable of Brian, who normally has no need to wear overalls, to assume that those provided by Refiners are in good condition. Also, as regards Refiners' breach of statutory duty, in *Westwood v Post Office* (1974) it was held that the fact that the plaintiff was a trespasser did not allow the defendants to act in breach of their statutory duty, and that the plaintiff was entitled to assume that the defendants would comply with their statutory obligations. Thus, *Westwood* would dispose of this argument (if it were to be decided that this case fell outside of *Gorris v Scott*). It is more likely that a defence of contributory negligence might succeed in reducing Brian's damages if it could be shown that Brian had taken insufficient care for his own safety: *Jones v Livox Quarries* (1952), and as there seems to be not emergency as in *Jones v Boyce* (1861), contributory negligence cannot be ruled out.

Question 15

Colin, Donald and Edgar are employed by Apex Manufacturing plc as maintenance workers. One of their jobs is to repair the ventilation system that is set close to the ceiling of Apex's premises. To do this they have to work on a cage which is supported by tall stilts and is moved via wheels at the base of the stilts and has a highly efficient braking system. Statutory regulations prohibit the moving of this piece of equipment while persons are in the cage. In order to save time Colin, who has the job of moving the cage, moves it along while Donald and Edgar are still in the cage. Colin does this twice without mishap but on the third occasion Donald sees that the cage is approaching a projection in the ceiling, panics and jumps out. Colin immediately applies the brakes and Edgar is thrown out of the cage.

Advise both Donald and Edgar who have suffered injuries.

Answer plan

This is a relatively straightforward breach of statutory duty question that also involves employer's liability, vicarious liability, *volenti* and *novus actus interveniens*.

The following aspects should be discussed:

• does breach give rise to a tort
• Apex's liability in employer's liability
• vicarious liability of Apex

Answer

Donald and Edgar have a number of possible causes of action against Apex, firstly, for breach of statutory duty, secondly, for breach of their common law employer's duties and, thirdly, as being vicariously liable for Colin's negligence.

Considering first any liability for breach of statutory duty, as the statutory regulations prohibit the moving of the cage whilst persons are in the cage there has been a clear breach of the regulations. It is, therefore, necessary to consider whether this breach gives rise to a cause of action in tort.

The correct test is to see whether the regulations on their true construction confer upon Brian a right of action in tort: *Cutler v Wandsworth Stadium* (1949). If the regulations address this point, eg Guard Dogs Act 1975 s 5(1), then that disposes of the matter, but if as is usual the statute (or regulations) is silent on the point then the court must ascertain the intention of Parliament. In the House of Lords in *Lonrho v Shell Petroleum* (1982) Lord Diplock stated that the initial presumption was that where the statute created an obligation together with a means of enforcing that obligation, eg by a criminal penalty then the obligation cannot be enforced in any other way. We are not told of any such means in the regulations, but even so the presence of a criminal penalty would not necessarily be fatal to Donald's and Edgar's cases: in *Atkinson v Newcastle Waterworks* (1877) the imposition of a fine for breach of a statutory duty was held to be exclusive, whereas in *Groves v Lord Wimborne* (1898) the provision in the regulations of a fine for breach was held not to deny the plaintiff a cause of action. It is worth noting in this respect that in *Groves*, as in the present case, the statute was enacted for the benefit of a class. The absence of any such provision would make it easier for Donald and Edgar to claim that a right in tort existed: *Thornton v Kirklees Metropolitan Borough Council* (1979). Lord Diplock continued to state that there were two exceptions to this general rule and one is relevant here, namely when the statute is enacted for the benefit of a class of persons and the plaintiff is a member of that class. As employees are regarded as a class of persons for whose benefit industrial safety legislation is enacted, as in *Groves*, it would seem that *prima facie* Donald and Edgar can sue in respect of Refiners' breach of statutory duty.

However, Donald and Edgar only cleared the first hurdle here; the next thing they must prove is the act which caused the damage is regulated by statute; that they were one of the persons the statute was intended to protect and that damage suffered was of a kind the statute was intended to prevent.

Prima facie none of these requirements should pose any problem for Donald and Edgar as the damage was caused by their presence in the cage whilst it was being moved. As employees of Apex plc they are persons the statute was intended to protect, see *Groves*, and the damage suffered was that of falling from the cage which is presumably the kind of damage that the statutory regulations were intended to prevent, so no problem of the ambit of the regulations arises as in *Gorris v Scott* (1874).

Next we should consider whether Donald and Edgar can sue Apex in negligence. As Donald and Edgar's employer, Apex owes Donald and Edgar a duty of care to provide a safe system of work; although Apex could argue that they did provide a safe system of work but that in this particular situation the normally safe system was improperly operated, this will not avail them because in *McDermid v Nash Dredging & Reclaimation* (1987) it was held by the House of Lords that the employer's duty did not consist of merely devising a safe system of work but also ensuring the operation of a safe system of work. This Apex have failed to do. This duty is non-delegable and it is no defence that Apex to show that they delegated performance to an employee whom the employer reasonably believed to be competent to perform it (per Lord Brandon in *McDermid*). Hence Apex will be liable for breach of their common law duty as employers.

Finally, as regards liability we should consider whether Apex are vicariously liable for Colin's negligence. It is clear that Colin himself owes Donald and Edgar a duty of care under normal *Donoghue v Stevenson* (1932) principles, in that he can reasonably foresee that any lack of care on his part may cause injury to them. There is no need to apply the modern formulation preferred by the House of Lords in *Caparo v Dickman* (1990) and *Murphy v Brentwood District Council* (1990). Indeed in *B v Islington Health Authority* at first instance Potts J stated that in personal injury cases the duty of care remained as it was pre-*Caparo*, namely the foresight of a reasonable person as in *Donoghue*, a finding that does not appear to have been disturbed on appeal (1992). Colin will be in breach of this duty if a reasonable person, placed in his position, would not have acted in this way: *Blyth v Birmingham Waterworks* (1856), and it is submitted that a reasonable person would not have moved the cage in a manner which exposed Donald and Edgar to danger. This breach must have caused Brian's damage, and the 'but for' test in *Cork v Kirby MacLean* (1952) proved the required causal connection. Additionally, the damage suffered by Brian must not be too remote in that it must be reasonably foreseeable: *The Wagon Mound* (1961). All that Colin need foresee is some personal injury; he need foresee neither the extent: *Smith v Leech, Brain* (1962) nor the exact manner in which the damage occurs: *Hughes v Lord Advocate* (1963). All these criteria are satisfied and so Colin has been negligent as regards his conduct to Donald and Edgar. As Colin is an employee of Refiners, and was acting in the course of his employment when this negligence took place, it follows that Refiners are vicariously liable for Colin's negligence, and any express prohibition on moving the cage whilst persons are present in it would not take him outside the cause of his employment: *Rose v Plenty* (1976), as he is merely carrying out an authorised act (moving the cage) in an unauthorised manner. It is submitted that a court would follow *Limpus v London General Omnibus* (1862) and *Rose v Plenty* rather than *Conway v Wimpey* (1951) (1). Hence Donald and Edgar could sue Apex plc as being vicariously responsible for Colin's negligence.

We must next consider whether any defences are available to Apex plc. From the facts given it seems that Colin and Donald have consented to being in the cage while it is being moved, giving rise to the question as to whether they are *volens* to the damage suffered. Normally the courts are most reluctant to hold that an employee is *volens* to an injury incurred during the course of his employment, *Smith v Baker* (1891), but may do so if the circumstances warrant. In this case as Donald, Edgar and Colin have consented to work in breach of statutory regulations the case does seem similar to *ICI v Shatwell* (1965) where two employees agreed to work in breach of statutory regulations and were held *volens* to the injuries caused. By analogy Donald and Edgar might be held *volens* (assuming Colin did not have the authority to order Donald and Edgar to remain in the cage) and, thus, unable to recover under any of the three causes of action previously discussed. However, the court might distinguish *Shatwell*'s case on the grounds that the danger there (testing detonators without using the shelter provided) was obvious and any reasonable employee would have complied with the regulations, whereas in the present case the danger is not so obvious and the reason for the breach was to perform the employers business more efficiently. In such a case the court might prefer to make a finding of contributory negligence against Donald or Edgar on the grounds in adopting an unsafe method of working that they failed to take sufficient care for their own safety, *Jones v Livox Quarries* (1952). Although the courts are reluctant to accept this defence for breach of statutory duty, *Westwood v Post Office* (1974), they will do so in appropriate circumstances and Colin and Donald's case is different from *Westwood*'s in that in *Westwood* the employers were in breach of statute, not the employee.

Hence it is submitted that Apex plc are liable for breach of statutory duty with a deduction for contributory negligence on Colin and Donald's part.

As regards the cause of action in negligence, both primary (employer's liability) and secondary (vicarious liability for Colin's actions) again *volenti* would not succeed but a defence of contributory negligence might. Edgar is contributory negligent in travelling in the cage in the first instant. Donald had the added problem in that he jumped from the cage, raising the possibility that this act is a *novus actus interveniens* that broke the chain of causation as in *McKew v Holland and Hammen & Cubitt* (1969) and this would be a valid defence for Apex for all three causes of action. However, to break the chain of causation the act would have to be unreasonable, as in *McKew*, and not a reasonable act carried out in the 'agony of the moment' and which with hindsight proved unnecessary -*Jones v Boyce* (1816) - it would seem that D has acted in the agony of the moment and so his action in jumping from the cage would not be a *novus actus interveniens* nor contributory negligence: *Jones v Boyce*.

Note

1   While this seems likely it should be noted that in recent years the
    courts have distinguished between careless and deliberate acts,
    and have taken a very narrow view of the course of employment
    where deliberate acts are concerned - see *Heasmans v Clarity
    Cleaning Ltd* (1989) and *Irving v Post Office* (1989). Perhaps the
    most dramatic example of this approach is to be found in *General
    Engineering Services v Kingston & St Andrews Corp* (1989) where
    firemen who drove very slowly to the scene of a fire were held
    not to be within the course of their employment in so doing, on
    the grounds that they were employed to travel to the scene of
    the fire as quickly as reasonably possible and in travelling as
    slowly as possible they were not doing an authorised act in an
    unauthorised manner, rather they were doing an unauthorised
    act. However, one of the grounds for the decision in *General
    Engineering Services* included the finding that 'this decision
    (ie the slow driving) was not in furtherance of their employer's
    business' per Lord Ackner. In Apex's case we are told that the
    reason for Colin's action was to save time, ie it was in
    furtherance of the employer's business. It is, thus, submitted that
    Colin's situation is legally distinguishable from that in *General
    Engineering Services*.

Chapter 5

Employers' Liability

Introduction

Questions on employers liability are often set in examinations: as the topic is only a specialised branch of the law of negligence it does introduce any new legal concepts but generally tests such areas as breach, causation, remoteness, contributory negligence and vicarious liability, and the topic may be combined with breach of statutory duty. Students should refer to Chapters 1, 3, 4 for examples of questions that involve an element of employer's liability. The non-delegable nature of employers duties should be noted, especially where independent contractors are involved.

Checklist

Students must be familiar with all of the above topics and especially:
- Provision of competent fellow employees
- Provision of safe plant and equipment
- Provision of safe place of work
- Provision of safe system of work

Question 16

Ken is employed by Lomad plc as an electrician. One day he is asked to repair a ceiling fan located in Lomad's workplace and is told to dismantle the fan and take it to the electrical workshop for repair. In order to save time Ken attempts to repair the fan whilst standing on a stepladder and whilst doing so he drops a pair of pliers which lands on Martin's head. Because Martin is of a rather nervous disposition he is off work for two months following this accident rather than the two days which would be normal for such an injury. Following this incident Ken decides to comply with his instructions and dismantles the fan but while he is doing this his screwdriver snaps and a piece of metal enters his eye.

Advise Martin and Ken of any remedies available to them.

Answer plan

This is a straightforward question on employers liability involving issues of both primary and secondary liability on the part of the employer.

Points that need to be discussed include:

- vicarious liability for Ken's action
- egg shell skull rule
- duty to provide a safe place of work

Answer

Martin will wish to sue Lomad plc for the damage that he has suffered, and he can sue them in respect of their primary liability to him as his employers and their secondary liability as being vicariously liable for the negligence of Ken. As regards Lomad's primary liability, Lomad have a duty to provide Martin with a safe place of work. (This is not an absolute duty but merely places on the employer the duty to take reasonable steps to provide a safe place of work: *Latimer v AEC* (1953), see also *Gitsham v Pearce* (1991), for a recent example.) We must decide, therefore, whether Lomad have taken such reasonable steps; they have, of course, instructed Ken to take the fan to the electrical workshop to repair it, but the problem for Lomad is that the duty to provide a safe place of work is non-delegable. In other words, the employer may entrust the performance of this work to an employee but he cannot thereby discharge his duty. In *McDermid v Nash Dredging & Reclaimation* Lord Brandon said 'The essential characteristic of the (non-delegable) duty is that, if it is not performed, it is no defence for the employer to show that he delegated its performance to a person, whether his servant or not his servant, whom he reasonably believed to be competent to perform it. Despite such delegation the employer is liable for the non-performance of the duty'.

Thus, following *McDermid* we can see that Lomad are in breach of their duty to provide a safe place of work. Considering now Lomad's secondary liability as Ken is employed by Lomad, Lomad will be liable for any tort committed by Ken in the course of his employment. It is clear that Ken himself owes Martin a duty of care under normal *Donoghue v Stevenson* (1932) principles, in that he can reasonably foresee that any lack of care on his part may cause injury to Martin. There is no need to apply the modern formulation preferred by the House of Lords in *Caparo v Dickman* (1990) and *Murphy v Brentwood District Council* (1990). Indeed in *B v Islington Health Authority* at first instance Potts J stated that in personal injury cases the duty of care remained as it was pre-*Caparo*, namely the foresight of a reasonable person as in *Donoghue*, a finding that does not appear to have been disturbed on appeal (1992). Ken will be in breach of this duty if a reasonable person, placed in his position, would not have acted in this way: *Blyth v Birmingham Waterworks* (1856), and it is submitted that a reasonable person would not have dropped a pair of pliers. This breach must have caused Brian's damage, and the 'but for' test in *Cork v Kirby MacLean* (1952) proves the required causal connection. Additionally, the damage suffered by Martin must not be too remote in that it must be reasonably foreseeable: *The Wagon Mound* (1961). All that Ken need foresee is some personal injury; he need foresee neither the extent: *Smith v Leech, Brain* (1962) nor the exact manner in which the damage occurs: *Hughes v Lord Advocate* (1963). All these criteria are satisfied and so Ken has been negligent as regards his conduct to Martin. As Ken is an employee of Lomad, and was acting in the course of his employment when this negligence took place, it follows that Lomad are vicariously liable for Ken's negligence. We are told that Ken is an electrician and in repairing the fan he is *prima facie* acting within the course of his employment. However, we need to see what is the effect of the express prohibition that he should not repair the fan *in situ* and whether by acting in contravention of this prohibition he has stepped outside the course of his employment. The authorities show that acting in contravention of a prohibition will not automatically take the act outside the course of the employment, eg *Rose v Plenty* (1976): *Limpus v London General Omnibus* (1862). What a prohibition can do is to limit those acts which lie within the course of the employment but it cannot restrict the mode of carrying out an act that does lie within the course of the employment - see eg *Limpus v London General Omnibus*. Thus, the question that must be decided is whether Ken in repairing the fan *in situ* has done an unauthorised act or whether he was merely carrying out an authorised act in an unauthorised manner. The court would have to decide whether the authorised act was repairing the fan (ie the wide approach to course of employment as in *Rose v Plenty* and *Limpus*) or whether it was to repair the fan in the electrical workshop (ie the narrow construction as in *Conway v Wimpey* (1951)). It is submitted that a court would take the former approach and, thus, Lomad would be liable for Ken's negligence. While this seems likely it should be noted that in recent years the courts have distinguished between careless and deliberate acts, and have taken a very narrow view of the course of employment where deliberate acts are concerned - see *Heasmans v Clarity Cleaning Ltd* (1989) and *Irving v Post Office* (1989). Perhaps the most dramatic example of this approach is to be found in *General Engineering Services v Kingston & St Andrews Corp* (1989) where firemen who drove very slowly to the scene of a fire were held not to be within the course of their employment in so doing, on the grounds that they were employed to travel to the scene of the fire as quickly as reasonably possible and in travelling as slowly as possible they were not doing an authorised act in an unauthorised manner, rather they were doing an unauthorised act. However, one of the grounds for the decision in *General Engineering Services* included the finding that 'this decision (ie the slow driving) was not in furtherance of their employer's business' per Lord Ackner. In Lomad's case we are told that the reason for Ken's action was to save time, ie it was in furtherance of the employer's business. It is thus submitted that Ken's situation is legally distinguishable from that in *General Engineering Services*.

We should now consider the extent of the liability as we are told that Martin is of a rather nervous disposition and that a normal person would not have suffered nearly as much damage. Fortunately for Martin, Ken and Lomad must take their victim as they find him.

The rule covering remoteness of damage for personal injury is that the defendant need only foresee some damage to the person - *The Wagon Mound* (1961) - the extent is irrelevant even if it was unforeseeable, *Dulieu v White* (1901); *Smith v Leech, Brain* (1961), ie Ken and Lomad must take their victim as they find him and are liable for all his damage - see eg *Brice v Brown* (1984) where a plaintiff with a hysterical personality disorder recovered a substantial sum for the extremely bizarre behaviour she suffered following her witnessing an accident to her daughter.

Turning now to Ken's damage, Lomad, as his employers are under a duty to provide Ken with safe equipment - *Smith v Baker* (1891). This they have not done, and it is no defence to Lomad to show that they purchased the screwdriver from a reputable supplier because by s 1(1) Employers Liability (Defective Equipment) Act 1969 where the defect is attributable to the fault of a third party it is deemed to be attributable to negligence on the part of the employer. Although this would appear to make life simple for Ken it would have to be shown that the defect was attributable to the manufacturer. If the screwdriver was relatively new, and it can be shown that nothing has happened since it left the manufacturers to cause the defect, then the defect can be attributed to the manufacturer: *Mason v Williams & Williams Ltd* (1956). Thus, by s 1(1) it will be attributed to negligence on the part of the employer. However, if the screwdriver had been in use for some time then it may be difficult to show the defect was due to fault on the part of the manufacturer - see *Evans v Triplex Glass* (1936) and as the duty to provide safe appliances is not absolute but merely to take reasonable care - see *Toronto Power v Paskwan* (1915), ie if for any reason the Employers Liability (Defective Equipment) Act 1969 does not apply then the situation is covered by *Davie v New Merton Board Mills* (1959), and Lomad will not be liable if they had not been negligent, eg if they had purchased the screwdriver from a reputable supplier and the defect was not discoverable on reasonable examination then no liability will arise.

Question 17

Iambic plc own some premises and decide to have its rather old fashioned central heating system replaced with a modern, efficient system. They engage Lead Ltd to carry out this work and Lead Ltd send two plumbers to Iambic's premises. While the plumbers are working one of them carelessly leaves a blowlamp running and the partition to an office catches fire and Jenny, who is working in the office, is burnt. Peter, who is an employee of Iambic plc, carelessly leaves a screwdriver on the floor of another office and Katherine trips over it and twists her leg. In the ensuing commotion caused by these two accidents an unknown thief enters the premises and steals a sheepskin coat belonging to Richard, another employee of Iambic plc. Richard kept his coat in a cupboard which was not provided with a lock.

Advise Jenny, Katherine and Richard.

Answer plan

This is a typical employers liability question in the sense that while mostly involving employers liability it also requires a discussion of vicarious liability.

The following issues must be examined:
- liability of Iambic plc for negligence of Lead Ltd
- liability of Iambic for negligence of its employees
- liability of Iambic for liability of Peter
- employers liability - limits on duty of care

Answer

Considering Jenny first, we need to see against whom any cause of action might lie.

It is clear that the plumber himself owes Jenny a duty of care under normal *Donoghue v Stevenson* (1932) principles, in that he can reasonably foresee that any lack of care on his part may cause injury to Jenny. There is no need to apply the modern formulation preferred by the House of Lords in *Caparo v Dickman* (1990) and *Murphy v Brentwood District Council* (1990). Indeed in *B v Islington Health Authority* at first instance Potts J stated that in personal injury cases the duty of care remained as it was pre-*Caparo*, namely the foresight of a reasonable person as in Donoghue, a finding that does not appear to have been disturbed on appeal (1992). The plumber will be in breach of this duty if a reasonable plumber, placed in his position, would not have acted in this way: *Blyth v Birmingham Waterworks* (1856), and it is submitted that a reasonable plumber would not have carelessly left a blowlamp running. This breach must have caused Jenny's damage, and the 'but for' test in *Cork v Kirby MacLean* (1952) proves the required causal connection. Additionally, the damage suffered by Jenny must not be too remote in that it must be reasonably foreseeable: *The Wagon Mound* (1961). All that the plumber need foresee is some personal injury; he need foresee neither the extent: *Smith v Leech, Brain* (1962) nor the exact manner in which the damage occurs: *Hughes v Lord Advocate* (1963). All these criteria are satisfied and so the plumber has been negligent as regards his conduct to Jenny.

As the plumber is an employee of Lead Ltd then Lead will be vicariously liable for any tort committed by the plumber in the course of his employment. As we are told that 'while the plumbers are working one of them carelessly ... ' it would seem that the plumber has been careless within the course of his employment, and the fact that the carelessness is gross and its consequences are obvious will not take the action outside the course of employment - see *Century Insurance v Northern Ireland RTB* (1942). Hence Jenny could sue Lead Ltd in respect of her injury.

From the facts of the problem there seems to be no reason for assuming that Lead Ltd are anything other than independent contractors. The normal rule is that an employer is not liable for the torts committed by an independent contractor during the course of the contractors duties: *Morgan v Girls Friendly Society* (1936); *D & F Estates v Church Commissioners* (1989). There are some situations where liability will arise, namely where the employer authorises the independent contractor to commit the tort: *Ellis v Sheffield Gas Consumers Co* (1853); where he negligently chooses an incompetent contractor: *Pinn v Rew* (1961); and where a non-delegable duty is imposed on him by common law, ie a duty the performance of which can be delegated but not the responsibility. The first two situations are not relevant here,but a non-delegable common law duty that may arise is that which exists where an independent contractor is employed to carry out work that is extra hazardous: *Honeywill & Stein v Larkin Bros* (1934); *Alcock v Wraith* (1991). In *Alcock* the Court of Appeal held that a crucial question was 'did the work involve some special risk or was it from its very nature likely to cause damage'. It is suggested that plumbing does not satisfy these criteria; the use of a blowlamp may carry some special risk, but Iambic could claim that the plumber's negligence was merely collateral to the performance of his work, and that as employers they are not liable for this collateral negligence: *Padbury v Holliday & Greenwood* (1912). If Jenny were to sue Iambic under the Occupier's Liability Act 1957 she would be met with the defence in s 2(4)(b) that Iambic acted reasonably in entrusting the work to an independent contractor and took such steps as were reasonable to satisfy itself that the contractor was competent and that the work had been properly done. As the work in question is technical there would be no requirement for Iambic to check that it had been properly done: *Haseldine v Daw* (1941).

If Jenny were to sue Iambic for breach of their common law duty as employers to provide her with a safe place of work, she would be met with the defence that Iambic had taken reasonable steps to do so, as this duty is not absolute but merely requires reasonable steps to be taken: *Latimer v AEC* (1953). This situation should be distinguished from that in *McDermid v Nash Dredging & Reclamation* (1987) as in this case it was held to be no defence to breach of a non-delegable duty to show that the employer had delegated performance to a person, whether his employee or not, whom he reasonably believed to be competent to perform it, per Lord Brandon. In Iambic's case they did not delegate the provision of a safe place of work to Lead Ltd, or to the plumber.

Jenny is, thus, advised to sue Lead Ltd in respect of her injuries.

Turning now to Katherine, and following the analysis we used with the plumber, we can see that Peter has been negligent as regards his conduct to Katherine as the necessary ingredients of duty, breach and damage are all present. We are told that Peter is an employee of Iambic, and assuming that when he left the screwdriver on the floor he was acting within the course of his employment, Iambic will be vicariously liable for his negligence. In addition to this secondary liability, Iambic as Katherine's employer has a primary duty to provide Katherine with a safe place of work. This is not an absolute duty, but merely requires Iambic to take reasonable steps to provide a safe place of work: *Latimer v AEC* (1953) and see also *Gitsham v Pearce* (1991) for a recent example. We need to decide, therefore, whether Iambic have taken such steps. Iambic have presumably instructed Peter not to leave any obstructions on the floor, but the problem for Iambic is that the duty to provide a safe place of work is non-delegable. In other words, an employer may entrust the performance of this duty to an employee but he cannot thereby discharge his duty. In *McDermid v Nash Dredging & Reclamation* Lord Brandon said 'The essential characteristic of the (non-delegable) duty is that, if it is not performed, it is no defence for the employer to show that he delegated its performance to a person, whether his servant or not his servant, whom he reasonably believed to be competent to perform it. Despite such delegation the employer is liable for the non-performance of the duty'. Thus, following *McDermid* we can see that Iambic are in breach of their duty to provide a safe place of work.

Thus, Katherine is advised to sue Iambic for breach of their primary duty to provide a safe place of work, and as being vicariously liable for Peter's negligence.

Finally, we must consider Richard's situation. The courts have held consistently that the duty which an employer owes is a duty to safeguard the employee's physical safety and does not extend to protecting the economic welfare of the employee. This whole area was considered extensively in *Reid v Rush & Tomkins* (1990) where this distinction was upheld. In *Deyoung v Stenburn* (1946) in a similar fact situation it was held by the Court of Appeal that no duty arose to protect the employee's clothing from theft (see also *Edwards v West Hertfordshire General Hospital Management Committee* (1957)); hence Richard cannot sue Iambic plc in the loss of his coat. On the facts given it seems most unlikely that he could sue either the plumber of Lead Ltd (as being vicariously liable) or Peter or Iambic plc (as being vicariously liable) for the loss of his coat and such loss is not reasonably foreseeable and no duty of care would arise in respect of this loss.

This situation differs from that in *Stansbie v Troman* (1948), where a contractor left a house empty and the front door unlocked, and was held liable for the subsequent theft of some property from the house, because in that situation it could be foreseen that a thief might enter and steal property from the house.

Question 18

To what extent, if any, does an employer's vicarious liability for the torts of his employees and his liability for breach of statutory duty add anything at all to the liability resulting from the employer's personal duty of care?

Answer plan

This is a question that requires careful thought. It would not be enough to merely list the main ingredients of vicarious liability, liability for breach of statutory duty and duty of care. What is required is a clear discussion of the limits of each of these doctrines and the extent to which any remedies which are not available through the duty of care route can be supplemented by the other two routes and vice versa.

Answer

The personal duty of care which an employer owes to his employee is to take reasonable care in all the circumstances for the employees' safety. Traditionally this is formulated as the duty to provide competent fellow employees, properly maintained plant and equipment and to provide a safe place and system of work: *Wilsons & Clyde Coal Co v English* (1938). Two points should be noted immediately before these duties are considered in detail, firstly, that these duties are non-delegable, by which we mean that an employer can delegate performance of these duties but by doing so he cannot thereby discharge those duties. In *McDermid v Nash Dredging & Reclamation* (1987) Lord Brandon stated that the essential duty of a non-delegable duty is that 'if it is not performed, it is no defence for the employer to show that he delegated performance to a person, whether his servant or not his servant, whom he reasonably believed to be competent to perform it. Despite such delegation the employer is liable for the non-performance of the duty'.

Secondly, the duty that an employer owes to an employee is owed to that employee personally, with all his faults and idiosyncrasies, and is not a duty owed to his employees as an amorphous body: *Paris v Stepney Borough Council* (1951).

Thus, in *Paris* the employers were held to be in breach of their duty when they failed to provide an employee who had sight in only one eye with safety goggles; although it was not usual practice to provide goggles for the work that the plaintiff carried out, the employers should have realised that in his particular case the consequences of an accident to his good eye would have been particularly disastrous.

To consider these personal duties in turn, the first duty is to provide competent fellow employees. An example of this can be seen in *Hudson v Ridge Manufacturing* (1957) where it was held that an employer was liable for the consequences of a practical joke played on one employee by a fellow employee who was known to perpetrate such jokes over a considerable period of time. In such a situation the employer might not be vicariously liable for the actions of the practical joker as they might well not lie within the course of his employment. Hence in such situations the personal duty of care of the employer goes further than his vicarious liability. This restriction on the employer's vicarious liability has become particularly important in recent years as the courts tent to take a much more restrictive approach to what constitutes the course of employment where the employee commits a deliberately wrongful act, as can be seen by the Court of Appeal decision in *Heasmans v Clarity Cleaning* (1987) and *Irving v The Post Office* (1987). In *Heasmans* an employer was held not to be vicariously liable for the actions of an employee who was employed to clean telephones, but who made unauthorised telephone calls costing some £1,400. The court noted that the employee was employed to clean the telephones and that in using them he had not cleaned them in an unauthorised manner, but had done an unauthorised act which had taken him outside the course of his employment. In *Irving* the employee, who worked for the Post Office and was employed to sort mail, wrote some racial abuse concerning the plaintiff upon a letter addressed to the plaintiff. The employee was authorised to write upon letters, but only for the purposes of ensuring that the mail was properly dealt with. It was held that the employers were not vicariously liable for the actions of the employee, as in writing a racial abuse he was doing an unauthorised act, and not an authorised act in an unauthorised manner. The court stated, per Fox LJ, that limits had to be set to the doctrine of vicarious liability, particularly where it was sought to make employers liable for the 'wilful wrongdoing' of an employee. Thus, in *General Engineering Services v Kingston and St Andrews Corp* 1(989) the firemen who drove very slowly to a fire were held not to be in the course of their employment in so doing as they were employed to travel to the scene of fires as quickly as reasonably possible, and in travelling as slowly as possibly they were not doing an authorised act in an unauthorised manner, but were doing an unauthorised act.

In such situations, as the vicarious liability of the employer may be limited, the primary duty to take reasonable care for the employees' safety may provide the employee with a remedy.

The next personal duty of the employer is to provide properly maintained plant and equipment: *Smith v Baker* (1891). This is a duty to do what is reasonably practicable: *Toronto Power Co v Paskwani* (1915) but by s 1(1) of the Employer's Liability (Defective Equipment) Act 1969 if an employee suffers personal injury in the course of his employment due to a defect in equipment provided by his employer and the defect is due wholly or partly to the fault of a third party (whether identified or not) the injury is deemed to be also due to negligence on the part of the employer. Hence an employer cannot discharge his duty to provide safe equipment by simply purchasing equipment from a reputable supplier, and his common law duty has been extended by statute from one which requires the exercise of reasonable care to what is in effect an absolute duty.

The employer is also under a duty to provide a safe place of work, again subject to taking steps that are reasonably practicable: *Latimer v AEC* (1953). Similarly, the employer must provide a safe system of work; the employer must not only provide such a system he must also ensure that it is operated safely: *McDermid v Nash Dredging & Reclamation* (1987).

The above duties extend only to safeguarding the employee's physical condition: in *Reid v Rush & Tomkins Group* (1989) it was held by the Court of Appeal that an employer had no duty to protect an employee's economic well-being, although there was a duty to warn prospective employees of any physical risks inherent in a job: *White v Holbrook Precision Castings* (1985).

It should also be noted that the courts are relatively ready to allow the defence of contributory negligence in cases involving breach of an employer's duty to an employee.

An employer is also vicariously liable for the torts committed by an employee in the course of his employment. Thus, where, by his negligence, an employee injures a fellow employee, the employer will also be liable providing that the act was in the course of the employment. There will often be an overlap between this ground of liability and that which arises from the employer's duty to provide competent fellow employees, but where a known practical joker causes damage to a fellow employee, as in *Hudson*, the joker may well be acting outside the course of his employment.

Finally, an employer may be liable for breach of statutory duty. As with the employers' personal duty of care this is non-delegable, and an employee who relies on this cause of action will have to show that the breach conferred a right of action in tort. This usually gives rise to few problems as the statute will have been enacted for the benefit of a particular class of person, namely employees: *Groves v Lord Wimborne* (1898). However, a problem may arise in that the damage suffered may not be of the type that the statute was intended to prevent, ie the *Gorris v Scott* (1874) situation. Thus, when considering a possible breach of s 14 of the Factories Act 1961 it has been held that the duty to fence dangerous machinery exists to protect the body of the worker and to prevent him being injured through having his clothing caught in the machinery but that is not relevant where a tool that a worker is using is caught in the machinery and the worker is thereby injured: *Sparrow v Fairey Aviation* (1964). In such a case, however, there would be a clear breach of the employers' personal duty of care, and indeed in *Fairey* the breach of this duty was admitted, and the case was only brought to the House of Lords to determine whether or not there had been a breach of s 14.

Statutory duties may be subject to the 'reasonably practicable' requirement when they may add little to the common law duty of care or they may be absolute requirements. In the latter case a breach is constituted when those requirements are not met, and the presence or absence of negligence is irrelevant.

Thus, to return to the statement under discussion, it can be seen that liability arising out of the employers' personal duty of care is often wider than vicarious liability or liability for breach of statutory duty. However, the three duties are separated and should not be confused. Obviously where a statutory obligation is absolute it will add to the employers' personal duty of care.

Chapter 6

Product Liability

Introduction

The passing of the Consumer Protection Act 1987 seems to have jolted examiners' minds on this topic, which has made a recent return to examinations. Essay questions on the effect of the Consumer Protection Act 1987 and the differences that it has made on product liability are a favoured mode of testing this area, but where problem questions are set the student must take care to consider the common law which has not been affected by the 1987 Act.

Checklist

Students must be familiar with the following aspects:

- Common law position - Dictum in *Donoghue v Stevenson*; intermediate examination; problems regarding defective product economic loss
- Position under Consumer Protection Act 1987 defects; persons liable; defences; loss caused; invalidity of exclusion clauses

Question 19

Discuss critically to what extent the Consumer Protection Act 1987 has changed the law on product liability in favour of the consumer.

Answer plan

This question is typical of the essays which examiners are currently setting. It requires a discussion of the main elements of Part I of the Act and a comparison of the statutory and common law regimes regarding product liability. Note, however, that the question requires candidates to discuss critically; it will not be sufficient merely to list the statutory requirements. These requirements must be compared with the still valid common law rules, and the effect of these changes from the consumer's point of view must be analysed.

In particular the following points must be discussed:

- position under the Consumer Protection Act 1987
- persons liable - s 2
- definition of defect and guidelines for assessing safety - s 3
- defences, especially the developments risks defence - s 4
- limitations on property damage
- position at Common Law
- Lord Atkin's dictum
- burden of proof
- requirement of causation and foreseeability

Answer

Part I of the CPA 1987 was introduced into English law to implement the European Community directive 85/734/EEC relating to product liability. The main provision of the Act is to be found in s 2(1) which states that where any damage is caused wholly or partly by a defect in a product then persons detailed in s 2(2) shall be liable for the damage. Section 2(2) lists the producer of the product, any person who holds himself out as the producer of the product, the importer of the product into the EC and by s 2(3) in certain circumstances the supplier of the product. A product is defined by s 1 as any goods or electricity, and includes a product which is comprised in another product.

The producer of the product is the manufacturer of the product, and a person holds himself out as being the producer if he puts his name or trade mark on the product or uses some other distinguishing mark, eg a supermarket chain which sells its own brand products. The supplier of the product will only be liable where is he asked to identify the producer of the product and fails to do so.

By s 3 a product contains a defect where 'the safety of the product is not such as persons generally are entitled to expect'. Thus, the 1987 Act only requires the product to be reasonably safe, it does not impose a requirement of absolute safety. As almost any product is capable of being unsafe if misused (eg an electric fire, a kitchen knife), the Act does not attempt to define safety, but instead provides a list of guidelines to be taken into account when considering what is meant by safety. So by s 3(2) all the circumstances shall be taken into account including a) the way and purposes for which the product has been marketed and any instructions and warnings provided, and b) what might reasonably be expected to be done with the product. The Act also provides for certain defences, including the fact that the defect did not exist in the product at the relevant time, and the development risks defence, namely 'that the state of scientific and technical knowledge at the relevant time was not such that a producer of products of the same description as the product in question might be expected to have discovered the defect if it had existed in his products while they were under his control'. This latter defence is likely to be heavily relied upon by drug manufacturers when sued in respect of side effects which cause damage (1).

One very important point which should be noted is that for all the defences contained within the Act the burden lies on the defendant to prove the defence.

To establish liability under the Act it is necessary for the plaintiff to show that the defect caused the damage, either wholly or partly. There is no requirement of foreseeability, only causation need be shown.

Finally, it should be noted that the Act covers death or personal injury or damage to property. The property in question must be of the type which is normally intended for private use and which was intended for private use by the plaintiff, ie damage to business property lies outside the scope of the Act. Damage to the product itself is excluded, and there is a minimum value of £275 for property damage below which damages cannot be awarded. By s 7 liability under the Act cannot be restricted or excluded.

To see to what extent this has changed the law it is necessary to study the (still existing) common law. In *Donoghue v Stevenson* (1932) Lord Atkin stated 'A manufacturer of products, which he sells in such a form as to show that he intends them to reach the ultimate consumer in the form in which they left him with no reasonable possibility of intermediate examination, and with the knowledge that the absence of reasonable care in the preparation or putting up of the products will result in an injury to the consumer's life or property, owes a duty to the consumer to take that reasonable care'.

The first problem that a consumer had was to identify the manufacturer. This may have been impossible, so that a donee of goods, as opposed to a purchaser, would be without a remedy.

In certain situations the common law extended liability from manufacturers to suppliers and other persons such as repairers, where the supplier or other person was under a duty to inspect the goods and failed to do so, see eg *Haseldine v Daw* (1941). However, this obligation does not arise in all cases, and where it does it requires a less thorough investigation than by the manufacturer and can even be discharged by a suitable exclusion clause, eg by selling the goods 'as seen and with all its faults and without warranty': *Hurley v Dyke* (1979). Thus, even where the supplier would be liable under common law principles the Act offers advantages as liability under it cannot be excluded or limited: s 7.

Additionally the remedy may have been in practice worthless where the manufacturer was based entirely outside the jurisdiction. In such a case under the 1987 Act the donee could proceed against the supplier or the importer of the goods into the European Community.

The next hurdle that a consumer had to overcome was to show the absence of reasonable care on the part of the manufacturer.

Although it is often stated that the 1987 Act has introduced a regime of strict liability the width of the state of the art defence is such that there will only be a small difference between an action in negligence and under the Act where this defence is invoked. The main difference is that by s 4 the burden of proving the defence lies on the defendant, and there is no requirement that the damage be reasonably foreseeable.

A problem that arose at common law was that it could be difficult to show that the defect arose in manufacture, especially where the product had left the manufacturer's control some time previously. Thus, in *Evans v Triplex Safety Glass* (1938), where the owner of a car claimed that the windscreen was defective, he failed in his claim as the windscreen had been in use in the car for about one year and the plaintiff could not show that the defect in the glass was due to negligence on the part of the manufacturers. On the other hand, in *Mason v Williams & Williams* (1955) the plaintiff succeeded in proving that the manufacturers were negligent by showing that nothing had happened to the product after it left the manufacturers possession that could have caused the defect.

This problem remains under the Act, as s 4(1)(d) provides that it is a defence for the manufacturer to show the defect did not exist in his product at the relevant time. Thus, causation remains a problem for the consumer, both at common law and under the Act but unlike the common law there is no requirement of foreseeability of damage under the Act. Liability under the Act does not extend to damage caused to the product itself, whereas at common law recovery for defective product economic loss was allowed by the House of Lords in *Junior Books v Veitchi* (1983). However, *Junior Books* has been subject to intense judicial criticism, and later cases have tended to confine it within its specific facts. Thus, it was not followed in *Aswan Engineering Establishment v Lupdine* (1987), *Simaan General Contracting v Pilkington Glass* (1988), *Greater Nottingham Co-operative Society v Cementation Piling & Foundations* (1987) or in *D & F Estates v Church Commissioners* (1989).

Perhaps the view of the courts to *Junior Books* can best be summed up by some judicial statement of high authority. In *D & F Estates* Lord Bridge stated that 'the consensus of judicial opinion seems to be ... that the decision cannot be regarded as laying down any principle of general application in the law of tort', and Lord Oliver stated that it was 'really of no use as an authority on the general duty of care'; in *Simaan General Contracting* Dillon LJ stated that *Junior Books* had been 'the subject of so much analysis and discussion with differing explanations of the basis of the case that the case cannot now be regarded as a useful pointer to any development of law ... indeed I find it difficult to see that future citation from *Junior Books* can ever serve any useful purpose'. In view of these dicta, it should come as no surprise to learn that the High Court recently refused to follow *Junior Books* in *Nitrigin Eireann Teoranta v Inca Alloys* (1992) holding that it was 'unique' and hence no plaintiff could nowadays reasonably be advised to rely on *Junior Books*. Practically, therefore, in this respect the common law and Consumer Protection Act are identical.

Unlike the common law the Act places a lower limit on property damage of £275, and by s 7 renders any exclusion or restriction of liability under the Act invalid.

Thus, overall it can be seen that the changes brought about by the Act do, on the whole, favour the consumer. Apart from the lower limit of £275 regarding property damage below which an action cannot be brought, the consumer under the Act is either no worse off than at common law, eg as regards causation, defective product, economic loss or is in an improved situation, eg the absence of any requirement of foreseeability of damage, the burden of proving any defence falling on the defendant and the invalidity of exclusion clauses.

Note

1   The state of the art defence permitted by s 4(1)(e) is much wider than that allowed in Article 7(e) of the original EC directive, and there is currently a disagreement between the European Community and the UK government as to whether the UK has enacted validly the directive, giving rise to the possibility that in appropriate cases a plaintiff could claim that a defendant could only rely on Article 7(e) and not s 4(1)(e) as the true state of the art defence.

Question 20

Alice buys a toaster to give to her son Bernard who has just moved into a new flat. Because Bernard is having the flat decorated he stores the toaster in a drawer in the kitchen and does not use it until the decorating is finished some four weeks later. Then he uses the toaster but due to the fact that it has been carelessly wired during manufacture it overheats and catches fire. Bernard suffers an electric shock when he attempts to put out the flames, his newly decorated kitchen is partially ruined and has to be re-papered, and the toaster is destroyed together with a pocket dictaphone that Bernard uses in his job as a self employed computer consultant.

Advise Bernard.

Answer plan

This problem calls for a discussion of Bernard's rights under the Consumer Protection Act 1987 and at common law.

The following aspects should be considered:

- persons liable under s 2(2) of the Consumer Protection Act 1987
- criteria for existence of a defect - ss 3(1) and 3(2)
- defences available under s 4 and burden of proof
- any restrictions on property damage set by s 5 - minimum value, business property and defective product economic loss
- common law action under *Donoghue* and differences between this action and the statutory remedy
- need to show foreseeability of damage
- restrictions on type of damage recoverable

Answer

Bernard should be advised of his rights under the Consumer Protection Act 1987 and at common law.

Under s 2(1) of the Consumer Protection Act 1987 the producer of the toaster will be liable for any damage caused by a defect in the toaster. Thus, the manufacturer of the toaster is liable as is any person who holds himself out as the producer, eg a shop who sold the toaster to Alice using its own brand name or trade mark or if the product has been manufactured outside the EC the importer into the EC of the product. If Bernard cannot identify any of these persons he can ask the supplier of the toaster to identify such persons and if the supplier fails to do so then the supplier will incur liability. Thus, Bernard should have no difficulty in identifying a potential defendant.

Next Bernard must show that there was a defect in the product and that this defect caused the damage. A defect is defined by s 3(1) as existing if the safety of the product is not such as persons generally are entitled to expect. The 1987 Act does not require the product to be absolutely safe, it is enough that it is reasonably safe. The Act does not define safety as such, but instead gives a number of guidelines which are to be taken into account in determining whether or not the product is safe. By s 3(2) all the circumstances are to be taken into account including the manner and purpose for which the product has been marketed, any instructions or warnings and what might reasonably be expected to be done with the product. As the product in question is a toaster and Bernard has used it for this purpose, and the toaster has overheated and caught fire because it has been carelessly wired during manufacture, it seems clear that it is unsafe and, thus, contains a defect. It seems clear also that this defect caused the damage which Bernard has suffered; under the 1987 Act it is sufficient for Bernard to prove causation and there is no requirement that the damage be reasonably foreseeable so *prima facie* all the damage suffered is recoverable.

A possible defence for the producer is contained in s 4(1)(d) in that the defect did not exist in the product at the relevant time, and as Bernard kept the toaster for four weeks prior to using it this defence must be considered. At common law this is usually proved by showing that nothing happened to the product after it left the defendant's possession that could have caused the defect. Thus, in *Evans v Triplex Safety Glass* (1938), where the owner of a car claimed that the windscreen was defective, he failed in his claim as the windscreen had been in use in the car for about one year and the plaintiff could not show that the defect in the glass was due to negligence on the part of the manufacturers. On the other hand, in *Mason v Williams & Williams* (1955) the plaintiff succeeded in proving that the manufacturers were negligent by showing that nothing had happened to the product after it left the manufacturers possession that could have caused the defect. As the time gap for Bernard is only four weeks and during that time the toaster lay in a drawer it should not be difficult for Bernard to demonstrate that the defect arose in the manufacture, and in any event the burden will be on the manufacturer to prove this defence: s 4(1).

Thus, under the Act Bernard can recover for the damage to his kitchen and the electric shock he suffered. By s 5(4) he can only recover in respect of property damage if the damage exceeds £275 but that seems likely on the facts that we are given. As regards the dictaphone it should be remembered that the Act is designed to benefit consumers and by s 5(3) liability does not arise in respect of property which is not obviously intended for private use or consumption and which is not intended to be used by the plaintiff mainly for his own private use or consumption. The dictaphone does not satisfy both of these requirements and so damage in respect of it cannot be recovered under the Act. Turning to the toaster itself, by s 5(2) damage to the product itself is excluded so Bernard cannot claim for the damage to the toaster.

At common law Bernard must rely on the diction of Lord Atkin in *Donoghue v Stevenson* that 'A manufacturer of products, which he sells in such a form as to show that he intends them to reach the ultimate consumer in the form in which they left him with no reasonable possibility of intermediate examination, and with the knowledge that the absence of reasonable care in the preparation or putting up of the products will result in an injury to the consumer's life or property, owes a duty to the consumer to take that reasonable care'. Thus, Bernard can proceed against the manufacturer of the toaster. Plaintiffs have sometimes been allowed to proceed against suppliers but that has been in cases where the supplier is under a duty to inspect the goods and fails to discharge this duty, eg *Haseldine v Daw* (1941). A supplier or retailer of electrical goods would not have such a duty imposed on him so Bernard could only sue the manufacturer.

As against the manufacturer Bernard would have, on the facts given, little difficulty in establishing a breach of duty due to the presence of the defect, as a reasonable manufacturer of toasters would not allow such a product into general circulation with such a defect: *Blyth v Birmingham Waterworks* (1856). If the manufacturer were to claim that the product did not exist in the toaster when it left his possession he would be met with arguments similar to those discussed under the Consumer Protection Act 1987, although at common law the burden would lie on Bernard to prove the breach. Bernard must prove that the breach or defect caused his damage, and the 'but for' test in *Cork v Kirby Maclean* (1952) shows the required causal connection. Finally, Bernard must demonstrate that the damage which flowed from the breach was not too remote in that it was reasonably foreseeable: *The Wagon Mound* (1961), and given the careless wiring the damage which occurred is reasonably foreseeable. Thus, Bernard can recover for the damage to his kitchen and for the electric shock, and no minimum value will apply to the common law action for property damage. As regards the damage to the toaster, this is defective product economic loss. At common law recovery for defective product economic loss was allowed by the House of Lords in *Junior Books v Veitchi* (1983). However, *Junior Books* has been subject to intense judicial criticism, and later cases have tended to confine it within its specific facts. Thus, it was not followed in *Aswan Engineering Establishment v Lupdine* (1987), *Simaan General*

Contracting v Pilkington Glass (1988), *Greater Nottingham Co-operative Society v Cementation Piling & Foundations* (1987) or in *D & F Estates v Church Commissioners* (1989).

Perhaps the view of the courts to *Junior Books* can best be summed up by some judicial statement of high authority. In *D & F Estates* Lord Bridge stated that 'the consensus of judicial opinion seems to be ... that the decision cannot be regarded as laying down any principle of general application in the law of tort', and Lord Oliver stated that it was 'really of no use as an authority on the general duty of care'; in *Simaan General Contracting* Dillon LJ stated that *Junior Books* had been 'the subject of so much analysis and discussion with differing explanations of the basis of the case that the case cannot now be regarded as a useful pointer to any development of law ... indeed I find it difficult to see that future citation from *Junior Books* can ever serve any useful purpose'. In view of this discussion, it should come as no surprise to learn that the High Court recently refused to follow *Junior Books* in *Nitrigin Eireann Teoranta v Inca Alloys* (1992) holding that it was 'unique'.

Thus, Bernard should be advised that there is little hope of a future court following *Junior Books* and that the damage to the toaster is irrecoverable at tort. The damage to the dictaphone, however, is recoverable for there is no common law requirement that the plaintiff be a consumer rather than a commercial user, the phrase 'consumer' in Lord Atkins' judgment now meaning 'user' - *Mason v Williams & Williams*.

Question 21

Hilary and Janet work together and Janet agreed to cut and dye Hilary's hair one evening. After cutting Hilary's hair Janet applied a dye which she bought from Blondie plc. After a few minutes, Hilary suffered an extremely painful allergic reaction to the dye and Janet washed the dye out. Several hours later large portions of Hilary's hair fell out and her scalp turned bright red. As a result Hilary cancelled a holiday that she was planning to take in Nepal which cost £2,000.

Answer plan

This is a question on product liability which requires an analysis of the position of Blondie plc at common law and under statute regarding product liability of Janet in negligence and any possible liability for the loss of the holiday.

The following points should be considered:

- Janet's liability to Hilary in negligence
- liability of Blondie plc to Hilary at common law and under the Consumer Protection Act 1987
- advantages of proceeding under the 1987 Act
- liability of Janet and Blondie plc in respect of the holiday

Answer

Let us first consider any liability that Janet might have incurred to Hilary. Janet will owe a duty of care to Hilary under normal *Donoghue v Stevenson* (1932) principles, in that she can reasonably foresee that any lack of care on her part may cause injury to Hilary. There is no need to apply the modern formulation of the test for the existence of a duty of care preferred by the House of Lords in *Caparo v Dickman* (1990) and *Murphy v Brentwood District Council* (1990). Indeed in *B v Islington Health Authority* (1991) at first instance Potts J stated that in personal injury cases the duty of care remains as it was pre-*Caparo*, namely the foresight of a reasonable person as in *Donoghue*, a finding that does not appear to have been disturbed on appeal (1992). We must next decide whether Janet is in breach of this duty, ie that a reasonable person, or rather a reasonable hairdresser, in Janet's position would not have acted in this way: *Blyth v Birmingham Waterworks* (1856); *Bolam v Friern Hospital Management Committee* (1957).

It is true that Janet is not a professional hairdresser, but as she has professed to have the skill of a hairdresser she will be judged by the standard of a competent hairdresser (1). We are not told whether or not the dye contained a warning regarding its application, eg that a small test should be made before general use, and if Janet disregarded any such warning she will be in breach of her duty. In any event it is submitted that a reasonably competent hairdresser (the standard by which Janet must be judged) would be aware that some persons might be particularly sensitive to hair dyes and would carry out a preliminary test. As Janet has apparently not done this she is in breach of her duty. Finally, it must be shown that this breach caused Hilary's injuries, and the 'but for' test in *Cork v Kirby MacLean* (1952) proves the required causal connection. In addition, the damage suffered by Hilary must not be too remote, ie it must be reasonably foreseeable: *The Wagon Mound* (1961). Certainly some allergic reaction is foreseeable if no pre-testing is carried out, and this will be sufficient to found liability for the painful reaction, the loss of hair and the discoloured scalp. There is no need for Janet to foresee the extent of the injuries suffered by Hilary, as the rule with personal injuries is that the defendant need only foresee the kind of injuries, not the extent: *Smith v Leech, Brain* (1962). Nor would it be any defence to Janet to show that Hilary had a particularly sensitive skin, as a tortfeasor must take his victim as he finds him (the egg-shell skull rule): *Dulieu v White* (1901); *Smith*. A problem may arise as regards Hilary's cancelled holiday and the loss that that entails - *prima facie* this is not a reasonably foreseeable consequence of Janet's negligence, and would only be recoverable if it was so, eg because Hilary had told Janet that she had arranged a holiday in the near future. In that case the cancelled holiday would be reasonably foreseeable and, hence, recoverable.

There is, however, a particular problem to suing Janet which is that she may not be able to satisfy judgment, so we need to consider whether Blondie plc are liable to Hilary. Considering first the common law situation, it was established in *Donoghue v Stevenson* (1932) that 'A manufacturer of products, which he sells in such a form as to show that he intends them to reach the ultimate consumer in the form in which they left him with no reasonable possibility of intermediate examination, and with the knowledge that the absence of reasonable care in the preparation or putting up of the products will result in an injury to the consumer's life or property, owes a duty to the consumer to take reasonable care' per Lord Atkin. This liability has been extended to include suppliers as well as manufacturers, so it will apply to Blondie plc whether they manufactured the dye or merely supplied it to Janet. A hurdle which needs to be overcome in holding Blondie liable is that common law liability will only arise where there is 'no real possibility of intermediate examination'. In *Kubach v Hollands* (1937) it was held that the presence of an adequate warning was enough to discharge this duty, so if the dye bottle supplied by Blondie contained a suitable warning this would exempt them from liability. If a suitable warning was not provided then Blondie could argue that the true cause of Hilary's damage was not their breach, but rather the negligent act of Janet in not carrying out a pre-test as a reasonably competent hairdresser would have been expected to, ie that Janet's negligent act is a *novus actus interveniens* which broke the chain of causation. Where it is alleged that the act of a third party over whom the defendant has no control has broken the chain of causation, then it must be shown that the act was 'something unwarrantable, a new cause which disturbs the sequence of events, something which can be described as either unreasonable or extraneous or extrinsic' per Lord Wright in *The Oropesa* (1943). The defendant will, therefore, remain liable if the act of the third party is not truly independent of his negligence. In *Knightley v Johns* (1982) the Court of Appeal held that negligent conduct was more likely to break the chain of causation than non-negligent conduct, and that in *Knightley* there were so many errors and departures from common sense procedures that the chain of causation had been broken. We have already decided, in considering Janet's possible liability that her actions in not carrying out a pre-test were negligent, and it is submitted that this negligent act was such a departure from common sense procedures as to break the chain of causation, and relieve Blondie of liability. The extent of Blondie's liability, should it exist at common law, will be governed by the reasonably foreseeable criterion, so they would not be liable for any loss as regards Hilary's aborted holiday.

We next need to consider if any liability arises under the Consumer Protection Act 1987. By s 2(1) of this Act where any damage is caused wholly or partly by a defect in a product then certain persons are liable for the damage. Those persons are the producer of the product, or anyone who holds himself out as the producer, eg if Blondie bought the dye from another company but put their own name to it, or possibly the supplier. The supplier will incur liability where he is requested to identify one of the preceding persons and fails to do so. Thus, it should be a simple matter for Hilary to identify a person to whom liability will attach under the 1987 Act, and we shall assume that that person is Blondie plc. Next, Hilary will have to show that the product contained a defect, if that its safety was not such as persons generally are entitled to expect: s 3(1). The Act does not attempt to define safety, but requires all the circumstances to be taken into account including any instructions or warnings provided: s 3(2). Thus, similar considerations will apply as in the earlier discussion above regarding common law liability, and a similar defence of *novus actus interveniens* will be available to Blondie as s 2(1) expressly requires causation to be proved. One advantage that accrues to Hilary in proceeding under the Act rather than at common law is that there is no requirement of foreseeability under the Act, and if Blondie were to be found liable then all the damage suffered by Hilary is recoverable. If Blondie wish to raise any of the defences open to them under s 4 they will have to prove these defences. The only relevant defence appears to be s 4(1)(e) that the state of scientific and technical knowledge at the relevant time was not such that a producer of products of the same description as the product in question might be expected to have discovered the defect if it had existed in his products while they were under his control. However, given the universal and sophisticated testing of hair products for allergic responses, this defence seems unlikely to succeed.

There is also a minimum value to actions under the Act, but this only applies to property damage and Hilary's action is a personal injuries one.

Overall, therefore, it seems that Hilary has a good case against Janet, but that he chances of success against Blondie plc are more problematical.

Note

1   From the facts of the question it seems that Janet is not a professional hairdresser. In *Philips v Whiteley* (1938) it was held that a jeweller who pierced ear for earrings was only under a duty to take the precautions which might reasonably be expected of a jeweller, and not meet the standards of cleanliness which would be expected of a surgeon. However, in *Wells v Cooper* (1958) it was held that a householder who did some work around the house must meet the standard of a reasonably competent carpenter. It is thus suggested that the earlier conclusion regarding Janet's duty of care is correct; her case is closer to *Wells* than *Philips*, in that in *Philips* there were two possible standards to apply which did not exist in *Wells* or in Janet's case.

Chapter 7

Occupiers' Liability

Introduction

Occupiers liability is a specialised branch of the tort of negligence and is tested in most examinations year after year. The area is governed by statute, namely the Occupiers Liability Act 1957 and the Occupiers Liability Act 1984. Thus, in addition to the common law concepts of duty, breach, causation and remoteness, attention must be paid to the statutes and the exact words used therein.

The 1984 Act is also frequently tested, and in moving around premises a person may well change in status from a visitor to a non-visitor, ie from being subject to the 1957 Act to being subject to the 1984 Act.

Checklist

Students must be familiar with the following areas:
- Who are occupiers, visitors and non-visitors
- Duty regarding children, warnings and independent contractors
- Exclusion of duty
- Circumstances under which a duty to a non-visitor arises and nature of this duty

Question 22

Arthur inherits a large and dilapidated house from his mother. He moves in and decides to have substantial renovations carried out by Askew Alterations Ltd, a local company who specialise in renovating old property. Whilst these alterations are in progress Arthur decides to hold a party to welcome his new neighbours.

i) Basil and his five-year old daughter Clara attend, but Clara becomes bored and wanders into a room marked 'Danger - do not enter' and is injured. Basil, while looking for Clara in that room turns on a light switch that has not been completely finished and suffers and electrical shock.

ii) Cedric, who is aware that Arthur's mother kept a good wine cellar, goes down the cellar intending to help himself to some wine, but slips on a cork on the steps and breaks both his legs.

Advise Basil, Clara and Cedric.

Answer plan

This is a standard occupier's liability question in that it involves the areas of independent contractors, children and visitors becoming non-visitors.

The following points need to be considered:

• occupiers and visitors
• Arthur's duty to visitors generally
• Arthur's duty to Clara
• effect of warning notice
• Arthur's duty to Cedric

Answer

Arthur is the occupier of his house as he has 'sufficient control over the premises that he ought to realise that any failure on his part to use care may result in injury to a person coming lawfully there' per Lord Denning in *Wheat v Lacon* (1966). Basil, Clara and Cedric are Arthur's visitors (*Wheat v Lacon*) and we must ascertain the nature of the duty Arthur owes to each of his visitors and decide whether he is in breach of that duty.

Arthur owes each of his visitors the common duty of care: s 2(1) Occupiers Liability Act 1957 and this duty is to take such care as in all the circumstances is reasonable to see that the visitor will be reasonably safe in using the premises to the purposes for which he is invited or permitted by the occupier to be there. It should be noted that it is the visitor who must be reasonably safe and not the premises, see eg *Ferguson v Welsh* (1987), so the fact that repairs are being carried out to Arthur's house, which is in a dilapidated condition does not, without more, constitute a breach of duty.

Turning now to Clara, by s 2(3)(a) of the 1957 Act Arthur must be prepared for children to be less careful than adults, and in *Latham v Johnson & Nephew Ltd* (1913) Lord Hamilton stated there may be a duty not to lead children into temptation. Having said this, if the danger is obvious, even to a child, then the occupier will not be liable: *Liddle v Yorkshire (North Riding) County Court* (1934). With very young children, of course, almost anything can be a danger, but here an occupier will be able to rely on the decision of

Devlin J in *Phipps v Rochester Corp* (1955) where it was held that reasonable parents would not allow small children to go unaccompanied to places which may be unsafe for them, that both parents and occupiers must act reasonably and each is entitled to assume that the other has so acted.

Considering all the circumstances of the case it should have been clear to Basil that Arthur's house was in the process of redecoration and would hence contain danger that might not be obvious to a small child. Following Phipps it would seem that Basil has not acted reasonably and that Arthur was justified in relying on Basil to act reasonably in respect of Clara. Arthur could also argue that the sign 'Danger - Do Not enter' is a warning which discharges his duty under 2(4)(a) but to achieve this the warning must in all the circumstances be enough to enable the visitor to be reasonably safe. The sign does not seem to be a warning at all in that it makes no attempt to describe the danger, but is rather a prohibition on the spacial extent to which the visitor is entitled to be on the premises which the occupier is entitled to do: *The Calgarth* (1927). In any event it would not be enough in all the circumstances to discharge the duty owed to a small child nor to turn the small child into a non-visitor.

In view of the decision of the House of Lords in *Edwards v Railway Executive* (1952) it is most unlikely that the Court would imply a licence in favour of Clara - see the judgment of Lord Goddard.

Hence, our advice to Clara is that she cannot sue Arthur, but that she could sue Basil in negligence. Basil owes Clara a duty of care under normal *Donoghue v Stevenson* (1932) principles, and as a duty of care has previously been established there is no need to go to the modern formulation of a duty of care that was preferred by the House of Lords in *Caparo Industries v Caparo* (1990) and *Murphy v Brentwood District Council*. Basil is in breach of his duty in allowing Clara to wander off in a house that was still being renovated, as this would not have been the action of a reasonable parent placed in Basil's position: *Blyth v Birmingham Waterworks* (1856). Finally, the damage that Clara has suffered was caused by Basil's breach of duty, as shown by applying the 'but for' test of Lord Denning in *Cork v Kirby MacLean* (1952), and this damage was reasonably foreseeable as required by *The Wagon Mound* (1961).

We have discussed the duty Arthur owes to Basil and must now consider whether Arthur is in breach of this duty. *Prima facie* it is a breach of duty to allow persons to come into contact with unsafe light switches, but Arthur has attempted to discharge his duty via the notice. The notice seems to be insufficient as a warning notice as it does not describe the nature of the danger in any way, and so by s 2(4)(a) would not be enough to make the visitor reasonably safe. In *Rae v Marks UK* (1989), it was held that where an unusual danger exists the visitor should not only be warned but a barrier or additional notice should be placed to show the immediacy of the danger, and Arthur has not complied with this condition. Overall, therefore, it seems that the notice is insufficient as a warning notice. However, Arthur could rely on s 2(4)(b) which states that where damage is caused to a visitor by a danger due to the faulty execution of any work of construction, maintenance of repair by an independent contractor employed by the occupier, the occupier is not to be treated without more as answerable for the danger if in all the circumstances he had acted reasonably in entrusting the work to an independent contractor and had taken such steps (if any) as he reasonably ought in order to satisfy himself that the contractor was competent and that the work had been properly done.

The renovation is covered by s 2(4)(b) as it is reasonable to entrust it to independent contractors and as we are told that Askew Alterations specialise in renovating old property it would seem that they are competent. The question, therefore, is what if any steps Arthur ought reasonably to have taken to satisfy himself that the work had been properly done. Despite the words 'had been properly done' it was held by the House of Lords in *Ferguson v Welsh* (1987) that it could apply where the work was still being done and had not been completed. The rule is that the more technical the work the less reasonable it is to require the occupier to check it, cf *Haseldine v Daw* (1941) and *Woodward v Mayor of Hastings* (1945). In Arthur's circumstances it would seem that as the work is technical there is no requirement to check the work had been properly done and Arthur has discharged his duty by employing reasonable independent contractors.

One could consider whether Askew Alterations are also occupiers, as although Arthur is an occupier, an independent contractor may also be an occupier for control need not be exclusive (see *Wheat v Lacon*). The question that has to be decided is whether the independent contractors have sufficient control as in *AMF International v Maquet Bowling* (1968). In the present case, although we are told that renovations are continuing, it seems unlikely that Arthur would hold a party while the contractors are physically present and working and although physical possession is not a necessary ingredient of control: *Harris v Birkenhead Corp* (1976), it would seem that at the relevant time Askew Alterations were not in sufficient control to make them occupiers.

Hence, our advice to Basil is that he cannot sue Arthur, but that he could sue Askew Alterations in negligence. Askew Alterations owe Basil a duty of care under normal *Donoghue v Stevenson* (1932) principles, and as a duty of care has previously been established there is no need to go to the modern formulation of a duty of care that was preferred by the House of Lords in *Caparo Industries v Caparo* (1990) and *Murphy v Brentwood District Council*. Askew Alterations are in breach of their duty in leaving the switch on in an unsafe condition, as this would not have been the action of a reasonable electrician placed in Askew Alteration's position: *Blyth v Birmingham Waterworks* (1856). Finally, the damage that Basil has suffered was caused by Askew Alteration's breach of duty, as shown by applying the 'but for' test of Lord Denning in *Cork v Kirby MacLean* (1952), and this damage was reasonably foreseeable as required by *The Wagon Mound* (1961).

Finally, we must consider advising Cedric. Although Cedric is initially a visitor, on entering the cellar he comes a non-visitor. An occupier may place a spatial limitation on the visitor's permission to enter: *The Calgarth* (1927) but in such a case the limitation must be brought to the visitor's attention: *Gould v McAuliffe* (1941). By implication Cedric must know that he has not Arthur's permission to enter his wine cellar and, thus, becomes a trespasser when he enters that part of the premises. Even if Cedric had permission to visit the wine cellar, as he went there to steal Arthur's wine then, on the authority of *R v Smith & Jones* (1978), Cedric must know that he is entering the cellar in excess of the premises given to him and then becomes a trespasser. Any duty now owed to Cedric is governed by the Occupiers Liability Act 1984. By s 1(2) of the 1984 Act an occupier will only owe a duty to a non-visitor if the occupier:

a) is aware of the danger or has reasonable grounds to believe it exists;

b) knows or has reasonable ground to believe that the non-visitor is in the vicinity of the danger or may come into the vicinity; and

c) the risk is one against which, in all the circumstances, he may reasonably be expected to offer the non-visitor some protection.

It seems unlikely that requirement a) is satisfied and requirement b) is not satisfied as Arthur has no reason to suspect that his guests will steal his property, hence no duty arises in respect of Cedric's accident in the cellar. In addition, Arthur would have against Cedric the defence of *ex turpi causa non oritur actio*: *National Coal Board v England* (1954), as to assist Cedric would be an affront to the public conscience: *Euro-Diam v Bathurst* (1988) per Kerr LJ; *Pitts v Hunt* (1990) per Beldam LJ, or take the test preferred by the majority in *Pitts* because Cedric's claim is based directly on the illegality, and is not merely incidental. Thus, Cedric cannot sue Arthur.

Question 23

Eric owns a waxworks museum in the seaside town of Westsea. He decides to have a new air conditioning system installed in the museum by Coolit plc, but Coolit can only carry out this work during the height of the tourist season. Rather than delay the job until the winter or shut down while the work is being done and lose income, Eric decides to allow the public into the museum while the new air conditioning system is being installed. He places notices around the museum stating 'Danger - Work in Progress'. While the employees of Coolit are working in one part of the museum, some scaffolding which they have erected in another part collapses and injures Florence, who paid to enter the museum and George who entered without paying via the open back door that Coolit's employees were using to bring in equipment.

Advise Florence, who has suffered a fractured skull and had her spectacles broken, and George, who has suffered a broken shoulder and has had his new suit ruined.

Answer plan

This is a straightforward Occupiers Liability question involving two occupiers, an independent contractor and a non-visitor.

The following aspects must be considered:

- likelihood of Eric and Coolit both being occupiers
- applicability of s 2(4)(1) Occupiers Liability Act 1957 to Eric
- liability of occupier to non-visitor
- damages recoverable

Answer

Eric is the occupier of the museum as he has, per Lord Denning, sufficient control over the premises that he ought to realise that any failure on his part to use care may result in injury to a person coming lawfully there: *Wheat v Lacon* (1968). In addition, Coolit plc may also be occupiers of the museum for there is no need for control to be exclusive (see *Wheat v Lacon*); the question is whether Coolit, as independent contractors, have sufficient control as in *AMF International v Magnet Bowling* (1968). This is, of course a question of fact and as presumably the installation of an air conditioning system in a waxworks museum would involve extensive work Coolit may well be held to be occupiers and so also liable together with Eric.

Florence is Eric's visitor: *Wheat v Lacon*, so Eric owes Florence the common duty of care by s 2(1) Occupiers Liability Act 1957 and by s 2(2) the duty is to take such care as in all the circumstances of the case is reasonable to see that the visitor will be reasonably safe in using the premises for the purposes for which he is invited or permitted by the owner to be there. It should be noted that it is the visitor who must be reasonably safe and not the premises, so the fact that renovations are taking place in the museum does not, by itself, constitute a breach of duty. The question as to whether the occupier is in breach of his duty is always a question of fact depending on the exact circumstances of the case, as can be seen by the differing decisions of the Court in the factually similar cases of *Murphy v Bradford Metropolitan Council* (1992) and *Gitsham v Pearce* (1992), but Eric will seek to rely on the defence contained in s 2(4)(b) of the 1957 Act, namely that where damage is caused to a visitor by a danger due to the faulty execution of any work of construction, maintenance or repair by an independent contractor employed by the occupier, the occupier is not to be treated without more as answerable for the danger if in all the circumstances he had acted reasonably in entrusting the work to an independent contractor and had taken such steps (if any) as he reasonably ought in order to satisfy himself that the contractor was competent and that the work had been properly done.

There is nothing in the facts of the problem to suggest that Coolit are anything but competent, so the question, therefore, is what, if any, steps Eric ought reasonably have taken to satisfy himself that the work had been properly done. Despite the words 'had been properly done' in the sub-section, it was held in *Ferguson v Welsh* (1987) that the obligation could arise where the work was still being done and had not been completed. The rule is that the more technical the work the less reasonable it is to require the occupier to check; cf *Haseldine v Daw* (1941) and *Woodward v Mayor of Hastings* (1945).

The work of installing an air conditioning system is certainly technical, but we are told that the damage was caused by a scaffolding collapsing, and if this danger was obvious by a reasonable observer from the floor, then Eric should have been aware of the danger and cannot bring himself within s 2(4)(b) as in *Woodward*, but if the careless work of Coolit was not apparent upon such examination then Eric will not be in breach.

Finally, we need to consider whether the notices stating 'Danger - Work in Progress' discharges any duty owed by the occupier. By s 2(4)(a) where damage is caused to a visitor by a danger of which he has been warned by the occupier, the warning is not to be treated without more as absolving the occupier from liability, unless in all the circumstances it was enough to enable the visitor to be reasonably safe. The notices do not indicate the nature of the danger and it is a question of fact whether they were thought to allow a visitor to be reasonably safe. In *Rae v Mars UK* (1989) it was held that where an unusual danger exists the visitor should not only be warned, but a barrier or added notice should be placed to show the immediacy of the danger. This has not been done and as the scaffolding fell on Florence it seems that in addition to the notice that area should have been roped off to keep visitors away from any possible danger.

Hence our advice to Florence is that Eric may be able to avail himself of this statutory defence, so she would be better advised to sue Coolit under the Occupiers Liability Act 1957 as occupiers and/or in negligence. Florence can recover for both the injury to her person and to her property: s 1(3)(b) Occupiers Liability Act 1957.

George is clearly not a lawful visitor of Eric or Coolit, and comes within the definition of a trespasser as laid down by Lord Dunedin in *Addie v Dumbreck* (1929) as a person who goes onto land without invitation ... and whose presence is either unknown to the proprietor or, if known, is practically objected to'.

The duty owed to George is covered by the Occupiers Liability Act 1984. By s 1(3) of this Act an occupier will only owe a duty to a non-visitor if:

a) he is aware of the danger or has reasonable grounds to believe it exists; and

b) he knows or has reasonable grounds to believe that the non-visitor is on the vicinity of the danger or may come into the vicinity; and

c) the risk is one against which, in all the circumstances, he may reasonably be expected to offer the non-visitor some protection.

If the duty does arise then by s 1(4) it is to take such care as is reasonable in all the circumstances to see that the non-visitor does not suffer injury.

In George's case requirement a) is satisfied as Eric was aware of the danger as can be shown by his placing of the warning notices: *Woolins v British Celanese* (1966). Requirement b) is not satisfied, as Eric has no reason to anticipate George's presence. In *White v St Albans City & District Council* (1990) it was argued that the very presence of a warning showed that the occupier had reason to suspect someone was likely to come into the vicinity of the danger, but this was rejected by the Court of Appeal. Thus, the duty under s 1(4) does not arise in George's case.

Even if the duty does arise it can be discharged by a reasonable warning: s 1(5) (but see above discussion) and by s 1(9) injury only includes personal injury and damage to property is expressly excluded: s 1(8), so in the unlikely event of George being able to establish liability under the 1984 Act the damage to his suit would be irrecoverable.

The question arises if George could establish any liability whether he would be met by the *ex turpi causa non oritur actio* defence as in *National Coal Board v England* (1954). The scope of this defence is difficult to ascertain from the decided cases. In *Euro-Diam v Bathhurst* (1988) it was said that the defence rests on a public policy that the courts will not assist a plaintiff who has been guilty of illegal or immoral conduct of which the courts should take notice. It applies if '... it would be an affront to the public conscience to grant the plaintiff the relief which he seeks ...' per Kerr LJ. Although this test was used in *Thackwell v Barclays Bank* (1986) and *Saunders v Edwards* (1987), and was used (by Beldon LJ) in *Pitts v Hunt* (1990), both Dillon and Balcombe LJJs stated in *Pitts* that they found this test difficult to apply and refused to allow the plaintiff to recover because his claim was based directly on the illegality rather than being incidental. Given these different approaches it is difficult to say whether such a defence would succeed against George.

Question 24

'Any sensible occupier will exclude the onerous duty of care he owes to visitors in respect of his occupation of premises.'

Discuss.

Answer plan

This question requires a discussion of the standard of care required of an occupier of premises and an assessment as to whether this duty is onerous, together with an assessment of the extent to which an occupier is free to exclude this duty.

The following points need to be considered:

* duty of care imposed on occupiers in respect of lawful visitors
  i) generally
  ii) in specific circumstances
  iii) extent to which this duty may be excluded
* duty of care imposed in respect of non-visitors, and the extent to which it may be excluded

Answer

We shall first consider the duty of care that an occupier of premises owes to his lawful visitors. This area is governed by the Occupiers Liability Act 1957, which by s 1(1) replaced the previous common law rules. By s 2(1) an occupier of premises owes the common duty of care to his visitors except in so far as he is free to and does extend, restrict, modify or exclude his duty by agreement or otherwise. This common duty of care is defined in s 2(2) as the duty to take such care as in all the circumstances of the case is reasonable to see that the visitor is reasonably safe in using the premises for the purposes for which he is invited or permitted by the occupier to be there. It follows from s 2(2) that it is the visitor that must be reasonably safe and not the premises - an occupier may maintain his premises in an unsafe state providing only that his visitors are safe. The duty contained within the Act is similar to the duty in a common law negligence action, as can be seen by a consideration of those cases which have decided whether or not there has been a breach of s 2(2): *Bell v Department of Health & Social Security* (1989); *Murphy v Bradford Metropolitan Council* (1991) to take some recent examples. Whether or not this is an onerous duty is in many ways a subjective decision: doubtless those persons who own a large number of properties might consider any duty owed in respect of those premises to be onerous, but it is submitted that a duty which goes no further than the standard *Donoghue* duty of care is not onerous.

One aspect in which the 1957 Act differs from the common law is that it makes specific provision for certain situations. Thus s 2(3)(a) states that an occupier must be prepared for children to be less careful than adults, but this would seem to add little to the *Donoghue* standard of care, for although an occupier must not place temptation in childrens' way: *Latham v Johnson & Nephew Ltd* (1913); *Glasgow Corp v Taylor* (1922), it has been held that an occupier will not be liable for dangers which are obvious even to children: *Liddle v Yorks (North Riding) County Council* (1934) and that as regards children of 'tender year', the occupier is entitled to assume that reasonable parents will not allow such children to be in dangerous situations without protection and is also entitled to assume that parents will act reasonably. As we have already suggested that a duty which goes no further than *Donoghue*, ie which depends on the foresight of a reasonable person and requires that person to act reasonably, is not onerous, s 2(3)(a) would not represent an onerous extension of the occupiers' duty. Section 2(3)(b) provides that an occupier may expect that a person in the exercise of his calling will appreciate and guard against any special risks ordinarily incident to it. Hence, an occupier may employ a person to carry out a hazardous activity on his premises and rely on this provision where that activity lies within that person's calling. This does not mean that merely because a visitor possess a particular skill, that that fact in itself is enough to discharge the duty of care owed to that visitor. Thus, in *Salmon v Seafarer Restaurants* (1983) and *Ogwo v Taylor* (1988) it was held that an occupier owes the same duty of care to a fireman as to any other visitor, and the question to be decided in all these cases was whether the injury to the visitor was reasonably foreseeable. An occupier is, of course, entitled to assume that the fireman will follow standard practice in fighting the fire. Again this provision does not appear to impose an onerous duty on an occupier, as it too adds little to the *Donoghue* type of duty.

Another situation for which the 1957 Act makes specific provision is that it enables the occupier to discharge his duty via a warning - s 2 (4)(a) states that where a visitor has been warned of a danger then that warning will not of itself be enough to discharge the occupiers' duty of care unless in all the circumstances t was enough to allow the visitor to be reasonably safe. Thus, an occupier may discharge his duty by a simple warning notice, providing that in all the circumstances it is sufficient; thus, in *Rae v Mars UK* (1989) it was held that where an unusual danger exists the visitor should not only be warned of the danger but a barrier or additional notice should be placed to show its immediacy. As, however, it is possible for an occupier to discharge his duty by the simple expedient of a suitable notice this supports our contention that duty not onerous.

Finally, the 1957 Act allows the occupier to discharge his duty by entrusting work to independent contractors: s 2(4)(b) provides that where damage is caused to a visitor by a danger due to the faulty execution of any work of construction, maintenance or repair by an independent contractor employed by the occupier, the occupier is not to be treated without more as answerable for the danger if in all the circumstances he had acted reasonably in entrusting the work to an independent contractor and had taken such steps (if any) as he reasonably ought in order to satisfy himself that the contractor was competent and that the work had been properly done. This sub-section has been liberally interpreted as regards the phrase 'work of construction, maintenance or repair': *AMF International v Magnet Bowling* (1968) it was held that the carrying out of some minor work was enough to bring the sub-section into operation, and in *Ferguson v Welsh* (1987) it was held that 'construction' included demolition. It was also held in *Ferguson* that although that sub-section requires the occupier to check that the work 'had been properly done' that the sub-section could apply where the work was still in progress and had not been completed. These decision may be seen as enlarging the circumstances in which an occupier owes a duty of care, but the courts are willing to find that entrusting work to an independent contractor is reasonable, and the wording of the sub-section contemplates that checking the work is not necessary in all circumstances. The guideline used by the courts is that the more technical the work, the less reasonable it is to require the occupier to check it. So in *Haseldine v Daw* (1942) it was held that an occupier need not check the work of a firm of lift repairers, whereas in *Woodward v Mayor of Hastings* (1945) it was held that the work of a cleaner should be checked. Thus, although the courts have widened the scope of the sub-section as regards circumstances in which the duty will arise, the actual duty still seems to be similar to the familiar *Donoghue* duty to take reasonable steps. We could not here that the 1957 Act has made life less onerous for occupiers in that prior to the Act it was held by the House of Lords in *Thomson v Cremin* (1956) that the duty an occupier owed to his visitors was a personal non-delegable duty that could not be discharged by employment competent independent contractors.

Having considered the nature of the occupiers' duty, we now need to see to what extent it can in fact be excluded. Section 2(1) allows an occupier to exclude his duty in so far as he is free to '... by agreement or otherwise'. A major restriction on the freedom of the occupier to do this is contained within the Unfair Contract Terms Act 1977. The 1977 Act controls (inter alia) the exclusion of liability for negligence, and by s 1(1)(c) of the 1977 Act this includes the common duty of care imposed by the 1957 Act. Section 2(1) of the 1977 Act renders void any attempt to exclude liability for death or personal injury resulting from negligence, and by s 2(2) attempts to exclude liability for other loss or damage are subject to the requirement of reasonableness. However the 1977 Act only applies to business liability: s 1(3), and so an occupier of (say) a private house may exclude the duty he would otherwise owe to his visitors by a suitable exclusion clause.

An occupier may be exonerated from liability for risks willingly accepted as his by the visitor: s 2(2) - *Simms v Leigh Rugby Football Club* (1969), and in deciding whether a visitor is *volens* to a danger the presence of warnings or exclusion notices may be relevant. Similarly, the liability of an occupier may be reduced by contributory negligence on the part of the visitor: *Stone v Taffe* (1974), and again the presence of such notices may be relevant.

Overall, therefore, it is difficult to agree with the statement that the duty that an occupier owes to his visitors is onerous. It is based on the requirement to act reasonably, and can be discharged relatively easily via warning notices or the use of independent contractors. As the duty is to take reasonable steps then it could be argued that the onerousness or otherwise of the duty will depend on what the courts consider to be reasonable conduct to expect from an occupier. In this context we might note the dicta in the House of Lords in *Smith v Littlewoods Organisation Ltd* (1987) where both Lord Goff and Lord Mackay were at pains to emphasise that no unreasonable burdens should be placed on occupiers, so it would seem unlikely that any more would be required of occupiers by the courts in the future than has been done in the past. In addition, a non-business occupier will be free to exclude his duty, whilst a business occupier will be free to exclude his liability for loss or damage other than death or personal injury in so far as his exclusion term satisfies the requirements of reasonableness.

Note

1   There is another possible restriction on the freedom of an
    occupier to exclude his duty - it has been argued by
    Winfield and *Jolowicz* that the standard of care imposed by
    the House of Lords in *British Railways Board v Herrington*
    (1972), which applied to trespassers, represents a minimum
    standard that cannot be excluded as it was based on a
    standard of common humanity, but there is no authority
    either for or against this proposition.

Nuisance

Introduction

Questions on nuisance are popular with examiners, possibly because nuisance is a complex topic with several unresolved areas. Much of this complexity is due to the fact that there are few hard and fast rules as to what constitutes a nuisance; instead there are a number of guidelines which the court may or may not decide are relevant in deciding whether a particular activity amounts to a nuisance.

Checklist

Students must have a good grasp of the following aspects:
- Types of activity capable of constituting a nuisance
- Factors indicating whether an interference is unreasonable and the relative importance of these factors inter se
- Possible defendants in a nuisance action
- Defences and especially invalid defences
- The undecided point regarding recoverability of damage for personal injury and economic loss
- Public nuisance

In addition a nuisance question may contain elements of negligence or *Rylands v Fletcher*.

Question 25

Sarah owns a house in a small village which she leases to May who owns four dogs which she keeps in kennels in the garden. The dogs spend large amounts of the day and night barking and this annoys her neighbours Terence and Ursula. Victor, another neighbour, finds the noise during the day particularly annoying as he works nights and has to sleep during the day. All the neighbours complain to May who refuses to do anything, so Ursula lights a large bonfire in her garden in the hope that the smoke will stop the barking. Terence, whose hobby is woodworking, takes the television suppressor off his electric drill and uses it in the evenings to interfere deliberately with the reception on May's television.

Discuss the legal situation.

Answer plan

The following areas should be addressed:

- is barking of dogs a nuisance?
- liability of landlord and tenant in nuisance
- is Victor a sensitive plaintiff?
- liability of Ursula in nuisance for bonfire
- liability of Terence in nuisance for interference with TV reception

Answer

We must first decide whether the barking of the dogs constitutes a nuisance. A nuisance is an unreasonable interference with a person's use or enjoyment of land, or some right over or in connection with it. It is well established that noise can constitute a nuisance: *Halsey v Esso Petroleum* (1961); *Tetley v Chitty* (1986), but not all interference gives rise to liability. There must be give and take between neighbours and the interference must be substantial, not fanciful: *Walter v Selfe* (1851). As we are told that the dogs spend large amounts of the day and night barking, this noise would amount to a nuisance, the duration of the interference being one of the factors that a court would take into account in deciding whether the noise amounts to a nuisance, as the shorter the duration of the interference, the less likely it is to be unreasonable: *Harrison v Southwark & Vauxhall Water Co* (1891).

Given that the barking of the dogs constitutes a nuisance we must next decide who is the proper defendant in respect of this nuisance. As May is responsible for the dogs she will be a defendant, but the landlord, Sarah, will not be liable: the nuisance did not exist before she leased the premises; the premises have not been let for a purpose which constitutes a nuisance (as in *Tetley v Chitty*); and any right Sarah has reserved to enter and repair is irrelevant as the nuisance has not arisen due to the disrepair of the premises. Hence May is the only defendant.

Finally, we must ascertain who can sue in respect of the barking. As nuisance is concerned with a person's use or enjoyment of land only persons with an interest in land can sue: *Malone v Laskey* (1907). Thus, if Terence and Ursula are owners or tenants of the property they can sue, but if, for example, Terence is the sole owner then Ursula will not have the requisite interest in the land to sue. Victor, assuming that he too has the necessary interest in land, may sue but may run into the problem that being a night worker he is a sensitive plaintiff. In *Robinson v Kilvert* (1884) it was held that the plaintiff could not recover where the damage was solely due to the sensitive nature of the plaintiff's property. However, in *McKinnon Industries v Walker* (1951) it was held that once a nuisance has been established a plaintiff can recover for interference with a sensitive use. Hence if Victor can establish that the barking constitutes an unreasonable interference with his use or enjoyment of property he will have full remedies.

The remedies available against May would be damages to compensate for past nuisance and an injunction to prevent further nuisance (1).

We must next consider the actions of Ursula and Terence. Ursula has lit a large bonfire in her garden. This of itself may not constitute a nuisance - the interference must be substantial and not merely fanciful: *Walter v Selfe* (1851). In deciding whether a particular interference is unreasonable or not the court will rely on a series of guidelines rather than on any rigid rules. In Ursula's case the court would consider the duration of the interference, as the shorter the duration of the interference the less likely it is to be unreasonable, as in *Harrison v Southwark & Vauxhall Water Co* (1891). In particular, it seems that an isolated event is unlikely to constitute a nuisance. In *Bolton v Stone* (1949) it was stated that a nuisance must be a state of affairs, however temporary, and not merely an isolated happening. Thus, although Ursula might claim that the bonfire is an isolated event, it does constitute a temporary state of affairs and is capable in law of being a nuisance. A possible argument that Ursula might employ is that she only lights a bonfire on rare occasions and that this is a reasonable use of her land, but the fact that a defendant is only making reasonable use of his land is not of itself a valid defence in nuisance: *Attorney-General v Cole* (1901); *Vanderpant v Mayfair Hotel* (1930). As regards any interference with health and comfort, the court will take into account the character of the neighbourhood: *Bamford v Turnley* (1860), as 'what would be a nuisance in Belgravia Square would not necessarily be so in Bermondsey'; *Sturges v Bridgman* (1879), per Thesiger LJ. Thus, as

Ursula lives in a rural area the occasional lighting of a bonfire might not constitute a nuisance as there must be an element of give and take between neighbours, but if Ursula by her lack of care allowed an annoyance from the bonfire to become excessive, she would become liable in nuisance: *Andreae v Selfridge* (1938). If, however, the smoke from the bonfire causes physical damage to the property (eg discolouration of paintwork, etc) then the character of the neighbourhood is not relevant: *St Helen's Smelting Co v Tipping* (1865). The real problem that Ursula faces, however, is that she is activated by malice, and although malice is not a necessary ingredient of nuisance, its presence is not only a factor to be taken into account: *Christie v Davey* (1893) but its presence may even turn an otherwise non-actionable activity into a nuisance as in *Hollywood Silver Fox Farm v Emnett* (1936) where it seems clear that in the absence of malice no action would have arisen. Hence May could sue Ursula in nuisance (May having the necessary interest in land being a tenant) and obtain damages and an injunction.

Terence is deliberately interfering with May's television reception. This interference is presumably not of limited duration, which is a factor mitigating against unreasonableness of any interference: *Harrison v Southwark & Vauxhall Water Co* (1981). Terence is clearly activated by malice as in *Hollywood Silver Fox Farm* and *Christie v Davey* so *prima facie* he would seem to have committed a nuisance. However, May has a problem in that in *Bridlington Relay v Yorkshire Electricity Board* (1965) Buckley J held that interference with purely recreational facilities such as television reception did not constitute an actionable nuisance, and following this May would have no cause of action against Terence (2).

Notes

1 The court does have power, under s 50 Supreme Court Act 1981 to award damages in lieu of an injunction, but this power is used very sparingly. In *Shelfer v City of London Electric Lighting Co* (1895) the Court of Appeal held that damages should only be awarded where
   i)   the injury to the plaintiff's legal rights is small;
   ii) the damage is capable of being estimated in money;
   iii) the damage can be adequately compensated by a small money payment;

iv) the case is one in which it would be oppressive to the defendant to grant an injunction.

On the fact that we are given there seems no good reason for the court to diverge from the normal practice and refuse to grant an injunction against May.

2   One might note here that this approach has not been followed in Canada. In *Nor-Video Services Ltd v Ontario Hydro* (1978) it was held that interference with television reception could found an action in nuisance, although the plaintiff in this case did suffer an interference with their business which May has not. In *Bridlington* Buckley J stated that he was not laying down a rule that in no circumstances could interference with recreational facilities ever constitute a nuisance, but that at present he did not regard the ability to receive interference free television as an important part of an ordinary householder's enjoyment of his property, particularly as the interference in question affected only one channel. It could be argued that things have changed since 1965, and that ordinary persons regard interference free television as important and that as *Bridlington* did not purport to lay down any absolute rule in this area, the fact that all the programmes are subject to interference and that Terence is acting maliciously should enable May to sue.

Question 26

Alban Manufacturing plc own a factory set in the centre of a manufacturing town in the Midlands and which employs a considerable number of people. One day the factory emits a quantity of acid smut which damages the paintwork of the neighbouring houses and some cars. In addition Alban have recently installed some machinery which is considerably more noisy than their previous machinery and which annoys their immediate neighbours.

Discuss any potential liability of Alban.

Answer plan

This is a deceptive question in that at first glance it only seems to cover a few issues of nuisance. However, a little careful study will show that it raises a number of issues.

The following areas must be discussed:

- utility of Alban's conduct
- relevance of neighbourhood to interference with health and comfort and physical damage
- can an isolated event constitute a nuisance?
- possibility of action in public nuisance
- additional actions in *Rylands v Fletcher* and negligence

Answer

We shall first consider whether Alban plc have incurred any liability in nuisance. A nuisance is an unreasonable interference with a person's use or enjoyment of land, or some right over or in connection with it. However, not all interference necessarily gives rise to liability and there must be give and take between neighbours - the interference must be substantial and not fanciful: *Walter v Selfe* (1851). The courts have developed a number of guidelines that are used to determine whether any particular interference is unreasonable, but each test is only a guideline and not a condition, and the court has to evaluate the defendant's behaviour in all the circumstances of the case. In Alban's case the court will consider whether the emission was an isolated event. In *Bolton v Stone* (1949) it was stated that a nuisance could not arise from an isolated happening but that it had to arise from a state of affairs, however temporary. Thus, in *Midwood v Manchester Corp* (1905) a gas explosion was held to be a nuisance because although it was an isolated event it was due to a pre-existing state of affairs, namely the build up of gas. On this basis it could be argued that the escape of acid smut was due to a build up of this material on Alban's premises and, thus, the emission can constitute an actionable nuisance. The damage suffered is not due to any sensitivity use of the neighbours property (as in *Robinson v Kilvert* (1889)) and although the premises are in the centre of a manufacturing town, the character of the neighbourhood is not to be taken into account where physical damage to property has been caused: *St Helen's Smelting Co v Tipping* (1865). We are told that Alban employ a considerable number of people but the utility of the defendant's conduct, although a factor to be taken into account seems to be a factor of lesser importance in the overall assessment - see *Adams v Ursell* (1913) and the Irish case of *Bellew v Cement Co* (1948).

Thus, the fact that Alban provide employment is not a conclusive factor. Note that it would not be necessary to show that Alban were negligent as negligence is not an essential ingredient of nuisance. Indeed it would be no defence to Alban to show that they took all reasonable care and even all possible care - provided that they caused the nuisance that is sufficient. Thus, taking all the circumstances into account a court would find that the emission constituted an actionable nuisance. The possible plaintiffs would be those persons whose property has been damaged, providing that they have an interest in the land in question: *Malone v Laskey* (1907), ie the owner and tenants could sue. Such persons could obtain damages for the loss they have suffered together with an injunction to prevent future emissions.

As regards the noisy machinery it is well established that noise can constitute a nuisance: *Halsey v Esso Petroleum* (1961); *Tetley v Chitty* (1986). In deciding whether the noise from the machinery amounts to a nuisance, it is clearly not an isolated event of limited duration, nor is there any evidence of sensitivity on the part of the neighbours. However, as the noise is an interference with health and comfort the character of the neighbourhood must be taken into account: *Bamford v Turnley* (1860). As Thesiger LJ stated in *Sturges v Bridgman* (1879) 'What would be a nuisance in Belgravia Square would not necessarily be so in Bermondsey'. As we are told that Alban's factory is in the centre of a manufacturing town then the neighbours would have to accept a certain amount of noise as part of everyday living. However, in *Roshner v Polsue & Alfieri Ltd* (1906) where a person lived in an area largely devoted to printing he obtained an injunction to prevent the use of a new printing machine which interfered with his sleep. Thus, it will be a question of act for the court to decide whether or not the increased noise amounts to a nuisance in all the circumstances of the case. Again only persons with an interest in land could sue in respect of this noise.

Alban might also, as regards the emission, be liable in public nuisance: *Halsey v Esso Petroleum*. Similar considerations will apply as for private nuisance, but it must additionally be shown, firstly, that the persons affected by the nuisance consist of the public or a section of the public: see *Attorney General v PYA Quarries* (1957) and, secondly, that the plaintiff suffered damage over and above that suffered by the public at large. In *Halsey* it was held that where acid smuts damaged washing hung out to dry and a car, that the owner of the car could sue in public nuisance. Thus, the car owners whose car paintwork is damaged could sue in public nuisance and they would not have to have any interest in land. Whether those persons whose house paintwork was damaged could sue would depend on their being able to prove damage over and above that suffered by the public at large.

An additional cause of action which might be against Alban is under the rule in *Rylands v Fletcher* (1868), ie that a person who for his own purposes brings onto his land and collects and keeps there anything likely to do mischief if it escapes, must keep it in at his peril, and, if he does not do so, he is *prima facie* answerable for all the damage which is the natural consequence of its escape. In addition there must be a non-natural user of land. Again in *Halsey* the defendants were liable under *Rylands* for the damage caused by the acid smuts to both the washing and the motor car. However, since *Halsey* was decided in 1961 the interpretation given to 'non natural' user has changed from 'there by nature' to 'ordinary' or 'usual' - see *British Celanese v Hunt* (1969) and the recent case of *Cambridge Water Co v Eastern Counties Leather* (1991), where factories in industrial parks were held to be a natural user of the land. In *Cambridge Water* it was held that factors to be considered included whether the activity was for the general benefit of the community and the character of the neighbourhood. Looking at all the circumstances, a court might well hold that a factory in a manufacturing town providing considerable employment opportunities does not constitute a non natural user and, therefore, despite *Halsey* a claim under *Rylands* might fail.

It would also be possible for those persons affected by the emission to sue in negligence, while those affected by the noise only would have to show damage, eg loss of a night's sleep: *Andreae v Selfridge & Co* (1938) or the loss of the opportunity to be quietly in bed of a Sunday morning: *Haddon v Lynch* (1911) (to take just two examples of damage in the law of nuisance).

The plaintiffs will have to show that Alban owes them a duty of care. In a novel fact situation the court will apply the test favoured by the House of Lords in *Caparo Industries v Dickman* (1990) and *Murphy v Brentwood District Council* (1990), namely to consider the foreseeability of damage, proximity of relationship and the reasonableness or otherwise of imposing a duty of care. If a duty is found to exist, it must be shown that Alban were in breach of their duty by failing to act as a reasonable factory owner would: *Blyth v Birmingham Waterworks* (1856), and that this breach caused the damage, and that the damage was not too remote in that it was reasonably foreseeable: *The Wagon Mound* (1961). The problem in a negligence action will be in proving that Alban were in breach of their duty for if they followed the standard procedures of their trade there is good evidence that they were not in breach, see eg *Knight v Home Office* (1990).

Question 27

The Eastway Council have run an adventure playground for children for many years. About a year ago several houses were built adjacent to the playground and the residents of the houses now complain of the noise emanating from the playground. In addition the Council has resurfaced the playground causing dust and fumes to enter the residents' properties. Several times a week footballs from the playground land in the residents' gardens, but the Council refuse to build a high fence round the playground on the grounds that they have insufficient funds.

Advise the residents of any remedies available to them.

Answer plan

This question covers a range of aspects on both liability and defences to actions in nuisance, together with the possibility that must always be considered in nuisance cases of alternative courses of action.

The following areas should be addressed:
- whether noise constitutes a nuisance
- whether dust and fumes constitute a nuisance
- liability of Council for any nuisance, private or public
- possible defences available for Council
- action in negligence
- action under *Rylands v Fletcher*
- action for trespass to land

Answer

Dealing first with the noise emanating from the playground it is well established that noise is capable of constituting a nuisance: *Halsey v Esso Petroleum* (1961); *Tetley v Chitty* (1986). A nuisance can be defined as an unreasonable interference with a person's use or enjoyment of land, or some right over or in connection with it. However, not all interference will necessarily constitute a nuisance; there must be give and take between neighbours and the interference must be substantial and not fanciful: *Walter v Selfe* (1851). There are a number of factors that the court takes into account in deciding whether an interference is unreasonable or not and we shall consider the application of these guidelines to the noise. One factor that needs to be considered is the duration of the interference, as if this is short the interference is not likely to be held unreasonable: *Harrison v Southwark & Vauxhall Water Co* (1891). However, we are told that the playground has been in operation for many years so this time factor is in favour of the existence of a nuisance. We are not told that the plaintiffs are especially sensitive to noise or that a reasonable person living in the area would not object to the noise which are capable of being possible defences, so we must consider the character of the neighbourhood. This is a relevant factor where the interference is with health and comfort: *Bamford v Turnley* (1860); as Thesiger LJ stated in *Sturges v Bridgman* (1879) 'What would be a nuisance in Belgravia Square would not necessarily be so in Bermondsey'. In *Halsey v Esso Petroleum* (1961) Veale J held that the standard was that of the ordinary and reasonable man living in the vicinity of the alleged nuisance. This would be a question of fact for the court to decide. The fact that the playground is socially useful is a factor to be considered, but it seems to be easily overridden: see *Adams v Ursell* (1913); *Bellew v Cement Co* (1948). Given that the noise can be shown to be unreasonable the next question is who can sue, and only those persons with an interest in the land affected can sue: *Malone v Laskey* (1907) - not their guests or other members of the family. We must next decide on an appropriate defendant - clearly there would be little point in suing the children and so the only practical defendant would be the Council. The owner of land may be liable for a nuisance committed on his land which he has not created where he allows the land to be used for a purpose and a nuisance is an 'ordinary and necessary' consequence of such use:

Tetley v Chitty per McNeill J. Thus, the neighbours could sue the Council for damages in respect of past noise, nuisance and for an injunction to stop future noise nuisance. It would be no defence to the Council to allege that the plaintiff came to the nuisance: *Sturges v Bridgman*, although the plaintiff must, of course, accept the standard of the neighbourhood to which he comes. Neither would it be possible for the Council to claim the defence of prescription, ie that the nuisance has been continued for twenty years, because time does not begin to run until the plaintiffs are aware of the nuisance: *Sturges v Bridgman*, nor would it avail the Council to claim that the public interest of providing a playground should prevail over the private rights of the residents: see *Pride of Derby v British Celanese* (1953) and *Kennaway v Thompson* (1981) where private interests were held to prevail over public interests (1). The remedies available would be damages for past nuisance and an injunction to prevent further infractions.

As regards the dust and fumes resulting from the resurfacing again this is capable of constituting a nuisance: *Matania v National Provincial Bank* (1936), if the interference is unreasonable. In this instance the duration of the interference is limited, which tends to show that the interference is less likely to be found to be unreasonable: *Harrison v Southwark & Vauxhall Water Co.* Attention may also be paid to the utility of the Council's conduct and this is especially true in construction cases where the interference is temporary, although as can be seen from the above discussion this factor is capable of being overridden. Overall, however, it would seem that the chances of the residents proceeding against the Council are slim in respect of the resurfacing work.

The landing of footballs in the gardens is also capable of constituting an actionable nuisance - see *Miller v Jackson* (1977) and the majority view of the CA.

From the facts given it seems unlikely that a sufficient number of persons are affected for the activities to amount to a public nuisance - see *Attorney General v PYA Quarries* (1957).

The neighbours could also sue the Council in negligence. The neighbours will have to show that the Council owes them a duty of care. In a novel fact situation the court will apply the test favoured by the House of Lords in *Caparo Industries v Dickman* (1990) and

Murphy v Brentwood District Council (1990), namely to consider the foreseeability of damage, proximity of relationship and the reasonableness or otherwise of imposing a duty of care. If a duty is found to exist it must be shown that the Council were in breach of their duty by failing to act as a reasonable council would: *Blyth v Birmingham Waterworks* (1856); that this breach caused the damage *Cork v Kirby MacLean* (1952), and that the damage was not too remote in that it was reasonably foreseeable: *The Wagon Mound* (1961). Although the neighbours could probably succeed in establishing that a duty of care was owed, and that those who are only complaining in respect of the noise suffered damage, it might be difficult to prove that the Council were in breach of their duty. Similarly as regards the damage from the resurfacing, the neighbours would again have to prove breach by the Council which might be difficult. In respect of the footballs landing in the garden *prima facie* it would be simpler to prove breach on the grounds that the Council could prevent this damage by building a high fence and they have refused to do this. The Council's defence to this would be lack of funds and in *Knight v Home Office* (1990), in holding that a prison hospital had not been in breach of their duty, Pill J stated that the court must take into account the fact that resources available for the public service are limited. However, as the cricket club in *Miller v Jackson* were held liable in negligence it would seem likely that the Council would also be found liable.

The neighbours should also be advised of the chances of mounting a successful action under the rule in *Rylands v Fletcher* (1868), which states that a person who for his own purposes brings onto his land and collects and keeps there anything likely to do mischief if it escapes, must keep it in at his peril, and, if he does not do so, he is *prima facie* answerable for all the damage which is the natural consequence of its escape. In addition the defendant must make a non-natural user of his land. Such an action would not lie against the Council as regards the noise, as this has not been collected and kept on their land by the Council. Similarly, the Council have not collected and kept the footballs on their land. It could be argued that the Council have incurred liability by allowing the playing of football when they could have banned such activity, but the neighbours would run into the problem of showing that the Council made a non-natural use of their land. The modern interpretation given to this phrase is 'ordinary' or 'usual'; in *British Celanese v Hunt* (1969) and the recent case of *Cambridge Water Co v Eastern Countries Leather* (1991)it was held that using industrial estates for manufacturing purposes was just what they were intended for, and so such use was not non-natural. By analogy, the Council could argue that the use of a childrens playground for the playing of football by children was its intended use and so was not non-natural. However, the Council might incur liability in respect of the duty and fumes from the resurfacing.

Finally, the residents in whose garden the footballs have landed could sue the children for trespass to land as this can be committed negligently: *League Against Cruel Sports v Scott* (1985) but there seems little point in suing children in respect of this.

Note

1   One could mention here the views expressed by Lord Denning in *Miller v Jackson* that public interests should prevail over private interests where there is a clash but this approach was not followed in *Kennaway* whose private rights were allowed to prevail. Lord Denning also stated that the reason for cricket balls coming into the plaintiff's garden was not the playing of cricket but the building of the houses, but the view was rejected by the majority of the Court of Appeal. It seems unsafe to advise the neighbours in the present case to rely on this dissenting judgment.

Question 28

In attempting to advise a client of his likely success in an action, there can be no area so fraught with difficulties as private nuisance.

Discuss.

Answer plan

This question calls for a discussion of some of the problems that would be encountered in successfully running an action in private nuisance.

In particular the following points need to be covered:

- guidelines in determining whether any particular interference is unreasonable
- possible defendants
- defences available to a defendant
- scope of the action as regards personal injury and economic loss

Answer

The law on private nuisance, or nuisance as we shall henceforth call it, gives rise to a number of difficulties in its application to factual situations. This is due not to any conceptual difficulty, but rather to the variety of circumstances in which nuisances have been held to exist and to the flexible approach which the courts adopt in deciding in any given case whether or not a nuisance exists. In addition the exact scope of the tort is shrouded in uncertainty. We shall examine, therefore, these uncertainties. A nuisance can be defined as all unreasonable interference with a person's use or enjoyment of land, or some right over, or in connection with it. It follows from this definition that only persons with an interest in the land affected can sue *Malone v Lasky* (1907),which should give rise to no difficulties in advising a client, but it seems from the decision in *Bridlington Relay Ltd v Yorkshire Electricity Board* (1965) that interference with purely recreational facilities lies outside the tort of nuisance. It is, however, instructive to note the exact words used by Buckley, J in his decision, viz, 'For myself, however, I do not think that it can at present be said that the ability to receive television free from occasional, even if recurrent and severe, electrical interference is so important a part of an ordinary householder's enjoyment of his property that such interference should be regarded as a legal nuisance ...'. Given the amount of television viewing that an ordinary householder undertakes in 1992 one might suggest that what was not an unreasonable interference in 1965 might be considered unreasonable in 1992, and that such interference might be actionable nowadays.

Moving on to what constitutes an unreasonable interference, we meet a major area of uncertainty. The courts have laid down a series of guidelines as to what constitutes an unreasonable interference, but as in any situation where it has to be decided whether or not some particular conduct is reasonable, the courts decisions cannot amount to binding precedents. The total circumstances of the case must always be taken into account in deciding this question. What gives rise to particular uncertainty in nuisance is that the courts seem willing, when the circumstances require it, to either disregard a particular guideline or to assign it less importance in some cases than in others. Nevertheless, there is one guideline that the courts seem willing to follow on almost all occasions, namely the rule that not all interference gives rise to liability, that there must be give and take between neighbours and that the interference must be substantial and not merely fanciful: *Walter v Selfe* (1851). When we consider the guidelines that the courts adopt we shall see that there are three that the courts tend to apply in the majority of cases, and three that the courts consider, but which they seem more willing to attach a lower importance to if the circumstances so require.

Turning now to the first category of criteria, we have the duration of the interference. The shorter the duration of the interference, the less likely it is to be found unreasonable. So in *Harrison v Southwark & Vauxhall Water Co* (1891) temporary work in sinking a shaft was held not to constitute a nuisance because of the temporary nature of the work. Given that a short interference is not likely to constitute an interference, the question arises as to whether an isolated event is capable of constituting a nuisance. In *Bolton v Stone* (1949) it was held that an isolated happening could not constitute a nuisance, but what was required was a state of affairs, however temporary. Thus, in *Midwood v Manchester Corp* (1905) a gas explosion was held to constitute a nuisance even though it was an isolated event because it was due to a pre-existing state of affairs, namely a build up of gas.*Castle v St Augustine's Links* (1922) is a similar example of an isolated event being held to constitute a nuisance as the occurrence was due to a pre-existing wrongful state of affairs. One factor which the courts seem to always take into account is whether the plaintiff is abnormally sensitive. The rule is that a person cannot increase his neighbour's possible legal liability just because he puts his land to some special use. Thus, in *Robinson v Kilvert* (1889) a plaintiff could not recover for damage caused by heat from the defendants heating pipes to his stock of 'exceptionally sensitive' brown paper, as the heat would not have interfered with a normal use of the property. However, once a nuisance has been established, then full remedies are available in respect of any unusually sensitive use the plaintiff makes of his property: *McKinnon Industries v Walker* (1952) The character of the neighbourhood is also a relevant factor where the interference is with health and comfort: *Bamford v Turnley* (1860). This is also illustrated by the famous statement of Thesiger LJ in *Sturges v Bridgman* (1879) where he said 'what would be a nuisance in Belgravia would not necessarily be so in Bermondsey'. It should not be thought that this criterion means that if an area is industrialised or built up that no nuisance can take place there - the question that has to he decided is whether the interference is unreasonable or not having regard to the general area. Thus, in *Roshmer v Polsue & Alfieri Ltd* (1906) a plaintiff who lived in an area which was mostly given over to printing successfully claimed that the noise of a new printing machine constituted a nuisance as it was held that the noise of this machine was excessive even for an area largely devoted to printing. Clearly, therefore, whether a particular interference with health and comfort is actionable will depend on the exact nature of the area and the interference in question, making advice on the chances of success at trial difficult to predict with any confidence. It should be noted, however, that the character of the neighbourhood is not relevant where property damage has been caused: *St Helens Smelting Co v Tipping* (1865).

Now we come to those guidelines to which the courts are ready to attach a lesser importance when the circumstances of the case demand it. Firstly, there is the utility of the defendants conduct, as the more useful it is the less likely it is that the resulting interference with the plaintiff's land is unreasonable. This would be especially true in, for example, construction work where in addition the interference will be temporary. However, if the circumstances so require, the court will override this guideline. So in the Irish case of *Bellew v Cement Co* (1948) the court decided that the only cement works in Ireland constituted a nuisance and granted an injunction which closed it down for a period of time despite the fact that the supply of cement was vitally important. In *Adams v Ursell* (1913) an English court also rejected the defence that the defendants activities were useful. Secondly, the courts may take into account any malice on the part of the defendant. Malice is not an essential ingredient of nuisance, but if the defendant is acting maliciously, any interference caused thereby is more likely to be unreasonable. Thus, in *Christie v Davey* (1893), where the defendants acts were totally malicious, they were held to constitute a nuisance. In *Christie* it is quite likely that the acts of the defendants would have been held to constitute a nuisance even in the absence of malice, but in *Hollywood Silver Fox Farm v Emmett* (1936) the presence of malice converted what would probably not have been a nuisance into a nuisance. There the defendant fired some guns at the boundary of his land adjacent to the plaintiff's land where foxes that were sensitive to noise were breeding. It was held that this constituted a nuisance, although it seems clear that in the absence of malice no nuisance would have been committed.

The final guideline to which the courts look is whether there has been some fault on the part of the defendant. Negligence is not an essential ingredient of nuisance, although it may often be present in practice, as it is no defence to an action in nuisance for the defendant to show that he took all reasonable care or even all possible care. Provided that the defendant caused (or continued) the nuisance he is liable. However, the defendants lack of care in allowing an annoyance to become excessive may give rise to liability in nuisance: *Andreae v Selfridge & Co* (1938).

It can be seen from the above discussion that whether the court will decide in any particular case that the interference suffered was unreasonable is difficult to predict, and tends to support the statement which forms this question. There are, however, additional areas of uncertainty within the law of nuisance. One problem concerns who can be sued in respect of any particular interference. There is no problem where the creator of the nuisance can be identified, but problems may arise where the occupier of land from which the nuisance emanates did not create the thing which causes the nuisance. If the relevant device was created by a trespasser then the occupier will only be liable if he continues or adopts the device: *Sedleigh-Denfield v O'Callaghan* (1940). If the occupier does neither of these things it may be impossible to identify the trespasser, leaving the plaintiff without a remedy. If the nuisance arose from an act of nature then by the authority of *Goldman v Hargrave* (1967) and *Leakey v National Trust* (1980) the occupier must take reasonable steps to minimise foreseeable damage to others. Again what a court will think is reasonable in any set of circumstances can be difficult to predict. If a tenant causes a nuisance on demised premises and is not worth suing because he will be unable to satisfy judgment, the landlord may be liable if he knew of the nuisance before the start of the tenancy, or if he let the purposes for which the tenancy was created would give rise to a nuisance as an 'ordinary and necessary' consequence of the use: *Tetley v Chitty* (1986).

It is generally not a valid defence to show that the plaintiff came to the nuisance: *Sturges v Bridgman* (1879). However, in *Miller v Jackson* (1977), where some houses were built at the edge of a village green on which cricket was played, and cricket balls landed in the plaintiff's gardens, Lord Denning stated that *Sturges* was no longer binding today, but this was not the view of the other members of the Court of Appeal. Lord Denning also stated in this case that where there was a conflict between public and private rights, that public rights should prevail. This was exactly opposite to the view taken in the earlier case of *Pride of Derby v British Celanese* (1953) where it was held that private rights should prevail. However, in the later case of *Kennaway v Thompson* (1981) the Court of Appeal refused to follow Lord Denning's dicta and held that where there was a clash between private and public rights that private rights should prevail. This represents a further area of uncertainty in the law of nuisance, but it is submitted that Lord Denning's dicta regarding the priority of public rights does not represent the correct view of the law at present, and that his dicta regarding *Sturges*, a long established case, must await confirmation by the House of Lords.

Finally, we should note that it. is still a debatable point of law whether recovery is possible in nuisance in respect of personal injuries or economic loss. In *Cunard v Antifyre* (1933) it was stated that recovery for personal injury is not possible, and dicta in *British Celanese v Hunt* (1969) and in *Ryeford Homes v Sevenoaks District Council* (1989) suggest that economic loss is recoverable.

Thus, taking an overall view of the law of nuisance we can see that there are a number of areas where either the law is uncertain, or where it would be difficult to predict with any confidence at all what decision a court would come to faced with a particular set of facts.

The Rule in Rylands v Fletcher and Fire

Introduction

Questions on *Rylands v Fletcher* are popular with examiners as there are a number of undecided aspects to the rule, and because it is very easy to combine a *Rylands* situation with elements of nuisance or negligence or animals.

Checklist

Students must be able to discuss the following topics:

* The elements of the rule itself with especial reference to
* The non-natural user requirement
* Whether personal injuries are recoverable under *Rylands*
* Defences and especially the independent acts of third parties

Question 29

Delta Manufacturing plc own and operate a factory situated in an industrial estate on the outskirts of a small town. One day the environmental control system malfunctioned for some unknown reason and large quantities of toxic fumes were emitted. These fumes damaged paintwork on some houses in the town and some inhabitants also suffered an allergic reaction to the fumes. As a result of the adverse publicity the town has seen a reduction in its normal tourist trade and the local shopkeepers are complaining of loss of business.

Advise Delta Manufacturing plc of any liability they might have incurred.

Would your advice differ if Delta operated their factory under statutory authority?

Answer plan

It is important in answering this question to consider the possible courses of action in detail, paying particular attention to *Rylands* and nuisance, and the possibility of a negligence action. The defence of statutory authority must also be considered for these actions.

The following points must be discussed:

- ingredients of *Rylands* with especial reference to non-natural user
- recoverability for property damage by landowners
- recoverability for property damage by landowners and non-landowners
- ingredients of nuisance
- negligence and the problem of proof of breach of duty
- statutory authority as a defence to the above actions

Answer

We shall first consider whether Delta have incurred any liability under the rule in *Rylands v Fletcher* (1868) which is that a 'person who for how own purposes brings onto his lands and collects and keeps there anything likely to do mischief if it escapes, must keep it in at his peril, and if he does not do so, he is *prima facie* answerable for all the damage which is the natural consequence of its escape'. In addition the defendant must have made a 'non-natural' use of his land.

The fumes have been brought onto Delta's land for Delta's purposes, and they have been brought onto Delta's land in the sense that they are not something that is there by nature such as thistles - *Giles v Walker* (1890), or rainwater - *Smith v Kenrick* (1849). The toxic fumes are clearly likely to do mischief if they escape and there has been an escape from Delta's premises as required by *Read v Lyons* (1947). Finally, we must determine whether or not there has been a non-natural user of land, an aspect that has given rise to much confusion. In *Rylands* itself the word natural was used to mean something on the land by nature, but later cases have construed the word as meaning 'ordinary' or usual. In *Rickards v Lothian* (1931) Lord Moulton said of the use of land required to bring *Rylands* into operation 'It must be some special use bringing with it increased danger to others, and must not merely be the ordinary use of ... or such a use as is proper for the general benefits of the community'. In *Read v Lyons* (1947) Viscount Simon described Lord Moulton's analysis of *Rylands* as 'of the first importance'. In *Mason v Levy Auto Parts* (1967) McKenna J held that in deciding whether there had been a non-natural user of land the factors to be taken into account were

(i) the quantities of material brought by the defendants onto their land (ii) the manner in which the material was stored, and (iii) the character of the neighbourhood. These factors seem to be moving *Rylands* in the direction of negligence. However, in *British Celanese v Hunt* (1969) Lawton J held that as the defendants factory was situated on an industrial estate the defendants were using the land for the very purpose for which it was intended. He also noted that the things being manufactured were for the general benefit of the community. More recently, in *Cambridge Water Co v Eastern Counties Leather* (1991) it was held by Kennedy J that the storage of toxic chemicals in a factory based in an industrial village was a natural use of the land. It was stated that it was necessary to consider whether the storage created special risks for adjacent occupiers, whether the activity was for the general benefit of the community, the amounts stored and the character of the neighbourhood. Thus, by analogy with *British Celanese* and *Cambridge Water*, as Delta are situated on an industrial estate they are not making a non-natural use of their land and so the rule in *Rylands v Fletcher* does not operate.

If the rule were to be applicable then the houseowners could recover for damage to their paintwork (*Rylands*) and both landowners (*Hale v Jennings Bros* (1938)) and non-landowners (*Perry v Kendrick Transport* (1956); *Halsey v Esso Petroleum* (1961)) could recover for the allergic reaction. The local shopkeepers have suffered economic loss and despite *Weller v Foot and Mouth Disease Research Institute* (1965) there seems to be no clear authority for recovery on their part.

We shall next consider whether any action will be against Delta in nuisance. As these landowners also suffered the allergic reaction it is an undecided point as to whether damage can be recovered for personal injury, although *Cunard v Antifyre* (1933) is against recovery. In any event those persons who do not have the requisite interest in land will be unable to recover: *Malone v Laskey* (1907). The shopkeepers may be able to recover for their economic loss: *British Celanese v Hunt*, though again this point is uncertain.

An action in public nuisance may also be against Delta. Here the plaintiff will have to show that the nuisance affected a section of the public: *Attorney-General v PYA Quarries* (1957) and that he suffered damage over and above that suffered by the public at large. The advantage to plaintiffs in public nuisance in that no interest in land is required and both personal injury and economic loss are recoverable: *Rose v Miles* (1815) so that those persons with no interest in land could sue in respect of the allergic reaction, which would constitute special damage, as could the shopkeepers.

Finally, Delta may also be liable in negligence. There would be no difficulty in showing the existence of a duty of care and causation and foreseeability, but there could be problems in proving breach as we are told that the emission occurred for an unknown reason. A possible plaintiff might seek to rely on *res ipsa loquitur* but this would not reverse the burden of proof which lies on the plaintiff throughout: *Ng Chun Pui v Lee Chuen Tat* (1988). If Delta could show that they had in place a proper system of inspection and control; *Henderson v Jenkins & Sons* (1970) this would be sufficient to negate liability. If negligence could be proved against D then of course any plaintiff who has suffered damage to property or to the person may sue but the shopkeepers would be unable to recover for their economic loss as the chances of a plaintiff now successfully relying on *Junior Books v Veitch* (1983) seems non-existent.

If the factory had been operated under statutory authority then liability would not arise either under *Rylands* or nuisance unless negligence on the part of Delta could be shown: *Green v Chelsea Waterworks* (1984); *Allen v Gulf Oil Refining* (1981).

Question 30

Edward owns a garden centre in a rural area. He specialises in growing and selling orchids which need to be reared in heated greenhouses, and he has an extremely large storage tank containing heating oil which he uses to heat the greenhouses. Due to internal corrosion of the tank the oil escapes and contaminates some vegetables growing on a farm belonging to Frank, Edward's neighbour. The oil also escapes onto the road and Frank, who is driving along the road at the time, skids and crashes his car. Frank cuts his head. As a result Frank cannot go to market and sell his cattle, and must feed them for another three months before he next has the chance to sell them.

Advise Edward.

Would your advice differ if the escape of oil had been caused by Jack, a rival of Edward's opening the tap of the oil tank?

Answer plan

Again this is a question involving a multiplicity of courses of action, viz *Rylands*, nuisance and negligence, and the ingredients and defences to this action must be considered.

The following points in particular need to be discussed:

- ingredients of *Rylands* and especially non-natural user
- types of damage recoverable under *Rylands*
- ingredients of nuisance
- damages recoverable under nuisance
- liability in negligence
- act of third party as defence to *Rylands*, nuisance, negligence

Answer

We shall first consider whether Edward has incurred any liability under the rule in *Rylands v Fletcher* (1868) which is that a 'person who for his own purposes brings onto his lands and collects and keeps there anything likely to do mischief if it escapes, must keep it in at his peril, and if he does not do so, he is *prima facie* answerable for all the damage which is the natural consequence of its escape'. In addition the defendant must have made a 'non-natural' use of his land.

The oil has been brought onto Edward's land for Edward's purposes, and has been brought onto Edward's land in the sense that it is not something that is there by nature such as thistles - *Giles v Walker* (1980) or rainwater - *Smith v Kenrick* (1849). The oil is clearly likely to do mischief if it escapes and there has been an escape from Edward's premises as required by *Read v Lyons* (1947). Finally, we must determine whether or not there has been a non-natural user of land, an aspect that has given rise to much confusion. In *Rylands* itself the word natural was used to mean something on the land by nature, but later cases have construed the word as meaning 'ordinary' or usual. In *Rickards v Lothian* (1931) Lord Moulton said of the use of land required to bring *Rylands* into operation 'It must be some special use bringing with it increased danger to others, and must not merely be the ordinary use of ... or such a use as is proper for the general benefits of the community'. In *Read v Lyons* Viscount Simon described Lord Moulton's analysis of *Rylands* as 'of the first importance'. In *Mason v Levy Auto Parts* (1967) McKenna J held that in deciding whether there had been a non-natural user of land the factors to be taken into account were (i) the quantities of material brought by the defendants onto their land (ii) the manner in which the material was stored, and (iii) the character of the neighbourhood. These factors seem to be moving *Rylands* in the direction of negligence. However, in *British Celanese v Hunt* (1969) Lawton J held that as the defendants situated on an industrial estate the defendants were using the land for the very purpose for which it was intended. He also noted that the things being manufactured were for the general benefit of the community. More recently, in *Cambridge Water Co v Eastern Counties Leather* (1991) it was held by Kennedy J that the storage of toxic chemicals in a factory based in an industrial village was a natural use of the land. It was stated that it was necessary to consider whether the storage created special risks for adjacent occupiers, whether the activity was for the general benefit of the community, the amounts stored and the character of the neighbourhood.

Given that the area in question is rural and that the storage of oil creates risks for adjacent owners it seems likely that the use is non-natural and that the rule in *Rylands v Fletcher* applies to the escape. Considering now the damage caused, it is clear from *Rylands* itself that Frank can recover the damage to his vegetables as Frank is a landowner who has suffered property damage on his land. As regards the damage to Frank's car, Frank is a landowner who has suffered property damage but at the time of the damage the property was not on his land. In *Halsey v Esso Petroleum* (1961) the plaintiff was allowed to recover under these circumstances. The cut to Frank's head is damage to the person, although not directly on the point the House of Lords in *Read v Lyons* is against recovery but recovery was allowed by the Court of Appeal in *Perry v Kendrick Transport* (1956) and the High Court in *Halsey v Esso Petroleum*, so it seems that recovery for personal injury is likely. The resulting additional expense for cattle feed to which Frank has been put is consequential on the cut to his head, and is similar to loss of earnings rather than pure economic loss and that too can be recovered.

We must next consider whether Edward has incurred any liability in nuisance. A nuisance is an unreasonable interference with a person's use or enjoyment of land, or some right over or in connection with it. However, not all interference necessarily gives rise to liability and there must be give and take between neighbours - the interference must be substantial and not fanciful: *Walter v Selfe* (1851). The courts have developed a number of guidelines that are used to determine whether any particular interference is unreasonable, but each test is only a guideline and not a condition, and the court has to evaluate the defendant's behaviour in all the circumstances of the case. In Edward's case the court will consider whether the escape was an isolated event. In *Bolton v Stone* (1949) it was stated that a nuisance could not arise from an isolated happening but that it had to arise from a state of affairs, however temporary. Thus, in *Midwood v Manchester Corp* (1905) a gas explosion was held to be a nuisance because although it was an isolated event it was due to a pre-existing state of affairs, namely the build up of gas. On this basis it could be argued that the escape of oil was due to a build up of this material on Edward's premises and, thus, the escape can constitute an actionable nuisance. The damage suffered is not due to any sensitivity use of the neighbours property (as in *Robinson v Kilvert* (1889)) and the character of the neighbourhood is not to be taken into account where physical damage to property has been caused: *St Helen's Smelting Co v Tipping* (1865). Note that it would not be necessary to show that Edward was negligent as negligence is not an essential ingredient of nuisance. Indeed it would be no defence to Edward to show that he took all reasonable care and even all possible care - provided that he caused the nuisance that is sufficient. Thus, taking all the circumstances into account a court would find that the escape constituted an actionable nuisance.

Again considering the damage caused, Frank can recover for the damage caused to his vegetables although as regards the damage to his car and the subsequent injuries Frank has the problem that he has no interest in the road. Nevertheless he could sue in public nuisance as the oil on the road would affect a section of the public. *Attorney-General v PYA Quarries* (1957) and Frank has suffered damage over and above that suffered by the public at large: *Rose v Miles* (1815). In public nuisance the plaintiff need have no interest in land and can recover for personal injury (and economic loss) so Frank could recover for the damage to his car and the cut to his head with its consequential damage.

Frank could also sue Edward in negligence and would have no difficulty with establishing a duty of care and causation and foreseeability. A problem might arise, however, with breach of duty as we are told that the leak arose from internal corrosion. Frank might seek to rely on *res ipsa loquitur* but this would not reverse the burden of proof which lies on the plaintiff throughout: *Ng Chun Pui v Lee Chuen Tat* (1988). If Edward could show that he had in place a proper system of inspection and control; *Henderson v Jenkins & Sons* (1970) that would be sufficient to negate liability.

If negligence could be proved against Edward then Frank could recover for all the damage that he has suffered as there seem to be no problems in causation and foreseeability.

If the leak had been caused by the deliberate actions of Jack that would provide a defence to Edward in an action in *Rylands*. In *Rickards v Lothian* it was held that the defendants were not liable because the cause of the damage was an unforeseeable independent act of a third party over whom the defendant had no control - see also *Perry v Kendrick Transport*. In nuisance the occupier is liable if he creates the nuisance, or is vicariously liable for its creation but where the nuisance is caused by the act of a trespasser the occupier is only liable if he continues or adopts the nuisance: *Sedleigh-Denfield v O'Callaghan* (1940). As Edward has neither adopted or created the nuisance he would not be liable in nuisance for Jack's actions. Similarly in negligence Edward would be under no duty of care to prevent Jack's actions: see *Smith v Littlewoods Organisation* (1987), and would not be liable for any damage flowing from them.

Question 31

Glenda, who owns a house in the centre of a large city, collects and cares for stray cats. She has ten of these cats which she keeps in cardboard boxes in the garden. One night the cats go into the next door garden belonging to Harriet and trample on some flowers which she hopes to exhibit at the local gardening show. The cats then howl for most of the night, keeping Harriet awake.

Advise Glenda on any liability she may have incurred.

Answer plan

This problem involves a number of possible causes of action, namely *Rylands*, nuisance, under the Animals Act 1971 and in negligence and trespass, and the relevant aspects of liability and defences should be discussed.

The following aspects need to be considered:

* liability under *Rylands* and whether there is a non-natural use
* damages recoverable under *Rylands*
* liability in nuisance and possible damages recoverable
* liability under the Animals Act 1971 with particular reference to s 2(2) and the damage covered by the Act
* liability in negligence and in trespass

Answer

We shall first consider whether Glenda has incurred any liability under the rule in *Rylands v Fletcher* (1868) which is that a 'person who for his own purposes brings onto his lands and collects and keeps there anything likely to do mischief if it escapes, must keep it in at his peril, and if he does not do so, he is *prima facie* answerable for all the damage which is the natural consequence of its escape'. In addition the defendant must have made a 'non-natural' use of his land.

The cats have been brought onto Glenda's land for Glenda's purposes, and they have been brought onto Glenda's land in the sense that they are not something that is there by nature such as thistles - *Giles v Walker* (1890) or rainwater - *Smith v Kenrick* (1849). The cats are clearly likely to do mischief if they escape and there has been an escape from Glenda's premises as required by *Read v Lyons* (1947). Finally, we must determine whether or not there has been a non-natural user of land, an aspect that has given rise to much confusion. In *Rylands* itself the word natural was used to mean something on the land by nature, but later cases have construed the word as meaning 'ordinary' or 'usual'. In *Rickards v Lothian* (1931) Lord Moulton said of the use of land required to bring *Rylands* into operation 'It must be some special use bringing with it increased danger to others, and must not merely be the ordinary use of ... or such a use as is proper for the general benefits of the community'. In *Read v Lyons* Viscount Simon described Lord Moulton's analysis of *Rylands* as 'of the first importance'. In *Mason v Levy Auto Parts* (1967) McKenna J held that in deciding whether there had been a non-natural user of land the factors to be taken into account were (i) the quantities of material brought by the defendants onto their land (ii) the manner in which the material was stored, and (iii) the character of the neighbourhood. These factors seem to be moving *Rylands* in the direction of negligence. However, in *British Celanese v Hunt* (1969) Lawton J held that as the defendants factory was situated on an industrial estate the defendants were using the land for the very purpose for which it was intended. He also noted that the things being manufactured were for the general benefit of the community. More recently, in *Cambridge Water Co v Eastern Counties Leather* (1991) it was held by Kennedy J that the storage of toxic chemicals in a factory based in an industrial village was a natural use of the land. It was stated that it was necessary to consider whether the storage created special risks for adjacent occupiers, whether the activity was for the general benefit of the community, the amounts stored and the character of the neighbourhood. Hence by analogy with *British Celanese* and *Cambridge Water*, as Glenda lives in the centre of a large city she is not making a natural use of her land, and the rule will operate assuming that cats are 'things'. The rule has been held to apply to caravan dwellers: *Attorney General v Cooke* (1933), and so by analogy it could apply to cats. The fact that Glenda does not have proper storage facilities for the cats, but rather keeps them in cardboard boxes, also tends to suggest that she is making a non-natural use of her land. Glenda will, therefore, be liable for the loss of Harriet's flowers, as this is property damage suffered on Harriet's land and as such is recoverable: *Rylands*. The lost night's, sleep is not damage which is recoverable under *Rylands* where actual physical damage to the plaintiff's property (or possibly person) is required. We must next consider whether Glenda has incurred any liability in nuisance. A nuisance is an unreasonable interference with a person's use or enjoyment of land, or some right over or in connection with it. However, not all interference necessarily gives rise to liability and there must be give and take between neighbours - the interference must be substantial and not fanciful: *Walter v Selfe* (1851). The courts have developed a number of guidelines that are used to determine whether any particular interference is unreasonable, but each test is only a guideline and not a condition, and the court has to evaluate the defendant's behaviour in all the circumstances of the case. In Glenda's case the court will consider whether the escape was an isolated event. In *Bolton v Stone* (1949) it was stated that a nuisance could not arise from an isolated happening but that it had to arise from a state of affairs, however temporary.

Thus, in *Midwood v Manchester Corp* (1905) a gas explosion was held to be a nuisance because although it was an isolated event it was due to a pre-existing state of affairs, namely the build up of gas. On this basis it could be argued that the escape was due to the keeping of a large number of cats on Glenda's premises and, thus, the escape is an actionable nuisance. The damage suffered is not due to any sensitivity use of the neighbours property (as in *Robinson v Kilvert* (1889)) and although the premises are in the centre of a manufacturing town, the character of the neighbourhood is not to be taken into account where physical damage to property has been caused: *St Helen's Smelting Co v Tipping* (1865).

It would not be necessary to show that Glenda was negligent as negligence is not an essential ingredient of nuisance. Indeed it would be no defence to Glenda to show that she took all reasonable or even all possible care - provided that she caused the nuisance that is sufficient. Thus, Glenda will be liable to Harriet in nuisance, and the damage recoverable will include both the property damage and damages in respect of the lost nights sleep. In addition Harriet could seek an injunction to prevent any future damage or disturbance.

We shall also consider whether any liability arises under the Animals Act 1971. By s 6(3) of the Act Glenda is the keeper of the cats which are a non-dangerous species. By s 2(2) of the Act the keeper will be liable for the damage if:

a) the damage is of a kind which the animal, unless restrained was likely to cause or which, if caused by the animal, was likely to be severe; and

b) the likelihood of the damage or of its being severe was due to characteristics of the animal which are not normally found in animals of the same species or are not normally found except at particular times or in particular circumstances; and

c) those characteristics were known to that keeper.

A cat is liable unless restrained to enter a neighbour's garden and trample on flowers, but whether this was due to characteristics in Glenda's cats not normally found in cats seems doubtful. It could be argued that stray cats are more liable to wander into other persons' property than house trained cats, but it seems more likely that a court would find that all cats wander, and so s 2(2)(b) is not satisfied and no liability will arise under the Animals Act 1971 (1).

Note

1   In addition there is the problem that 'damage' is defined in s 11 of the Act in terms of personal injury and property damage is not expressly included, although it has been suggested that the defence is not exhaustive and causes damage to property: *Winfield v Jalowicz* on Tort, 13th Edition 458.

Glenda could also be liable to Harriet in negligence. Glenda will owe Harriet a duty of care and in keeping a large number of cats in her garden in cardboard boxes with no attempt to restrict their movements out of her property Glenda is in breach of her duty and the damage is caused by this breach and is foreseeable.

Glenda could also be liable to Harriet in trespass to land as this form of trespass can be committed negligently: *League against Cruel Sports v Scott* (1985).

Question 32

One evening Henry lights a bonfire in his garden in order to burn some garden rubbish. The smoke and smell from the bonfire annoys his neighbours who are watching television with the windows open, and sparks from the fire damage some clothing that one of his neighbours has hung out in his garden to dry. The smoke from the bonfire drifts onto the road and is so thick that it obstructs the vision of a passing motorist who as a result runs into a lamp-post. Henry goes indoors to listen to the radio and some time later the bonfire spreads to his neighbour's property and destroys a garden shed.

   Advise Henry of his legal liability.

Answer plan

This is a question that requires a discussion of Henry's liability in nuisance, the relationship of nuisance to an action in *Rylands v Fletcher*, and any liability Henry might incur in negligence and under the special rules that govern fires.

The following points should be addressed:

- liability in nuisance for the smoke and smell
- liability in nuisance for the damage to clothing
- possibility of liability arising under the rule in *Rylands v Fletcher*
- liability in negligence
- liability for fire under the Fires Prevention (Metropolis) Act 1774

Answer

We shall first consider any liability that Henry may have incurred in private nuisance (which we shall henceforth simply refer to as nuisance) for the smoke and smell from his bonfire. A nuisance consists of an unreasonable interference with a person's use or enjoyment of land, or of some right over, or in connection with it. However, not all interference will necessarily give rise to liability - the interference must be substantial and not merely fanciful: *Walter v Selfe* (1851). In deciding whether a particular interference is unreasonable or not the court will rely on a series of guidelines rather than on any rigid rules. In Henry's case the court would consider the duration of the interference, as the shorter the duration of the interference the less likely it is to be unreasonable, as in *Harrison v Southwark & Vauxhall Water Co* (1891). In particular, it seems that an isolated event is unlikely to constitute a nuisance. In *Bolton v Stone* (1949) it was stated that a nuisance must be a state of affairs, however temporary, and not merely an isolated happening. Thus, although Henry might claim that the bonfire is an isolated event, it does constitute a temporary state of affairs, and is capable in law of being a nuisance. A possible argument that Henry might employ is that he only lights a bonfire on rare occasions and that this is a reasonable use of his land, but the fact that a defendant is only making reasonable use of his land is not, of itself, a valid defence in nuisance: *Attorney General v Cole* (1901); *Vanderpant v Mayfair Hotel* (1930). As regards any interference with health and comfort, the court will take into account the character of the neighbourhood, as 'what would be a nuisance in Belgravia Square would not necessarily be so in Bermondsey': *Sturges v Bridgman* (1865), per Thesiger LJ. Thus, if Henry lives in a suburban or rural area the occasional lighting of a bonfire might not constitute a nuisance as there must be an element of give and take between neighbours, but if Henry by his lack of care allowed an annoyance from the bonfire to become excessive he would become liable in nuisance: *Andreae v Selfridge & Co* (1938). Hence as regards the smoke and smell from his bonfire, whether Henry will be liable in nuisance will depend on whether, taking all the circumstances into account, the interference is unreasonable. As nuisance protects a person's use or enjoyment of land, then only those neighbours with an interest in the land can sue: *Malone v Lasky* (1907) and not mere members of their family and guests. It was also held in *Bridlington Relay v Yorkshire Electricity Board* (1965) that interference with purely recreational facilities, such as television reception, would not constitute an actionable nuisance, but whatever the status of that decision today, the interference suffered by Henry's neighbours is not with the reception of their television programmes but rather with their enjoyment of their property, for had they wished to just sit in their houses with the windows open they would not have been able to do so without the discomfort from the smoke and smell of Henry's bonfire.

Turning now to the damage to the neighbour's clothing, where physical damage to property has been caused the character of the neighbourhood is not relevant: *St Helens Smelting Co v Tipping* (1965), and a court would be far more likely to find that an interference is unreasonable where physical damage to property has occurred. Even if the bonfire did not originally constitute a nuisance. Henry's lack of care in allowing the interference to become unreasonable would make him liable in nuisance: *Andreae v Selfridge*. It, therefore, seems likely that Henry would be liable for the damage to his neighbours clothing, providing of course that his neighbour has the required interest in land. Henry could also incur liability for the damage to his neighbours clothing in negligence. Henry will owe his neighbour a duty of care under normal *Donoghue v Stevenson* principles, for as a duty of care has already been held to exist in such circumstances there is no need to go to the modern formulation of the test for a duty of care that was preferred by the house of Lords in *Caparo v Dickman* (1990) and *Murphy v Brentwood District*

Council (1990). In allowing sparks to damage his neighbours property Henry has not acted as a reasonable person would and so is in breach of his duty: *Blyth v Birmingham Waterworks* (1865), and the 'but for' test of Lord Denning in *Cork v Kirby MacLean* (1965) shows the required causal connection. Finally, the damage suffered by the neighbour is not too remote as it is reasonably foreseeable; *The Wagon Mound* (1962). Thus, Henry would be liable for the damage to the clothing and there would be no requirement in negligence for the neighbour to have any interest in land. As regards the passing motorist, he could not sue Henry in nuisance as he has no interest in the land. He could sue Henry in negligence as the required elements of duty, breach and damage appear to be present (see the above discussion regarding the neighbour and his damaged clothing). The motorist may also have a cause of action in public nuisance in that Henry has created a danger close to the highway: *Tarry v Ashton* (1876); *Castle v St Augustine's Links* (1922).

We shall next consider whether Henry has incurred any liability for the fire and the damage it has caused to the garden shed. Liability could arise in a number of ways; the first possibility is an action under the rule in *Rylands v Fletcher* (1868), but in *Mason v Levy Auto Parts* (1967) MacKenna J held that liability for fire cannot be based on *Rylands* because the 'thing' has not escaped from the defendants land as required by *Rylands*. Instead Henry may be liable under common law liability for fire in which the plaintiff will have to show, firstly, that Henry brought onto his lands things likely to catch fire, and kept them there in such conditions that if they did ignite the fire would be likely to spread to the plaintiff's land; secondly, that he did so in the course of some non-natural use of the land; and, finally, that the things ignited and the fire spread. Although these are different criteria to those used in *Rylands,* similar considerations will apply in deciding whether these criteria have been satisfied in any particular case. The only element that would appear to give rise to any problems here is the requirement that the use of land be non-natural. The original meaning given to this phrase in *Rylands* was something that was there by nature, but in *Rickards v Lothian* (1931) Lord Moulton stated that the use must be 'some special use bringing with it increased dangers to others, and must not merely be the ordinary use of the land or such a use as is proper for the general benefit of the community'. This approach was also used in *British Celanese v Hunt* (1969) where again the general benefit to the community of the use to which the land was put was stressed, and most recently in *Cambridge Water Co v Eastern Counties Leather plc* (1991) in determining whether a use was natural Ian Kennedy J held it was necessary to consider whether the activity was for the general benefit of the community and whether it created any special risks for adjacent occupiers. Using these criteria, as Henry's activity in lighting a bonfire is not for the general benefit of the community and it creates special risks for adjacent occupiers, it is a non-natural use of land, and, thus, the elements described in Mason are fulfilled. Henry would, thus, be liable in a common law action for fire. In addition Henry would also incur liability at common law in nuisance as the fire has damaged his neighbours property: *Goldman v Hargrave* (1967), assuming that his neighbour has the necessary interest in the land, and liability could also attach in negligence as there is no problem in establishing a duty of care, causation and damage that is not too remote, and by leaving the fire to go indoors and listen to the radio Henry has failed to take reasonable care to prevent the fire from causing damage: *Musgrove v Pandelis* (1919); *Ogwo v Taylor* (1987). Now we must consider whether Henry could escape liability by relying on the provisions of the Fires Prevention (Metropolis) Act 1774. Section 86 of that Act provides that 'no action, suit or process whatever, shall be had, maintained, or prosecuted against any person in whose house, chamber, stable, barn or other building, of whose estate any such fire shall ... accidentally begin, nor shall any recompense be made by any such person for any damage suffered thereby, any law, usage, or custom to the contrary notwithstanding'. So Henry will not be liable for the consequences of the fire if it began accidentally. The meaning of 'accidentally' was considered in *Filliter v Phippard* (1847) where the defendant deliberately lit a fire to burn some weeds and then neglected the fire which spread to the plaintiff's land and damaged his hedge. It was held that the defendant could not rely on the Act because the fire did not begin 'accidentally' - it began negligently. The court held that a fire only began accidentally where it began by mere chance or was incapable of being traced to any cause. As *Filliter* is legally indistinguishable from Henry's situation it follows that Henry cannot rely on the 1774 Act as defence.

Thus, Henry should be advised that he will be liable for the damage to the clothing, to the shed and for the damage suffered by the motorist.

Chapter 10

Animals

Introduction

Questions involving animals may arise in examinations in a number of ways. A question whose main ingredient is nuisance or *Rylands v Fletcher* or negligence may involve animals, but we are concerned in this Chapter with questions where the topic being tested is mainly the Animals Act 1971 and related common law issues.

Checklist

To attempt a question on animals students must be aware of:
- The common law situation
- Definition of a dangerous species
- Liability for damage caused by dangerous and non-dangerous species
- Defences
- Definition of a keeper of an animal
- Straying livestock

Question 33

Graham owns a large Alsatian dog which he lets roam in his garden to deter unwelcome visitors. One day the dog jumps over the low garden fence to chase a cat and the cat runs into the road to escape and is run over. Helen, who owns the cat, is told of this incident by a neighbour of Graham's who witnessed it, and later that evening Helen goes to Graham's house to demand compensation for her cat. Before she can enter Graham's garden the dog jumps over the fence and bites Helen, who in an attempt to escape further attack runs into the road. Fiona who is driving along the road at the time swerves to avoid Helen and runs into a lamp post and is injured.

Advise Graham of any liability that may have arisen.

Answer plan

This is a relatively straightforward question (though the position with Helen's cat is rather tricky) that requires a discussion of the following points:

- is s 2(3) satisfied with respect to Helen and her cat?
- does the Animals Act 1971 cover property damage?
- extent of Graham's liability for Helen's damages
- extent of Graham's liability for Fiona's damages
- any defences available to Graham
- other courses of action open to Helen and Fiona

Answer

The Animals Act 1971 divides animals into dangerous and non-dangerous species. An Alsatian dog is a non-dangerous species, because by s 6(2) of the 1971 Act a dangerous species is one which is not commonly domesticated in the British Isles and whose fully grown animals normally have such characteristics that they are likely, unless restrained, to cause severe damage and that any damage that they may cause is likely to be severe. By s 2(2) of the Act the keeper will be liable for the damage caused by an animal which does not belong to a dangerous species if:

a) the damage is of a kind which the animal, unless restrained, was likely to cause or which, if caused by the animal, was likely to be severe; and

b) the likelihood of the damage or of its being severe was due to characteristics of the animal which are not normally found in animals of the same species or are not normally found except at particular times or in particular circumstances; and

c) those characteristics were known to that keeper ...

By s 6(3) Graham is the keeper of the dog as we are told he is the owner. He will be *prima facie* liable if s 2(2) is satisfied. Considering first the position with Helen's cat, s 2(2)(a) is satisfied as it is damage of the kind which the dog unless restrained is likely to cause. This wording is wide enough to cover damage by a dog running into the road or chasing a cat into the road.

Section 2(2)(b) is not so straightforward because it requires the damage to be caused due to characteristics not normally so found in Alsatian dogs or only at particular times or in particular circumstances (1). The problem for Helen is that it is normal for dogs to chase cats, see eg *Buckle v Holmes* (1926), (decided under the common law prior to the act where there was a single requirement),where it was held that no liability attached where a cat killed some pigeons. Hence s 2(2)(b) is not satisfied. Section 2(2))(c) is presumably satisfied as Graham would know of these tendencies. Hence as 2(2)(b) remains unsatisfied, no liability arises with Helen's cat (2).

Turning now to Helen, again s 2(2)(a) is satisfied as the damage caused by a bite from an Alsatian is likely to be severe. Section 2(2)(b) is satisfied because Alsatians are not normally vicious except in the particular circumstances as being kept as guard dogs and we are told that Graham keeps his dog to deter unwelcome visitors. Section 2(2)(c) is also satisfied as Graham must know of the characteristics in his dog (see *Cummings v Grainger* (1977). Thus, Graham is liable to Helen for the bite subject only to any defences contained within the Act. Section 5(1) and s 10, namely that the damage was due wholly to Helen's fault or that Helen was contributarily negligent do not apply on the facts we are given. Graham cannot rely on s 5(3), for although that exempts a keeper from liability for damage caused by an animal kept for protection of persons or property where keeping it for that purpose was not unreasonable, it only covers damage caused to trespassers and Helen never entered Graham's property and was never a trespasser. The *volenti* defence contained in s 5(2) is also clearly inapplicable (3).

Turning now to Fiona, s 2(2)(a) is satisfied because as we have argued earlier, the wording of s 2(2)(a) is wide enough to cover a dog running into the road. It is submitted that s 2(2)(b) is satisfied as an Alsatian dog would not normally run into the road except in the particular circumstances of a guard dog chasing a perceived intruder from the premises it was guarding, and s 2(2)(c) is satisfied as Graham knows of this characteristic. Thus, s 2(2) is satisfied in respect of Fiona and as the damage was caused by the dog, under s 2(2) there is no requirement of foreseeability so Graham is liable, subject only to the defences in the Act. These have been considered with respect to Helen, and none could be relied on by Graham who is then liable for the damage suffered by Fiona.

Graham could argue that the damage to Fiona was caused not by the dog, but by Helen running into the road rather than along the pavement so that Helen's action was a *novus actus interveniens* which broke the chain of causation. The act of a third party may break the chain of causation where it is something unwarrantable, a new cause which disturbs the sequence of events, something which can be described as either unreasonable or extraneous or intrinsic, per Lord Wright in *The Oropesa* (1943). In Fiona's case as the act of Helen was an involuntary one and not unreasonable, it will not break the chain of causation - see *Scott v Shepherd* (1733).

Helen and Frank could also sue Graham in negligence for not taking reasonable steps to confine the dog within the limits of his property, and possibly in *Rylands v Fletcher* (1868) although whether liability exists in Rylands for the escape of an animal is debatable - see *Read v Lyons* (1947). However, Rylands has been held to cover the escape of caravan dwellers: *Attorney General v Cooke* (1933), so arguably it could cover animals.

Notes

1 In *Curtis v Betts* (1990) it was stated that s 2(2)(b) should be read as if it referred simply to 'the damage' rather than to 'the likelihood of the damage or of its being severe'.
2 One might also consider whether liability under the Animals Act 1971 extends to property damage. By s 11 damage is defined as including death or personal injury and property damage is not expressly covered. However, it has been argued in Winfield & Jolewicz on Tort that as s 11 is not exhaustive then property damage is included, and it seems to have been allowed at common law: *Buckle v Holmes* (1926).
3 There may also have been a breach of s 1 Guard Dogs Act 1975 but s 5(1) of that Act expressly provides that breach shall not confer a civil right of action.

Question 34

Henry owns a large dog which has a tendency to attack people in uniforms. Henry keeps the dog chained in his garden with a substantial chain. Unfortunately there is a latent defect in one link of the chain and when Pat the postman goes to the front door of the house to deliver some letters the dog attempts to attack Pat, the chain breaks and the dog bites Pat. Pat is taken to hospital and given an anti-tetanus injection to which he suffers a rare and unforeseeable allergic reaction and his leg has to be amputated. Richard, a policeman, calls to investigate the situation and the dog jumps over the garden fence and bites Richard. While Richard is doubled up in pain on the pavement Steven, who Richard arrested for a drug offence a little while ago, sees Richard on the floor and kicks him on the head.

Advise Henry.

Answer plan

This question ranges over a number of aspects of liability for animals both under the Animals Act 1971 and under other causes of action.

The following points need to be considered:
- Henry's liability under s 2(2) to Pat
- defences available to Henry in respect of Pat
- Henry's liability under s 2(2) to Richard
- defences available in respect of Richard
- Henry's liability for action of Steven

Answer

Under the statutory classification of the Animals Act 1971 Henry's dog is a non-dangerous species because it is commonly domesticated in the British Isles - see s 6(2). By s 6(3) Henry is the keeper of the dog as he is the owner. By s 2(2) the keeper of an animal belonging to a non-dangerous species is liable for the damage caused by the animal if:

a) the damage is of a kind which the animal, unless restrained, was likely to cause or which, if caused by the animal, was likely to be severe: and

b) the likelihood of the damage or of its being severe was due to characteristics of the animal which are not normally found in animals of the same species or are not normally found except at particular times or in particular circumstances; and

c) those characteristics were known to that keeper ...

Considering now Henry's liability to Pat, s 2(2)(a) is satisfied because the bite from a large dog is likely to be severe, the tendency to attach persons in uniform is not a characteristic of dogs (see eg *Kite v Napp* (1982), so s 2(2)(b) is satisfied and s 2(2)(c) is satisfied as this characteristic would be known to Henry (see *Cummings v Grainger* (1977) for liability under s 2(2) generally). Thus, Henry is liable for the damage caused to Pat subject only to the defences within the 1971 Act.

These defences include *volenti*, s 5(2), contributory negligence, s 10, or that the damage was wholly due to the fault of the person suffering it, s 5(1). Section 5(3) also provides a defence against trespassers but this would not apply to Pat (see s 2(6) Occupiers Liability Act 1957). It should be noted that neither the act of a stranger nor an act of God provide a defence to s 2(2) as they are not mentioned in the Act. Thus, the fact that the dog broke free from the chain due to a latent defect in the chain is not a defence, as liability under s 2(2) does not require negligence: *Curtis v Betts* (1990). Henry is liable for the bite suffered by Pat, and he is also liable for the medical consequences of the anti-tetanus injection because liability under the Act is strict and subject only to the defences contained within the Act. There is, thus, no necessity for the damage suffered to be reasonably foreseeable, it merely has to be a direct consequence of the action of the animal, ie *Re Polemis* (1921) is the appropriate test of recovery of damage. In any event even if the foreseeability was required as Henry must take his victim as he finds him, *Dulieu v White* (1901), ie with an allergy to tetanus injections, or if the need for such an injection is foreseeable, Henry will be liable for its consequences: *Robinson v Post Office* (1974). Hence Henry will be liable for both the bite and the loss of Pat's leg.

Turning now to Richard, following our discussion above, Henry will be liable to Richard for the bite and none of the statutory defences are valid (NB Richard is not a trespasser in this case because he has not entered Henry's property). The question arises as to whether Henry is liable for the kick perpetrated by Steven. Section 2(2) states that the keeper is liable for damage caused and as we have seen there is no requirement of foreseeability, merely directness. However, Henry could argue that the kick by Steven is a *novus actus interveniens* which breaches the chain of causation so that the damage from the kick was not caused by his dog, therefore, that damage does not come within s 2(2). In *Re Polemis* where directness was considered, Scrutton LJ stated that indirect damage meant damage caused by the 'operator of independent causes having no connection with the ... act, except that they could not avoid its results'. Where it is alleged that the act of a third party, over whom the defendant has no control, has broken the chain of causation, then it must be shown that the act was something unwarrantable, a new cause which disturbs the sequence of events. It must be something which can be described as either unreasonable or extraneous or extrinsic, per Lord Wright in *The Oropesa* (1943). Thus, the defendant will remain liable if the act of the third party is not truly independent of the defendant's act. In *Knightley v Johns* (1982) the Court of Appeal held that negligent conduct was far more likely to break the chain of causation than non-negligent conduct, so it would follow that a deliberate act is even more likely to break the chain and be found to be truly independent of the defendant's original act.

In the circumstances the act of Steven is unreasonable, extraneous, extrinsic and deliberate and would breach the chain of causation so that Henry would not be liable for those consequences.

Henry could not be sued by Pat in negligence as there has been no breach of duty on his part as we are told that the chain was substantial but had a latent defect. Henry could be sued in negligence by Richard, as once the dog broke free Henry would have been negligent in not securing the dog if he was aware of the broken dog chain.

Richard could possibly sue Henry under *Rylands v Fletcher* although whether liability exists for the escape of an animal is debatable: see *Read v Lyons* (1947). However, the rule in Rylands has been held to be applicable in the case of an escape of caravan dwellers: *Attorney General v Cooke* (1933) so arguably it could cover the escape of animals. But even if Rylands did apply to the escape of an animal, it seems not completely certain whether Rylands covers personal injuries; although recovery was allowed in *Hale v Jenning Bros* (1938) and *Perry v Kendricks Transport* (1956), it was doubted obiter in the House of Lords in *Read v Lyons* whether such an award was possible.

Question 35

Jenny, who lectures in zoology, has a pet South African monkey called Nigel. Nigel has been hand reared since he was born and is quite tame. One day Nigel opened a window catch and climbed out of Jenny's house and went through an open window in her neighbour, Angela's, house. Angela's mother, Maria, was visiting at the time and as Maria has a phobia about monkeys because she was bitten by one as a child, Maria panicked and ran through the glass back door, cutting herself extensively. She went to hospital by ambulance and while she was at the hospital a thief entered by the broken back door and stole some of Angela's property.

Advise Angela and Maria.

Answer plan

The question is a little different from the standard animals question in that it involves a dangerous species, together with a consideration of the damage for which its keeper is liable.

The following points need to be discussed:

- definition of a dangerous species
- liability for damage caused - extent and limitations
- other causes of action

Answer

We first have to decide whether Nigel belongs to a dangerous or non-dangerous species. By s 6(2) Animals Act 1971 a dangerous species is a species.

a) which is not commonly domesticated in the British Islands; and
b) whose fully grown animals normally have such characteristics that they are likely, unless restrained, to cause severe damage or that any damage that they may cause is likely to be severe.

It should be noted that by s 6(2) it is the species which must be dangerous and not the particular animal in question. Thus, the fact that Nigel is tame does not take him out of the category of dangerous species. In addition s 6(2) requires that the animal be of a type which is not commonly domesticated in the British Isles - the fact that Nigel might belong to a species which is commonly domesticated in South Africa again will not take Nigel out of his classification. Thus, s 6(2)(a) is satisfied. Section 6(2)(b) is satisfied as eg the bite from a fully grown monkey is likely to be severe or it is likely to cause severe damage to property for example. Thus, both heads of s 6(2) are satisfied and Nigel belongs to a dangerous species. By s 2(1) the keeper is liable for any damage caused except where the Act provides a defence. There is no restriction on the damage caused by Nigel or the damage Nigel is likely to cause, or whether or not that damage is severe. It is also clear from the wording of the Act that there is no requirement that the damage be foreseeable, it is enough that it is caused by the animal. Jenny is the keeper of the animal by s 6(3) as we are told that Jenny owns Nigel.

From s 2(1) it follows that Jenny is liable for the damage caused by Nigel. The only defences available to Jenny are those contained within the act, namely *volenti* s 5(2), contributory negligence, s 10, the defence with regard to trespassers and guard dogs, s 5(3) and s 5(1) where the damage is wholly due to the fault of the person suffering it. Clearly ss 5(2) and 5(3) are not relevant to Maria, but could Jenny claim that the damage suffered by Maria was wholly due to her fault in running through the glass door. As s 2(1) makes the keeper liable for the damage caused (subject to the statutory defences) s 5(1) covers the situation where the victim causes the damage wholly by himself. We should, thus, ask whether Maria's act of running through the door was a *novus actus interveniens* which broke the chain of causation, ie that the appearance of Nigel merely provided the opportunity for Maria to be the author of her own misfortune. The problem for Jenny in running this defence is the well established rule that a tortfeasor takes his victim as he finds him (*Dulieu v White* (1901)), and in this case the victim has a phobia about monkeys. No question of foreseeability arises under s 2(1) (though even if it did it would be disposed of by the above rule - see *Robinson v Post Office* (1974); *Bradford v Robinson Rentals* (1967)). The act of the plaintiff may break the chain of causation where his act is so careless that his injury cannot be attributed to the fault of the defendant. Comparing *McKew v Holland and Hannen & Cubitts* (1969) with *Wieland v Cyril Lord Carpets* (1969) it seems clear that to constitute a *novus actus interveniens* on the part of the plaintiff the act must be unreasonable. As Jenny must take Maria as she finds her, ie with a phobia about monkeys, Maria's acts are not likely to be found so unreasonable as to constitute a *novus actus interveniens*. Again it is settled law that if a person in the agony of the moment causes himself damage the act causing the damage will not necessarily break the chain of causation: *Jones v Boyce* (1816). Hence it is submitted that Maria's action will not constitute a *novus actus interveniens* but that contributory negligence under s 10 would be a more appropriate defence (if any).

As regards the theft of property the damage has been caused by a third party so the question arises as to whether or not the act of the thief caused the damage rather than Nigel, ie was the theft a *novus actus interveniens*. Where it is alleged that the act of a third party, over whom the defendant has no control, has broken the chain of causation, then it must be shown that the act was something unwarrantable, a new cause which disturbs the sequence of events. It must be something which can be described as either unreasonable or extraneous or extrinsic, per Lord Wright in *The Oropesa* (1943). Thus, the defendant will remain liable if the act of the third party is not truly independent of the defendant's act. In *Knightley v Johns* (1982) the Court of Appeal held that negligent conduct was far more likely to break the chain of causation than non-negligent conduct, so it would follow that a deliberate act is even more likely to break the chain and be found to be truly independent of the defendant's original act. The problem facing Jenny is that we are told that the thief entered by the broken back door, which suggests that the act of the thief may not be truly independent of Jenny's original act in that the thief may not have entered the premises had the back door not been broken. If the court were to make such a finding then Jenny would be liable for the loss resulting from the theft. It is not likely that Jenny would succeed in claiming that the true cause of the theft was a *novus actus interveniens* by Maria in failing to secure the back door before going to hospital, as Maria's actions seem reasonable in the 'agony of the moment' caused by Jenny's original tort, and would not break the chain of causation: *Jones v Boyce* (1816). Although in *Stansbie v Troman* (1948) it was held that the act of a thief did not break the chain of causation, this was explained by Lord Goff in *Smith v Littlewoods Organisation* (1987) as being due to the contractual relationship between the parties in question.

Jenny could also be liable to Maria in negligence; there would be no difficulty in establishing a duty of care and breach of that duty, and the problem of causation, ie did Maria herself cause her injuries has already been considered above. Similarly with Angela it would be straightforward enough to show the existence of a duty of care and breach of that duty, and again we have considered the problem of causation above.

Jenny might also be liable under the rule in *Rylands v Fletcher* (1868) for the escape of Nigel if the rule applies to animals. This was doubted in *Read v Lyons* (1947), but the rule has been held to cover the escape of caravan dwellers: *Attorney General v Cooke* (1933), so by analogy it could cover the escape of an animal. However, even if Rylands does cover the escape of an animal, it is not certain whether Rylands applies to personal injuries; recovery was allowed in *Hale v Jennings Bros* (1938) and *Perry v Kendricks Transport* (1956) but it was doubted obiter in the House of Lords in *Read v Lyons* whether such an award was possible. Jenny could also be liable to Angela in nuisance. Although the escape of Nigel was an isolated event, in *Bolton v Stone* (1949) it was stated that although a nuisance could not arise from an isolated happening, it could arise from a state of affairs, albeit temporary. Thus, in *Midwood v Manchester Corp* (1905) a gas explosion was held to be a nuisance because although it was an isolated event it was due to a pre-existing state of affairs, namely the build up of gas. Hence Angela could argue that the escape of Nigel was due to a wrongful state of affairs on Jenny's property, namely that Nigel was not kept within Jenny's property. Maria could not sue in nuisance as she lacks the requisite interest in land: *Malone v Lasky* (1907).

Chapter 11

Defamation

Introduction

Questions on defamation appear regularly in examination papers. Defamation is a major topic and encompasses a considerable volume of law, but in practice examiners tend to concentrate on several specific topics, notably the defences of fair comment and qualified privilege, although students also will have to have a good grasp of the elements of liability.

Checklist

Students must be familiar with the following areas:

- Distinction between libel and slander
- Defamatory statements and innuendoes
- Reference to plaintiff
- Publication
- Defences with especial references to fair comment and qualified privilege

Question 36

Alfred a well known and successful businessman, held a large party at his country house. Beryl, who once worked for Alfred in public relations, but was dismissed and is now a reporter, writes an article in the Daily Globe in which she says 'Alfred, who makes his money by rationalising companies, ie by throwing people out of work, held a party at his house for the sycophants who work for him. Whether they would be so happy if they were aware of his bizarre view of business ethics during his recent takeover bid for Alpha plc, is uncertain. Certainly, the investigation by the takeover panel will make 'interesting reading' '. The next day, as Alfred is walking into his office, Cedric, who was recently made redundant during Alfred's takeover of Alpha, sees him and shouts 'You are a villain who thinks only of himself. I hope they put you in jail for years over your takeover.'

Advise Alfred and his guests of the legal situation.

Answer plan

This is a typical defamation question - typical in that it involves the element of both liability and defences.

The following aspects need to be considered:

- is Beryl's statement defamatory of Alfred
- is Beryl's statement defamatory of the guests - problem of class defamation
- defences available to Beryl, especially justification and fair comment
- is Cedric's statement defamatory of Alfred
- defences available to Cedric

Answer

We must consider whether Alfred and his guests have been defamed by Beryl and the Daily Globe and whether Alfred has been defamed by Cedric.

The newspaper article by Beryl is in permanent form and so any defamation will take the form of libel and be actionable without any need to prove special damage. To succeed in an action for defamation, Alfred must prove that the statement complained of was defamatory, that it could reasonably be understood to refer to Alfred and that it was published to a third party.

The usual test for a statement being defamatory is that it tends to lower the Plaintiff in the estimation of right thinking members of society generally: *Sim v Stretch* (1936) or which expose him to hatred, contempt or ridicule: *Parmiter v Coupland* (1840). The statement regarding Alfred contains three possible defamatory elements, namely the allegation that Alfred employs sycophants, that he has a bizarre view of business ethics and that he is being investigated by the takeover panel.

The first allegation may well be defamatory and Alfred could plead a false innuendo ie that the words contain a secondary meaning that he is incapable of choosing employees correctly which would be defamatory of an eminent businessman. This would be a question for the jury to decide and in *Hartt v Newspaper Publishing* (1989), the Court of Appeal held that the approach to adopt was that of the hypothetical ordinary reader who was neither naive nor unduly suspicious but who might read between the lines and be capable of loose thinking. The statement that Alfred has a bizarre view of business ethics is defamatory, *Angel v Bushell & Co* (1968) as it is suggesting a lack of honesty or probity.

The final part of Beryl's statement concerning the investigation by the Takeover Panel needs careful consideration. In *Lewis v Daily Telegraph* (1964) it was held by the House of Lords that to say a person was being investigated for fraud was not the same as saying that he was guilty of fraud and so to say that Alfred is the subject of an investigation by the Takeover Panel is not, without more, defamatory.

It should, perhaps, be noted here that the test of the defamatory nature of a statement is its effect on right thinking members of society; the fact that Beryl's statements might not cause Alfred's friends or business colleagues or employees to think any the less of him is not relevant: *Byrne v Deane* (1937).

Next we shall consider the guests: the allegation that they are sycophants is defamatory as it would expose them to ridicule or contempt: *Parmiter v Coupland*.

The statement has clearly been published to a third party but the problem for the guests is that we are told that it was a large party, so the problem arises as to whether a group or class can sue when it has been defamed as an entity. In *Knupffer v London Express Newspapers* (1944), the House of Lords held that in class defamation, a member of the class could only sue if the words point particularly to the plaintiff or the class was so small that the words must necessarily refer to each member of it. Beryl's words do not particularly point to any guest so whether the guests can sue in the statement will depend on the size of the class, ie the number of guests. Unfortunately, we are given no indication of this in the facts of the question, but should the class be small enough then again the necessary elements of the tort of defamation would be present for the guests.

Let us now consider any defences which are available to Beryl and the Daily Globe.

Considering the statement concerning Alfred, Beryl and the Daily Globe could rely on the defence of justification, ie truth. This would be a valid defence for the allegation regarding the investigation by the Takeover Panel (assuming it is true). It would seem that it would be an extremely difficult defence to establish in respect of the allegation that Alfred employs sycophants, and as regards the business ethics allegation difficulties of proof could arise for the defendants unless the Takeover Panel investigation substantiated these claims. Thus, their defence would be limited to the investigation allegations (if such an allegation were held to be defamatory which is unlikely as we previously submitted).

The defendant may also raise the defence of fair comment, ie that the statement is fair comment based on true facts made in good faith on a matter of public interest.

The courts define public interest widely: *London Artists v Littler* (1969) and the activities of a prominent businessman would be a matter of public interest. But the comments must be based on true facts and as we have seen, this truth may be difficult to establish for the comments concerning sycophants and business ethics. An additional problem arises in that the statements must be one of opinion and not of fact. It may be that a court would find the statement that Alfred employs sycophants to be a statement of opinion - see *Dakhyl v Labouchere* (1908) (though it must still be based on true facts see *Merivale v Carson* (1887)) but the statement regarding business ethics does appear to be more of a statement of fact. By fair we mean that the defendant honestly believed the opinion expressed: *Slim v Daily Telegraph* (1968) and not that a reasonable person would agree with the opinion: *Silkin v Beaverbrook Newspapers* (1958). Although Beryl's comment may be fair in this respect, the defence can be rebutted by showing that the defendant acted out of malice: *Thomas v Bradbury Agnew* (1906). The burden of proving malice will be on the plaintiff, *Telnikoff v Matusevich* (1991), although the defendant will still have to show that the facts on which the comment was based were true and the comment was objectively fair in that anyone, however prejudiced or obstinate, could honestly have held the views expressed. In view of the fact that Beryl was dismissed by Alfred, malice may be found on her part, but providing that the Daily Globe did not act maliciously, it will not be tainted with Beryl's malice: *Lyon v Daily Telegraph* (1943).

Overall, therefore, it seems unlikely that either Beryl or the Daily Globe could rely on the defence of fair comment. The Daily Globe could rely on an apology as a defence under the Libel Acts 1843 *ant !!*

and 1845 if the statement was published with malice and without gross negligence, an apology was published as soon as possible and a payment has been made into court by way of amends.

Turning to the guests and the allegation that they are sycophants (assuming the guests can overcome the reference problem) the only defences available to Beryl and the Daily Globe would appear to be fair comment but as we have seen from our discussion regarding Alfred, this defence is unlikely to succeed. The Daily Globe would also have available the apology defence under the Libel Acts 1843 and 1845.

Finally, we must consider Cedric's statement. This is in transient form and so it is slander, and normally special damage would have to be shown for it to be actionable. However, where the words impute a crime punishable by imprisonment *Hellwig v Mitchell* (1910) or are calculated to disparage the plaintiff in any office, profession, calling, trade or business carried on by him, s 2 Defamation Act 1952, then there is no need for the plaintiff to prove special damage. As Cedric's words fall into both categories, they are *prima facie* actionable. However, spoken words are not actionable where they amount to mere abuse or insult: *Parkins v Scott* (1862): *Lane v Holloway* (1968). The test seems to be whether the statements would have been taken by a listener as those made in the heat of the moment or whether they did contain a serious allegation.

In applying this test it is submitted that no liability arises in respect of Cedric's statement.

Question 37

The Westfield Chamber of Commerce decides to set up a fund to allow a promising young businessman to spend some months in Europe studying European Business Methods. A committee consisting of Diana, Edward and Fenella is set up to consider applications. An application is received from George and Diana circulates a memo to Edward saying 'I understand that George is on the point of insolvency. He does not seem to be a suitable candidate'. Edward also circulates a memo stating 'George is incompetent and not fit to represent Westfield in Europe'. Edward types this himself but leaves a copy on the photocopying machine where it is seen by Henry. Edward's company recently tendered for some business with George's company but failed to obtain the contract.

Advise George.

Answer plan

Again a standard defamation question requiring mostly a discussion of the defence of qualified privilege and fair comment.

The following aspects need to be addressed:
- is Diana's statement defamatory
- can Diana claim qualified privilege or fair comment
- effect of possible malice on Edward's defences
- possible evasion of qualified privilege defence by using negligent mis-statement as cause of action

Answer

The statements by Diana and Edward are in permanent form so any defamation that has occurred will take the form of libel and be actionable without proof of any special damage.

In order to succeed in an action for defamation George will have to prove that the relevant statement was defamatory, that it referred to him and was published to a third party.

The usual test for a statement being defamatory is that it tends to lower the plaintiff in the estimation of right thinking members of society generally: *Sim v Stretch* (1936) or which expose him to hatred, contempt or ridicule: *Parmiter v Coupland* (1840). Diana's statement appears at first sight to meet this criterion: in *Read v Hudson* (1700), it was held to be defamatory to impute insolvency to a trader even though there was no suggestion of discreditable conduct, and if the statement contains the false innuendo that George is not competent in his business or profession that will clearly be defamatory: *Capital & Counties Bank v Henty* (1882). The fact that George's friends or business colleagues might regard insolvency as something that might happen to even the most talented a businessman these days is not relevant to the issue of whether the statement is defamatory as the statement must be judged by the standard or right thinking members of society generally, not just the plaintiff's friends: *Byrne v Deane.*

Edward's statement is clearly defamatory, reflecting adversely, as it does, on George's competence. Both Diana's and Edward's statements refer to George by name and Diana has published the name to a third party, namely Edward and Fenella. Edward has published the name both to Diana and Edward and also to Henry, as negligent publication to a third party is sufficient publication: *Theaker v Richardson* (1952) (1).

Prima facie, therefore, George can establish the elements of the tort of defamation against Diana and Edward, so we shall next consider any defences available.

Diana may be able to avail herself of the defence of justification ie truth, providing that George is, in fact, close to insolvency. If this is not the case, Diana may seek to rely on the defences of fair comment and qualified privilege. The first of these defences applies where the statement is fair comment based on true facts made in good faith on a matter of public interest. The Courts define public interest widely: *London Artists v Littler* and the award in question would be a matter of public interest. The comment must be based on true facts which are stated in the comment. The problem for Diana is that the comment that George is not a suitable candidate is based on a fact (that he is close to insolvency), but we do not know whether that fact is true.

By fair comment, we mean that Diana must have honestly believed the opinion: *Slim v Daily Telegraph* (1968) and not that a reasonable person would agree with the opinion: *Silkin v Beaverbrook Newspapers* (1958). Although Diana's comment may be fair in this respect, the defence can be rebutted by showing that the defendant acted out of malice: *Thomas v Bradbury Agnew* (1906). The burden of proving malice will lie on the Plaintiff: *Telnikoff v Matusevich* (1991), although the defendant will still have to show that the facts on which the comment was based were true and the comment was objectively fair in that anyone, however prejudiced or obstinate, could honestly have held the views expressed.

Although Diana may well be able to establish that the comment was fair as there seems to be no evidence of malice, she still has to overcome the hurdle of basing the comment on true facts.

It seems that Diana's best defence would be to rely on qualified privilege, namely that she was under a duty to make the statement to Edward and Fenella and they were under a corresponding duty to receive it: *Watt v Longsden* (1930). The requisite duty would exist in this case and Diana could rely on this defence unless she was acting maliciously. By malice is meant that the defendant had no honest belief in the truth of her statement: *Horrocks v Lowe* (1975) and there is not reason to impute malice to Diana.

Edward could rely on the defence of justification if his statement were true. As regards fair comment, Edward's problem is that his statement seems to be one of fact rather than opinion and there is no sub-stratem of fact as in *Kemsley v Foot* (1952) (2). If it were a comment it would have to be fair in the sense discussed above, but George might well be able to show malice in Edward's part which would destroy the defence.

If Edward were to seek to rely on qualified privilege, then although he would be able, like Diana, to show the required reciprocal duty regarding Diana and Fenella, this defence too can be destroyed by showing that Edward was actuated by malice. In any event, Edward could not rely on qualified privilege as regards the publishing to Henry as Edward is under no duty to make the statement to Henry and Henry is under no duty to receive it: *Watt v Longsden*.

It would then seem that George has a good case against Edward but that Diana may be able to rely on qualified privilege as a defence (3).

Notes

1 This is assuming of course, that Henry understands the defamatory nature of the statement and its reference to George: *Sadgrove v Hole* (1901).

2 Edward could argue that his statement should be interpreted as 'George is incompetent and, therefore, not fit to represent Westfield in Europe' and, thus, is comment based on fact. He would then have to show that the statement George is incompetent is a true fact which would be difficult to prove.

3 One could point out that in *Lawton v BOC Transhield* (1987) a plaintiff was allowed to sue as regards a reference using the tort of negligent mis-statement as a cause of action. Had the Plaintiff sued in defence he would have been met with the defence of qualified privilege and would have failed because

he could not have shown that the defendant acted maliciously. Although Lawton has been subject to much criticism, it was followed recently in *Spring v Guardian Assurance* (1992) (although Spring involved a reference which was obligatory under the LAUTRO rules). It may, thus, be possible for George to sue Diana in negligence.

Question 38

Ian is a sports commentator for Eastland TV. He decides to make a programme on Eastleigh Rovers, a local amateur football team that has reached a regional cup final. In the programme there is a shot of the team in a public house with the comment from Ian 'This is how the team prepares on Friday night, for its cup final match on Saturday.' In fact, the scene was shot on a Saturday night after a previous game. This film also shows John, the centre-forward eating a hamburger with the comment from Ian 'As a bachelor, John has to do his own cooking so he eats out a lot.' John is in fact married to Jane, who is most upset at this comment.

Eastleigh Rovers lose their cup final and Ian in his post match summary, states 'They played appallingly badly, even by the standards of an amateur team'. The Eastland Gazette reviews the programme and match, repeats Ian's comments regarding the team playing badly and wonders whether this was due to John's poor diet.

Advise John, Jane and Eastleigh Rovers of any action they might have in defamation.

Answer plan

This is a wide ranging question of defence which covers the areas of innuendo, references to Plaintiff and republication.

The following aspects should be discussed:

- commentary and Slander Defamation Act 1952
- Jane's ability to sue despite not being expressly referred to
- Eastleigh Rovers and class defamation
- liability of Eastland TV for repetition of defamatory statement

Answer

The statements made by Ian in the TV programme are deemed to be publication in a permanent form by s 1 Defamation Act 1952. They may, thus, constitute libel and be actionable without proof of special damage.

For any of the potential plaintiff to sue in defamation, they must show that the statement complained of was defamatory, that it referred to them and that it was published to a third party.

Considering first John, the statement that he is a bachelor is not *prima facie* defamatory. However, when coupled with the true innuendo that John is married to Jane, the statement that he is a bachelor might lead people who know that he lives with Jane to assume that they are not in fact married: *Cassidy v Daily Mirror* (1929). Thus, the statement is defamatory as it would tend to lower John in the estimation of right thinking members of society generally, *Sim v Stretch* or expose him to hatred contempt or ridicule, *Parmiter v Coupland*. The fact that John's friends might not think any the less of him for living with a woman to whom he is not married, is not relevant, as the standard is that of right thinking members of society: *Byrne v Deane* (1937) (1).

Turning to Jane, Ian's statement concerning John obviously also carries the suggestion that Jane is living with John without being married to him: *Cassidy v Daily Mirror*. This is defamatory and the fact that Jane is not referred to by Ian is no bar to her suing: *Cassidy; Morgan v Odhams Press*. The fact that Ian is innocent in this matter (eg because he was mistaken or was even told that John was unmarried) is, of itself, no defence, as defamation depends on the fact of defamation not the intent of the defamer: *Cassidy: Hulton v Jones* (2).

In both John and Jane's case, there would be no problem in showing the statement referred to them and had been published to a third party.

The next question is whether the team, Eastleigh Rovers, can sue in defamation. The statement that the team prepares for a cup final by drinking the night before and the statement concerning how badly they played are both *prima facie* defamatory and these statements were published to third parties. However, the statements concerning the team are an example of class or group defamation and in *Knupffer v London Express Newspapers* (1944), it was held by the House of Lords that in class defamation, a member of the class could not, unless the words pointed particularly to the Plaintiff or that the class was so small that the words must necessarily refer to each member of it. It is submitted that a football team is such a small class that the individual member can sue.

Having established Ian's (and Eastland TV's) liability to these statements we need to consider whether Ian can raise any successful defences. In respect of John and Jane, no common law defences seem available. However, both Ian and the TV company could make use of s 4 of Defamation Act 1952 which covers unintentional defamation, ie where the words were not defamatory on the face of them and the publisher did not know of circumstances by virtue of which they might be understood to be defamatory, s 4(5)(b) and the publisher took all reasonable care. In these circumstances the publisher must make an offer of amends ie publish a correction, plus apology. If such an offer is accepted, no action will lie and if the offer is successful, it is a defence to show the words were published innocently, the offer was made as soon as practicable and has not been withdrawn and the statement was made without malice.

Considering the statement made about the team, there seems to be no defence to the allegations regarding drinking. As regards the allegation that they played appallingly badly, the defences available are justification ie truth and fair comment. To establish the defence of fair comment it will have to be shown that the statement was fair comment based on true facts made in good faith on a matter of public interest. The courts interpret public interest widely: *London Artists v Littler* (1969) and a televised football match would certainly come under this heading. the comment must be one of opinion and not of fact, which is the case here. The comment must also be based on true facts which must be either stated in the comment or be capable of being inferred from the comment: *Kemsley v Foot* (1952). In a case such as the present the comment is an opinion based on the fact in Ian's commentary - Ian does not have to set these all out again in detail before he gives his opinion: *McQuire v Western Morning News* (1903). By fair comment is meant that Ian must have honestly believed the opinion expressed: *Slim v Daily Telegraph* (1968) and not that a reasonable person would agree with the opinion: *Silkin v Beaverbrook Newspapers* (1958). Although Ian's comment may be fair in this respect, the defence can be rebutted by showing that the defendant acted out of malice: *Thomas v Bradbury Agnew* (1906). The burden of proving malice will be on the Plaintiff, *Telnikoff v Matusevich*, although the Defendant will still have to show that the facts on which the comment was based were true and the comment was objectively fair in that anyone, however prejudiced or obstinate, could honestly have held the views expressed. Hence overall, it would seem that a defence of fair comment would be likely to succeed in the post match comments.

The review in the Eastland Gazette constitutes a republication of the comments regarding the team and by implication republishes the statement regarding John and Jane. The question is whether any liability for this republication attaches to Eastland TV or whether liability is solely that of the Eastland Gazette. In *Slipper v British Broadcasting Corp* (1991) the Court of Appeal held that in republishing defamation the question was had there been a breach in the chain of causation, ie was the republication of a *novus actus interveniens*. In *Slipper's* case the court held that where the BBC broadcast a programme which was alleged to be defamatory it could be liable for subsequent reviews which reproduced the libel as it was a natural and predictable consequence of the programme that it would be reviewed and the libel repeated.

Hence the TV company could also be liable for the subsequent repetition of the story of their allegations in the Eastland Gazette.

Notes

1   It could be argued by Ian that the standard of right thinking members of society alter with time, so that for example it is no longer defamatory to call a person a German as in *Slazengers v Gibbs* (1916) or a Czech as in *Linklater v Daily Telegraph* (1964). Given this, Ian could argue that to say that an adult male lives with a woman is no longer defamatory. As, however, it is still defamatory to make this allegation of a woman, s 1, The Slander of Women Act 1891, it seems most illogical that it would not also be defamatory of a man.

2   Jane could also argue that the film of John eating out plus the commentary suggesting that she does not do any cooking for John, which would also be defamatory, it is submitted, using the test in *Byrne v Deane*.

Question 39

To what extent do you think that the law of defamation represents an unwarrantable restriction on the freedom of speech?

Answer plan

This essay calls for a discussion of the elements of liability for defamation, together with those defences which are relevant to preserving freedom of speech.

The following points should be considered:

- elements of liability
- position with dead persons, companies, local authorities
- relevant defences - consent
- justification
- absolute privilege
- qualified privilege
- fair comment
- defence under s 4 Defamation Act 1952

Answer

To consider whether the law of defamation represents any restriction on free speech we must consider what constitutes defamation and what defences to defamation exist in law.

Let us start by looking at those persons who can sue in defamation. The basic rule is that only living persons can sue, so no restrictions exist at all on freedom of speech as regards dead persons. However, in law a company is a person, and they can sue for defamatory statements affecting their business: *Metropolitan Saloon Omnibus Co v Hawkins* (1859). But it has recently been held by the Court of Appeal in *Derbyshire County Council v Times Newspapers* (1992), overruling *Bognor Regis UDC v Campion* (1972), that a local authority cannot sue for libel as regards its governing reputation. In view of the question being answered it is interesting to note that the Court of Appeal decided that to hold otherwise would impose a substantial and unjustifiable restriction on freedom of speech. We next need to consider what constitutes defamation. The standard test is that proposed by Lord Atkin in *Sim v Stretch* (1936), namely that a statement is defamatory if the words are 'words which tend to lower the plaintiff in the estimation of right thinking members of society generally'. In *Hartt v Newspaper Publishing plc* (1989), the Court of Appeal held that in determining the meaning of the words the approach adopted should be that of the hypothetical ordinary reader who was neither naive nor unduly suspicious, but who might read between the lines and be capable of loose thinking. The effect of this is to make a great many statements potentially actionable, but it should be remembered that the standard is the objective one of the right thinking member of society. Another factor which tends to widen the possible scope of liability is that there is no need for the plaintiff to be referred to by name - it is sufficient that the statement could be understood to refer to him: *Cassidy v Daily Mirror* (1929); *Morgan v Odhams Press* (1971). In addition, the maker of a statement may be held liable for the republication of that statement, where such republication is reasonably foreseeable: *Slipper v British Broadcasting Corp* (1991). It can, thus, be seen that defamation is a tort of potentially very wide scope, so we must turn to the defences that will limit liability and preserve freedom of speech.

A person may consent to the publication of what would otherwise be defamatory material, eg the 'My Wicked Life' type of newspaper interview. Another defence which probably prevents the bringing of a number of libel actions is that of justification or truth. It is sufficient in this respect to show that the substance of the allegation is true - it is not necessary to show that the statement is true in each and every particular. If more than one allegation is made against the plaintiff then by s 5 of the Defamation Act 1952 the defence will not fail merely because one allegation is untrue if that allegation does not materially affect the plaintiff's reputation having regard to the true allegation. Statements made on certain occasions carry absolute privilege, ie no liability will attach to them no matter how false or malicious.

Such occasions include statements made in Parliament, in judicial proceedings and in official communications. It can, thus, be seen that there are virtually no restrictions on freedom of speech on such occasions. There additionally a number of situations to which qualified privilege attached. This defence can be destroyed by showing that the defendant was actuated by malice, ie that the defendant has no honest belief in the truth of his statement: *Horrocks v Lowe* (1975). Perhaps the most important situation to which this defence attaches are the statements made by A to B concerning C where both A and B have an interest in the statement: *Watt v Longsden* (1930). The absence of the requisite interest on the part of either party is fatal to this defence: *Watt*. This is a defence that could be relevant in a variety of situations, and from the point of view of preserving freedom of speech it should be noted that malice cannot be inferred merely because the maker of the statement is unreasonable or prejudiced or unfair: *Horrocks* (1). Another widely used defence in defamation actions is that of fair comment based on true facts made in good faith on a matter of public interest. The courts tend to define public interest very widely: *London Artists v Littler* (1969), and as in justification it is the sting of the allegation that has to be true rather than each and every allegation. However, the statement must be comment, ie it must be opinion rather than a factual statement, and distinguishing between opinion and fact can sometimes be difficult. Finally, the comment must be fair, which means that the defendant must have honestly believed the opinion: *Slim v Daily Telegraph* (1968).

Because of the strictness of the common law rules regarding reference to the plaintiff and the relevance of extraneous matters which may not be known to the maker of the statement s 5 of the Defamation Act 1952 provides a defence in cases of innocent defamation, ie those cases in which the publisher did not intend to refer to the plaintiff and was unaware if circumstances whereby his words might be understood to do so, or where the words were not defamatory on the face of them, and the publisher was unaware of circumstances whereby they might be understood to be defamatory. In either case, providing that the publisher was not negligent he will have a defence if he makes an offer of amends, ie publishes a correction plus an apology and notifies the recipients of the statement that is alleged to be defamatory.

In the law of defamation a balance must be struck between protecting the reputation of persons and infringing freedom of speech: *Derbyshire County Council v Times Newspapers*. Liability if defamation is wide, but a number of defences are available which have the effect of protecting free speech. given the variety and scope of these defences it is difficult to claim that the restrictions imposed by the law of defamation are unwarrantable.

Notes

1   Although the defence of qualified privilege applies to references, in *Lawton v BOC Transhield* (1987) a plaintiff was allowed to bring an action as regards an allegedly negligent reference in the tort of negligent mis-statement. Had he brought the action in defamation he would have been met with the defence of qualified privilege, and would have to have shown that the defendants acted out of malice to succeed, which in the circumstances of the case he could not have done. *Lawton* has been criticised as allowing plaintiffs to sidestep the defence of qualified privilege by bringing their case in negligence. However, in the recent case of *Spring v Guardian Assurance* (1992) such an action was allowed.

Chapter 12

Trespass to the Person, to Land and to Goods

Introduction

Trespass is an area which may be tested by the examiner, either in its own right or as part of a question, mostly involving for example occupiers liability or nuisance.

There have, however, been a number of recent developments in the law of trespass such as hostile touching, trespass to air space and false imprisonment of prisoners, which may jog the examiner's mind on the topic of trespass.

Checklist

Students should have a good grasp of the following topics:

- Definition, elements and defences for battery. Note the divergence of opinion as to whether the tort can be committed negligently and on the requirement of hostility
- Definition, elements and defences for assault
- Definition, elements and defences for false imprisonment and note the recent judgment concerning the residual liberty of prisoners
- The rule in *Wilkinson v Downton*
- Definition, elements and defences to trespass to land ie especially trespass to airspace
- Definition, elements and defences to trespass to goods, and in particular title to lost goods and the allowance for improvement of goods

Question 40

Javid, who was conducting a market survey, entered Keith's property in order to ask him some questions. Keith came to the door and said to Javid 'If you have come to try to sell me anything you can clear off' and raised his fist to Javid. This frightened Javid, who ran away but tripped over and broke his leg. Keith immediately rant to help Javid. While he was bending over Javid, and trying to help him, Lionel came along, assumed that Keith had hit Javid and took Keith to a Police Station where he said

'This man has hit an innocent man'. Keith was keep in custody in a very damp cell while enquiries were made and was later released.

Advise Javid and Keith.

Answer plan

This question covers assault and false imprisonment. The test for recovery of damages in this lot needs to be discussed, together with the relevant provision of Police and Criminal Evidence Act 1984.

The following areas should be considered:

- status of Javid - visitor or trespasser
- assault by Keith
- Keith's liability for Javid's fall
- false imprisonment by Lionel
- defamation by Lionel
- false imprisonment by the police

Answer

We should perhaps, first consider the legal status of Javid ie when Javid entered Keith's property whether he was a visitor or a trespasser. In *Robson v Hallett* (1967) it was held that when a person enters premises for the purpose of communicating with the occupier, he is treated as having the occupier's implied permission to be there until the visitor knows or ought to know that his permission has been revoked. Once this permission has been revoked, the visitor has a reasonable time to leave before he becomes a trespasser. Thus, Javid is a visitor as Keith's permission has not been revoked (1).

When Keith raises his fist to Javid, this is an assault. An assault is an attempt or threat to apply force to a person whereby that person is put in fear of immediate physical contact. In *Thomas v NUM (South Wales Area)* (1985) it was held by the High Court that where the plaintiff has no reasonable belief that the defendant can affect his purpose there is no assault, even if the conduct is frightening. However, in Javid's case, even if Javid is by nature exceptionally timid, it would seem that he has a reasonable belief that Keith can affect his purpose. Hence Keith has committed an assault on Javid so we must consider whether Keith is liable for Javid's broken leg. The rule for remoteness of damage in trespass to the person is that the defence is liable for all the direct consequences of the trespass: *Nash v Sheen* (1953), ie the test in *Re Polemis* (1921). Thus, Keith will be liable for Javid's broken leg; it seems unlikely that Keith could claim Javid's carelessness amounted to a *novus actus interveniens* (2) and it would be more realistic of Keith to allege contributory negligence on Javid's part. This defence has been held to be applicable to battery: *Barnes v Nayer* (1986), and the reasoning of the Court of Appeal would also seem to be appropriate to assault.

When Lionel takes Keith to the police station, he commits *prima facie*, false imprisonment as Lionel presumably restrains Keith in some way. False imprisonment is the total deprivation of the freedom of a person for any period, however short, without lawful justification. The only justification Lionel could claim is under the provisions of the Police and Criminal Evidence Act 1984. By s 24(4) anyone, ie a private citizen or a police offer, may arrest without warrant anyone who is in the act of committing an arrestable offence or anyone who he has reasonable grounds for suspecting of committing such an offence. However, s 24(4) does not apply where that offence has been committed, but by s 24(5) where an arrestable offence has been committed any person may arrest without warrant anyone who is guilty of the offence or anyone who he has reasonable grounds to suspect to be guilty of it. This means, of course, that where an offence has been committed, there is a defence to false imprisonment, even if the person arresting arrests an innocent person. If an offence has not been committed s 24(6) allows a police officer to arrest without warrant anyone he reasonably suspects to have committed an offence. Thus, PACE 1984 preserves the trap in *Walters v Smith* (1914) where it is necessary for a private person to prove that the offence is question has been committed by someone. The recent case of *R v Self* (1992) is an example of the trap in action.

Lionel's problem is that as no arrestable offence has in fact been committed he cannot invoke s 24(5) and falls in the trap of *Walters v Smith* and will be liable for false imprisonment.

Lionel's statement that Keith has hit Javid is defamatory, refers to Keith and has been published to a third party. This contains all the necessary elements of defamation but will be covered by qualified privilege as he is under a moral duty to make the statement and the police officer is under a legal duty to receive it: *Watt v Longsden* (1930).

When Keith was kept in custody this was a lawful imprisonment under s 24(6) of the 1984 Act, and even if the conditions of imprisonment become or are intolerable, that does not render the detention unlawful - see *R v Deputy Governor of Parkhurst Prison ex P Hague: Weldon v Home Office* (1991) where the House of Lords expressly disapproved of dicta to the contrary in *Middleweek v Chief Constable of Merseyside* (1990). However, in *Hague's* case, the House of Lords did state that such detention might give rise to a remedy in public law, and if the prisoner suffered an injury to his health, a remedy might lie in negligence. So Keith cannot sue the police for false imprisonment, though if he had suffered any injury due to the dampness of the cell he could sue in negligence.

Notes

1   One might point out here that even if Javid were to be a trespasser, although reasonable force may be used to eject him, *Green v Goddard* (1704) this can only be done after he has been asked to leave the premises and been allowed a reasonable opportunity to do so: *Tool Metal Manufacturing v Tungsten Electric* (1955). Neither of these requirements have been met in Javid's case.

2   It might be possible for Keith to argue that the true cause of Javid's damage was his carelessness rather than Keith's original assault. In *Re Polemis* (1921) it was held that the defendant was liable for all the damage directly resulting from his act; Keith would not be liable for any damage indirectly resulting ie damage due to the 'operation of independent causes having no connection with the act, except they could not avoid its result' per Scrutton LJ. This gives rise to the possibility that he could claim that Javid's carelessness in tripping was a *novus actus interveniens* which broke the chain of causation. A comparison of *McKew v Holland and Hannen and Cubitts* (1969) with *Wieland v Cyril Lord Carpets* (1969) suggests that a subsequent act of the plaintiff will only be treated as breaking the chain of causation where the act is unreasonable, and it is not unreasonable for a person subject to an assault to run away and concentrate on escaping rather than anything else.

Question 41

Martin owns a house with a very large garden. Neil takes his dog for a walk along the road bordering Martin's house when the dog jumps over Martin's fence and runs into his garden to eat some flowers. Neil enters the garden to retrieve his dog who by now has run into Martin's greenhouse. While Neil is in the greenhouse, Martin sees him and shuts the door, saying 'stop there, you thief, I am phoning the Police'. Neil, who knows that he can explain his presence to the police, is quite happy to stay in Martin's greenhouse and admiring Martin's collection of exotic plants. The police arrive in a few minutes, and no charges are brought against Neil. Neil leaves his jacket in Martin's greenhouse, but Martin refuses to return it to Neil until Neil pays Martin compensation for damage Martin claims was done to the plants in his garden by Neil.

Advise Martin and Neil of any legal consequences of their actions.

Answer plan

This question covers trespass to land and false imprisonment. The question as to whether trespass to land can be committed negligently, must be discussed together with the elements and defences to false imprisonment.

Thus, the answer should consider:

- Neil's trespass via the dog
- Neil's trespass on Martin's property
- false imprisonment by Martin, and the provisions of PACE 1984 and common law defences
- distress damage feasant
- other causes of action eg negligence, nuisance, Animals Act 1971, defamation

Answer

When Neil's dog enters Martin's property, Neil has committed trespass to land via his dog, and it seems from *League Against Cruel Sports v Scott* (1985) that trespass to land via animals can be committed negligently. When Neil enters Martin's land to retrieve the dog, he too has committed trespass to land, as clearly Neil intended to enter upon Martin's land which is sufficient - there is no need to show that Neil intended to trespass: *Conway v Wimpey* (1951).

When Martin shuts Neil in the greenhouse, Martin has committed the tort of false imprisonment which consists of the total deprivation of the freedom of a person for any period however short, without lawful justification. The fact that Neil is quite happy to remain in the greenhouse is not relevant to liability though it would be relevant to any issue of damages, should this arise. Two defences are relevant to Martin's actions here, namely the provisions of the Police and Criminal Evidence Act 1984 (PACE) and the common law defences. By s 24(4) anyone, ie a private citizen or a police officer may arrest without warrant anyone who is in the act of committing an arrestable offence or anyone who he has reasonable grounds for suspecting of committing such an offence. However, s 24(4) does not apply where the offence has been committed, but by s 24(5) where an arrestable offence has been committed any person may arrest without warrant anyone who is guilty of the offence or anyone who he has reasonable grounds to suspect to be guilty of it. This means of course, that where an offence has been committed there is a defence to false imprisonment even if the person arresting arrests an innocent person. If an offence has not been committed s 24(6) allows a police officer to arrest without warrant anyone he reasonably suspects to have committed an offence. Thus, PACE 1984 preserves the trap in *Walters v Smith* (1914) where it is necessary for a private person to prove that the offence in question has been committed by someone. The recent case of *R v Self* (1992) is an example of the trap in action.

However, as Neil is a trespasser, for he has entered Martin's land without invitation and his presence is objected to, *Addie v Dumbreck* (1929), Martin may use a reasonable degree of force to control his movement, *Harrison v Rutland* (1893), *Alderson v Booth* (1969).

As regards Martin's retention of Neil's jacket, this is a conversion of Neil's goods, as Martin is performing a positive wrongful act or dealing with the goods in a manner which is inconsistent with the rights of the owner: *Maynegrain v Campafina Bank* (1984). Neil can, therefore, sue Martin in conversion and by s 3(2) Torts (Interference with Goods) Act 1977, the remedies available are an order to deliver the goods to Neil or to pay damages or an order to deliver with the alternative of paying damages. The defence of distress damage feasant makes it lawful for an occupier of land to seize any chattels which are unlawfully on his land and have done damage therein, and to detain them until payment of compensation for the damage. The problem for Martin is that Neil's jacket has not caused actual damage and, thus, his jacket cannot be lawfully distrained: *R v Howson* (1966).

A number of other causes of action are disclosed by the facts of the problem. When Martin says 'Stop there, you thief, I am phoning the police' this is a defamatory statement. Although it is slander as it imputes a crime punishable by imprisonment, it is actionable without proof of special damage: *Hellwig v Mitchell* (1910). It refers to Neil but the question arises as to whether it has been published to a third party. If any person heard Martin's statement then Neil can sue Martin in defamation, but if no one other than Martin or Neil heard the statement, there is no publication. When Martin alleged to the police that Neil was a thief, then publication would be covered by qualified privilege as Martin is under a moral duty to make the statement and the police are under a legal duty to receive it: *Watt v Longsden* (1930).

Martin could also sue Neil in nuisance as there has been an unreasonable interference with Martin's use or enjoyment of his land, and although this was an isolated event, it was due to a wrongful state of affairs, ie the dog not being on a lead or not being properly controlled: *Pitcher v Martin* (1937).

Martin could also sue Neil in negligence and under the Animals Act 1971. Under s 2(2) of the 1971 Act it would have to be shown:

a) the damage is of a kind which the animal, unless restrained, was likely to cause or which, if caused by the animal, was likely to be severe;

b) the likelihood of the damage or of its being severe was due to characteristics of the animal which are not normally found in animals of the same species or are not normally found except at particular times or in particular circumstances; and

c) those characteristics were known to that keeper.

As we are told that Neil owns the dog then by s 6(3) he is the keeper.

The damage to plants will come under s 2(2)(a) and a tendency to eat plants is a characteristic not usually found in dogs and Neil is presumably aware of this characteristic, satisfying both ss 2(2)(b) and (2)(2)(c). Thus, all the requirements of s 2(2) have been met. There is no need to show any negligence on Neil's part: *Curtis v Betts* (1990).

Question 42

Oliver is employed as a salesman. He calls on Peter's shop to sell them some office stationery when he sees a gold watch on the floor. He picks it up and hands it to Peter who takes his name and address. Some three months later, Oliver is passing Peter's shop when he sees the watch in the window for sale. Oliver goes in and takes the watch from the window, but Peter grabs the watch from Oliver and there is a scuffle in which Oliver is injured.

Advise Oliver.

Would your advice differ if Oliver found the watch behind the counter of Peter's shop?

Answer plan

This is a relatively straightforward question of title to lost goods and also involves an element of trespass to the person.

The following aspects should be discussed:
- Oliver's right to the watch as against peter's
- Oliver's right to the watch as against Oliver's
- rules regarding supervening possession
- necessary intention present in non public part of shop
- effect of Oliver being a trespasser

Answer

Oliver will wish to sue Peter for conversion of the watch and for trespass to the person.

Conversion has been defined as being 'committed wherever one person performs a positive wrongful act of dealing with goods in a manner inconsistent with the rights of the owner' *Maynegrain v Campafina Bank* (1984) per Lord Templeman. The tort is one of strict liability in that provided that the defendant intends to deal with the goods in a manner which is inconsistent with the owner's (or someone with a superior right to the goods) rights, the fact that the defendant is ignorant of these rights is no defence. So, for example, the innocent purchaser from a thief of stolen goods, commits a conversion against the owner: *Moorgate Mercantile v Twitchings* (1977). It hence follows that Peter has committed a conversion of the watch in offering it for sale.

To sue in conversion Oliver must show that he had the right to possession: *Marquess of Bute v Barclays Bank* (1955). The owner of the watch, of course, remains the owner but as he has not claimed his property the normal rule is that the finder, ie Oliver in our case, has a right to them against everyone except the true owner, if he has reduced the goods into his possession. Thus, in *Armory v Dalaminie* (1721), the finder of a jewel was held to be able to recover it from a jeweller to whom it had been handed and who refused to return it.

All this, however, assumes that the finder was the first person to reduce the goods into his possession and the possession counts as title: *The Winkfield* (1902). However, we must decide whether someone other than Oliver had obtained earlier possession of the goods when Oliver found them in which case, that person and not Oliver has the right to the goods. This can occur in two ways. Firstly, if an employee finds goods in the course of his employment then the employees possession is deemed to be that of his employer and the employee gains no possessory right against his employer: *Parker v British Airways Board* (1982). The important element here is that the goods must be found in the course of employment ie the employment must the the cause of the finding of the goods and not merely the occasion of the finding of the goods, *Byrne v Hoare* (1965). We are told that Oliver is a salesman and that he calls on Peter's shop to sell some stationery. Oliver was undoubtedly going about his employer's business when he found the watch, but it seems that Oliver's employment was the occasion of his finding the watch rather than the cause and so it is submitted that Oliver's employer does not have a right of possession to the watch. Secondly, if goods are found on land not occupied by the finder, in certain situations, the occupier's occupation will confer upon him a possession of the lost goods, which is earlier in time than the finder and this previous possession can exist even though the occupier was unaware of the presence of the lost goods on his land. Such earlier possession will arise where the goods are buried on the land or attached to the land in such a manner as to suggest that the occupier is exerting exclusive control over the relevant area: *South Staffordshire Water Co v Sharman* (1896). Where the goods are found just lying on the premises and the public have access to the premises, the finder generally allows a superior right to the occupier: *Bridges v Hawkesworth* (1851): *Hannah v Peel* (1945) unless the occupier has 'manifested an intention to exercise control over the building and things which may be in or on it': *Parker v British Airways Board* per Donaldson MR. In *Bridges*, the finder of some cash in a shop was held to be entitled to it as against the shopowner and the more modern case of *Parker* shows that the required intention is not easy to establish. In *Parker*, the finder of a bracelet in an airport lounge was held entitled to it as against the occupiers of the lounge. Thus, the weight of authority would allow Oliver a superior right to the watch as against Peter. By s 3 Torts (interference with Goods) Act 1976, Oliver may obtain a court order to the watch or damages or delivery with the alternative of damages.

As Oliver is entitled to the watch, he is entitled to recover it from Peter using reasonable force if necessary to protect his property. As Peter has directly and intentionally applied hostile touching to Oliver's person, Oliver can sue Peter in battery and in assault if he was first put in reasonable fear of immediate physical contact.

If the watch was found behind the counter, Peter will find it easier to establish the intention described in *Parker*, as it would be easier to show that Peter intended to exercise control of the area behind the counter and any things in it. In addition, if Oliver was trespassing when he went behind the counter as it was not part of the premises to which he was invited, *The Calgarth* (1927), then as a trespasser he would acquire no rights as against the occupier: *Parker v British Airways Board*.

It seems likely that Peter did evince the required intention in respect of as the area behind the counter. He, thus, has a right to the goods as against Oliver and when Oliver removed the watch from the window, Oliver was committing an conversion of the goods. Peter was entitled, therefore, to use reasonable force to protect his property and he would be able to sue Oliver in Battery and possibly assault as regards the ensuing struggle.

Question 43

George is walking along the road when he slips and falls, and Frank sees this and goes to help George. While he is helping George to his feet Ian comes along and, thinking that Frank is trying to rob George, Ian grips Frank by the arm and says 'I am taking you to the police, you thief'. George struggles to free himself and pushes Ian to the ground. Ian sees a passing policeman and tells him that Frank has tried to rob George and has hit him (Ian). The policeman arrests Frank and takes him to the police station where is he released after a few hours.

Advise Frank of the legal situation.

Answer plan

This question calls for a discussion of the various forms of the tort of trespass to the person, namely assault, battery and false imprisonment, together with the defence of lawful arrest. The tort of defamation also needs to be considered.

The following aspects need to be considered:
- Ian's liability to Frank for assault, battery and false imprisonment
- possible defence of lawful arrest and trap in *Walters v Smith*
- defamation by Ian on two occasions, and possible defence of qualified privilege
- liability of policeman to Frank for assault, battery and false imprisonment and defence of lawful arrest
- liability of policeman for defamation and defence of qualified privilege
- liability of Frank to Ian for assault or battery and defence of self-defence

Answer

We need to advise Frank of any torts that may have been committed by Ian or the policeman, and of any liability that Frank may have incurred to Ian.

Considering first Ian's behaviour, Ian may have committed an assault upon Frank. An assault is an attempt or threat to apply force to a person whereby that person is put in fear of immediate physical contact. The test is an objective one in that the plaintiff must have a reasonable belief that the defendant can carry out his purpose: *Thomas v NUM (Sough Wales Area)* (1985). Ian may well have been guilty of an assault but we are not given enough facts to be certain, for if Ian approached Frank from behind and gripped his arm before saying anything then the tort of assault would not have taken place as Frank would not have been put in fear of immediate physical contact (1).

When Ian gripped Frank by the arm, he committed the tort of battery. Battery consists of a direct act of the defendant which causes contact with the plaintiff's body without the plaintiff's consent. The act must be both direct: *Scott v Shepherd* (1773) and intentional: *Stanley v Powell* (1891); *Letang v Cooper* (1965), and Frank would have no difficulty in showing either of the requirements. There must be some contact with the plaintiff's person, however trivial: *Cole v Turner* (1704), and contact has clearly occurred. Finally, the touching must be hostile: *Wilson v Pringle* (1987), which does not mean that Frank need show any ill-will or malevolence but he must show hostility. This requirement has been doubted by Lord Goff in an obiter statement in *F v West Berkshire Health Authority* (1989), but as Lord Goff argued that a touching could amount to a battery in the absence of hostility and that the fundamental question was did the plaintiff consent to the touching, even if Lord Goff's approach were to be used Ian's act in gripping Frank's arm would constitute a battery.

We should next consider whether in restraining Frank, Ian has committed the tort of false imprisonment which consists of the total deprivation of the freedom of a person for any period of time, however short, without lawful justification. When Ian grips Frank by the arm he deprives him of his freedom for a short period and so all the elements of this tort are present.

Given that, *prima facie*, these torts have taken place, we need to consider whether Ian has any defences available to him. The only defence relevant to Ian is available for all three torts, namely the defence of lawful arrest under the provisions of the Police and Criminal Evidence Act 1984. By s 24(5) where an arrestable offence has been committed any person, ie a private citizen or a police officer, may arrest without warrant anyone who is guilty of the offence or anyone who he has reasonable grounds for suspecting to be guilty of the offence. This means that where an offence has been committed that s 24(5) provides a defence where the person arresting arrests an innocent person. If an offence has not been committed then by s 24(6) a police officer may arrest without warrant anyone who he reasonably suspects to have committed an offence. Thus, the 1984 Act preserves the trap in *Walters v Smith* (1914) where it is necessary for a private citizen to prove that the offence in question has in fact been committed by someone. The recent case of *R v Self* (1992) is an example of the trap in action where a person was reasonably suspected of a theft and was arrested by a private citizen. He resisted arrest and was later convicted of assault to resist lawful arrest, but acquitted of theft. It was held by the Court of Appeal that the conviction for assault to resist lawful arrest could not stand, because s 24(5) required as a condition precedent that an arrestable offence had been committed, and that as the appellant had been acquitted of the alleged offence a private citizen could not carry out an arrest under s 24(5) which did not operate under these circumstances. As Frank has not committed the arrestable offence of which Ian suspected him, his arrest of Frank is not lawful and Ian cannot avail himself of the defence of lawful arrest. The fact that Ian might have had reasonable grounds to suspect Frank of the offence is irrelevant: s 24(5): *R v Self*, if the offence has not in fact been committed.

We should also advise Frank whether in struggling with Ian and pushing him to the ground Frank himself has committed any torts against Ian. From our discussion above it is clear that Frank may be guilty of assault and/or battery although on the facts that we are given there does not appear to have been any false imprisonment of Ian. The defence that would be appropriate for Frank to invoke is that of self-defence, for as Ian's attempted arrest is not lawful Frank is entitled to protect himself against Ian's assault and battery. The rule is that in self-defence the steps taken to protect oneself must not be out of all proportion to the harm threatened: *Lane v Holloway* (1968), and provided that Frank satisfies this criterion he will have a valid defence to any action by Ian.

In calling Frank a thief Ian has defamed Frank. To succeed in an action for defamation Frank will have to show that Ian made a defamatory statement that could reasonably be understood to refer to him and that this statement was published to a third party. As the statement in question was spoken then it was in the form of slander and normally in slander the plaintiff will have to prove special damage. However, where the statement imputes a crime punishable by imprisonment then the statement is actionable *per se*: *Hellwig v Mitchell* (1902). The test for the defamatory nature of a statement is whether it would lower the plaintiff in the estimation of right thinking members of society: *Sim v Stretch* (1936), which Ian's allegation does. It also seems clear from what we are told that Ian could not avail himself of the defence that the slander was mere abuse: *Parkins v Scott* (1862); *Lane v Holloway* (1968), as it could be intended to be taken seriously. The statement obviously refers to Frank and has been published to a third party, namely George. Thus, all the elements of defamation are present, and there are no defences on which Ian could rely in respect of this statement. When Ian makes his allegations to the policeman then again the elements of defamation are present, but Ian will be able to rely on the defence of qualified privilege. This defence operates where (inter alia) one person has a legal, social or moral duty to make a statement to another and that other has a corresponding interest to receive it: *Watt v Longsdon* (1930). Ian has such a duty as regards criminal acts and the policeman has a duty to receive such statements. Thus, Ian could rely on the defence of qualified privilege which Frank could only destroy by showing that Ian was actuated by malice when he made the statement, which in the circumstances seems unlikely.

When the policeman arrests Frank he may commit an assault or battery, but he can rely on s 24(6) of the Police and Criminal Evidence Act 1984 as a defence because, as discussed above, this sub-section allows a police officer to make a lawful arrest where he reasonably suspects that someone has committed an arrestable offence, and the policeman has such reasonable grounds. This lawful arrest will also, of course, be a valid defence to any action for false imprisonment, and if the policeman makes any statements to his colleagues at the police station regarding Frank's alleged criminal acts, such statements would be protected by the doctrine of qualified privilege as both the policeman and his colleagues have the required interests as discussed above.

Thus, Frank could sue Ian for assault, battery, false imprisonment and defamation, but could not sue the policeman. Frank could not be sued by Ian in respect of the struggle.

Note

1   If Ian said 'I am taking you to the police, you thief' before gripping Frank, it is submitted that this would constitute a battery. In *R v Meade & Belt* (1823) it was said that words cannot amount to an assault, but this case has been subject to both academic and judicial criticism: *R v Wilson* (1955), although it is supported by Salmond and Heuston, *Law of Torts*, 20th edition.

Economic Torts

Introduction

Questions on the economic torts are popular with examiners as not only is it an important topic but also it has been the subject of recent important developments. In addition, the exact scope of some of the torts is subject to some uncertainty calling for a careful analysis of some decisions of the courts. This is a complex area, and candidates should only attempt questions if they have a reasonably good and up to date knowledge of the topics.

Checklist

Students should have a good grasp of the following aspects:

- Conspiracy involving lawful and unlawful acts, defences to lawful act, conspiracy
- Inducing a breach of contract - mental state required and defences
- Intimidation
- Interference with trade by unlawful means - note the uncertainty regarding the ingredients and extent of this tort
- Deceit, malicious falsehood and passing off

Question 44

Alfred runs a grocery business which supplies packed lunches to several nearby factories. Brian and Charles run a nearby sandwich bar and feel that Alfred's competition, as he is able to purchase foodstuffs at reduced prices via his grocery business, is unfair. They, therefore, falsely tell the Personnel Officer at the factory that they believe that the local Food Inspector is unhappy with the state of hygiene at Alfred's premises, and as a result, the factory ceases to use Alfred as a supplier.

When Alfred becomes aware of the activities of Brian and Charles, he immediately informs David, who supplies bread to both Alfred and Brian and Charles, but he (Alfred) feels he cannot do business with a person who supplies his rivals and that David must choose to do business with Alfred or Brian and Charles, but not both.

Advise Alfred as to the legal situation.

Answer plan

This is a typical problem on the economic torts in that the facts disclose a range of possible causes of action, which must all be discussed. In this type of question, the student should not neglect the possibility of an action arising in the traditional tort areas of deceit, malicious falsehood and passing off.

The following areas should be considered:
- Alfred's competition via his grocery business
- Brian and Charles' report to the factory
- conspiracy by unlawful means
- inducement to breach contract
- interference with trade by unlawful means
- malicious falsehood
- Alfred's dealing with David
- inducing breach of contract
- intimidation
- interference with trade by unlawful means

Answer

Alfred should be advised as to whether Brian and Charles have committed any torts and whether he himself has committed any torts in his dealings with Brian and Charles and with David.

As regards Alfred's competition with Brian and Charles, via his grocery business, this does not give rise to any course of action. Competition, however vigorous or unfair, is not unlawful: *Mogul Steamship v McGregor Gow* (1892) and despite the modern development in the area of the economic torts, Hoffman J, recently held that there is no tort of unfair trading: *Associated Newspapers Group v Insert Media* (1988).

When, however, Brian and Charles made their statement to the personnel Officer of the factory a number of possible courses of action arise.

Firstly, Brian and Charles may be guilty of conspiracy to commit an unlawful act. Conspiracy has been defined as the agreement of two or more persons to do an unlawful act or a lawful act by unlawful means: *Mulcahy v R* (1868) per Willes J. Although the word 'agreement' was used in this definition, the word combination is now preferred reference as there is no need for a contractual agreement merely that the persons conspire together with a common purpose: *Belmont Finance Corp v Williams Furniture* (1980). The conspiracy must cause damage to the plaintiff for the tort is not actionable *per se*, and this has clearly happened as the factory has ceased to trade with Alfred. Before we can conclude that all the ingredients of the tort are present, we should consider what constitutes an unlawful act. A tort is unlawful for this purpose: *Sorrel v Smith* (1925) and as Brian and Charles are committing the tort of malicious falsehood and also conspiring to induce a breach of contract this is sufficient. In the recent house of Lords decision in *Lonrho v Al-Fayed* (1991) it was held that the tort of conspiracy to injury could be established by showing that an intent to injure the plaintiff's business interest was the predominant purpose, even though the means were lawful and would not have been actionable, if carried out by an individual, or by showing that unlawful means were used. But where there was an intent to injure and unlawful means were used it was no defence for the defendants to show that their predominant purpose was to protect their own interest - it was sufficient that they had used unlawful means to constitute the tort. Hence Brian and Charles could not avail themselves of the defence that their predominant purpose was to defend their interest rather than to injure Alfred's interests.

Secondly, Brian and Charles may have committed the tort of inducing a breach of contract: *Lumley v Gye* (1853). Following the classification of Jenkins LJ in *DC Thomson v Deaking* (1952) Brian and Charles' action is that of direct persuasion to breach the contract between the factory and Alfred. The court needs to find some persuasion to breach the contract and in *Square Grip Reinforcement v MacDonald* (1968), Lord Milligan stated that where a defendant was 'desperately anxious' to achieve a particular result then the court would be likely to want a statement made by the defendant as persuasion, and that appears to be the case here. It must also be shown by Alfred that Brian and Charles knew of the contract between Alfred and the factory and acted with the intention of bringing about a breaking of this contract and on the facts of the problem Alfred would seem to have little difficulty here, and Alfred should be able to establish that this tort has been committed.

Thirdly, Brian and Charles may have committed the tort of interference with trade by unlawful means. This now seems to be established as a tort in its own right: *Merkur Island Shipping v Laughton* (1983): *Hadmor Productions v Hamilton* (1983), in *Lonrho v Fayed* (1989) in the Court of Appeal it was held that it was not an essential ingredient of the tort that the defendant's predominant purpose was to injure the plaintiff rather than to further his own interest, but it was necessary to prove that the action was directed against the Plaintiff or intended to harm the plaintiff. Alfred should have no problem in establishing this, but there seems to be considerable uncertainty as to just what constitutes unlawful means. In *Lonrho v Shell Petroleum* (1982) the breach of a penal statute has held to be insufficient to found a cause of action and in *Chapman v Honig* (1963) a criminal contempt of court was also held insufficient. However, in the later case of *Acrow v Rex Chainbelt* (1971) such a contempt was held sufficient and in *Associated British Ports v TGWU* (1989) in the Court of Appeal it was held that a non-actionable breach of a statute could constitute unlawful means if it was coupled with an intent to injure the Plaintiff. In the light of these later cases, it is submitted that as Brian and Charles have committed at least the tort of malicious falsehood, that, in common with other economic torts, the commission of a tort is sufficient unlawful means allowing Alfred to sue.

Finally, Brian and Charles have committed the tort of malicious falsehood. To establish this Alfred most prove that Brian and Charles have made a false statement to someone other than Alfred; that that statement was made maliciously and that the statement has caused damage to Alfred. There is no problem in showing that the statement is false statement of fact - it is clearly not opinion or trade puff (see the judgment of Walton J, in *De Beers Products v Electric Co of New York* (1975). To show malice Alfred must prove that Brian and Charles acted out of spite or with a desire to injure him and on the facts we are given, Alfred should have no problem here. Finally, Alfred must show that he has suffered damage which can be shown by the loss of business: *Ratcliffe v Evans* (1982). In addition by s 3(1)(b) Defamation Act 1952, if the words are calculated to cause pecuniary damage to the Plaintiff in any trade or business carried on by him, there is no need to prove special damage.

Turning now to Alfred's dealings with David, Alfred himself has committed a number of torts. Firstly, Alfred has committed the direct form of the tort of inducing a breach of contract, as all the elements identified in the earlier discussion are present. Secondly, Alfred may have committed the tort of interference with trade by unlawful means; again the problem of what constitutes unlawful means arises and whether a breach of contract is sufficient when combined with an intent to harm Brian and Charles' business. Finally, Alfred may have committed the tort of intimidation, ie a threat to a third party that the defendant will use some unlawful means against the third party unless the third party does or refrains from doing some act he is entitled to do and consequently the plaintiff suffers loss: *Rookes v Barnard* (1964). Alfred has issued a threat to David but the question is whether he has used unlawful means. In Rookes, it was held that for the purpose of this tort a breach of contract constitutes unlawful means. Provided that David submits to Alfred's threat and Brian and Charles suffer damage as a result all the ingredients of intimidation are present.

Question 45

George owns a small engineering business and replies to a tender issued by Gamma Manufacturing plc for the supply of some components. He mentions this to Henry who owns a similar business and when Henry says that he might also tender for the components, George tells Henry that Gamma have a reputation for delay in paying their suppliers. Gamma do not have such a reputation and George knows that Henry's cash-flow situation is delicate and that he cannot afford to deal with very slow payers. As a result, Henry does not submit a bid to Gamma and George obtains the contract.

Advise Henry.

What would be the legal situation if prior to Gamma contracting with George, Henry called on Gamma and claimed that his components were superior to those that Henry supplied and this obtained the contract in preference to Gamma, when in fact, Henry knows that his components and George's are of a similar quality.

Answer plan

This is a question on the economic torts which is a little unusual in that it gives greater emphasis to the 'traditional' economic torts of deceit and malicious falsehood than to the more 'modern' torts of conspiracy, including a breach of contract, intimidation and interference with trade by unlawful means. These 'traditional' economic torts are still important and when candidates encounter a question that seems to be testing the more 'modern' economic torts, the facts of the problem should be read carefully to see if they disclose the possible existence of the 'traditional' economic tort.

The following aspects should be discussed:

- elements of conspiracy, inducing a breach of contract and intimidation not present
- interference with trade by unlawful means by George
- deceit by George
- malicious falsehood by Henry
- discussion of fact v puff
- inducement
- damage and s 3 Defamation Act 1952

Answer

We need to advise Henry as to whether he has any course of action in respect of George's false statement concerning Gamma manufacturing plc. Henry can have no course of action in conspiracy as George has acted alone. If he had conspired with his company (assuming that his business has been incorporated as a company) that would be sufficient, *Belmont Finance Group v William Furniture*, but there is no evidence to that effect. George cannot be liable for inducing a breach of contract for when George made the statement to Henry, there was not contract between Henry and Gamma. Neither can George be liable in the tort of intimidation as that requires a threat to be made to a third party. *Rookes v Barnard* and the statement, which does not seem to be a threat anyway, was made to the Plaintiff Henry.

However, George may have committed the tort of interference with trade by unlawful means. This now seems to be established as a tort in its own right: *Merkur Island Shipping v Laughton* (1983):

Hadmar Productions v Hamilton (1983). In *Lonrho v Fayed* (1989) in the Court of Appeal it was held that it was not an essential ingredient of the tort that the defendants predominant purpose was to injure the plaintiff rather than to further his own interests, but it was necessary to prove that the act was directed against the plaintiff or intended to harm the plaintiff. Henry should have no problem in establishing this, but there seems to be a considerable uncertainty as to just what constitutes unlawful means. In *Lonrho v Shell Petroleum* (1982) the breach of a penal statute was held to be insufficient to found a cause of action and in *Chapman v Honig* (1971) a criminal contempt of court was also held insufficient. However, in the later case of *Acrow v Rex Chainbelt* (1971) such a concept was held sufficient and in *Associated British Ports v TGWU* (1989) in the Court of Appeal it was held that a non-actionable breach of a statute could constitute unlawful mans if it was coupled with an intent to injure the Plaintiff. In the light of these later cases, it is submitted that as George has committed at least the tort of deceit that in common with other economic torts, the commission of a tort is sufficient unlawful means allowing Henry to sue.

Finally, George has committed the tort of deceit: this tort has five elements: *Pasley v Freeman* (1789). Firstly, that the defendant made a false representation of fact. Henry's statement that Gamma are slow payers is a representation and we are told that it is false. The statement seems to a representation of fact: Henry could argue that as he has stated that Gamma have a reputation as slow payers this is not a fact but an opinion as in *Bisset v Wilkinson* (1927). However, if Henry could not have honestly held that opinion or was warranting that he knew facts to justify this opinion, then his statement will be treated as one of fact: *Smith v Land & House Property Corp* (1884). We shall treat George's statement as being a statement of fact and we are told that it is false. Secondly, the defendant must know that the statement is false, have no belief in its truth or be recklessly careless whether it be true or false: *Derry v Peek* (1889) and in *Angus v Clifford* (1891) Bowen LJ stated in the Court of Appeal that careless meant indifference to the truth or wilful disregard of the importance of the truth.

In view of George's knowledge of Henry cash-flow situation, it seems likely that at the least George was recklessly careless whether his statement was true or false.

Thirdly, the defendant must have intended that his statement be acted upon, as as George made the statement directly to Henry, no problem arises here. Fourthly, the defendant's false statement must have been relied upon by the Plaintiff. It need not be the sole or decisive factor in causing the plaintiff to act as he did: *Edgington v Fitzmaurice* (1885) it is sufficient if it was one of the reasons. Provided that Henry did not undertake his own investigations into George's speed of paying and rely on George's investigations: *Atwood v Small* (1838) it is irrelevant that Henry had the means to discover that these statements were false: *Redgrave v Hurd* (1881). Finally, Henry must show that he suffered damages as a result of George's false statement, which he has done by losing the chance of the contract.

In the event of Henry claiming to Gamma that his component was superior to George's, when Henry knew that this was not true, then Henry commits the tort of malicious falsehood.

Malicious falsehood consists of making a false statement by the defendant with malice, to a third person as a result of which the plaintiff suffers damage. If George wishes to sue Henry in this tort he must first show that Henry made a false statement to a third party. The false statement must be one of fact and not mere opinion or puff. Where a defendant makes a statement which boosts his own goods that is mere puff: *White v Mellin* (1895). However, where the defendant makes disparaging remarks about the plaintiff's goods then the statement is more likely to be treated as a statement of fact *Lyne v Nichols* (1906): *De Beers Products v Electric Co of New York* (1975). This is particularly so where the defendants statement is intended to be taken seriously *Lyne v De Beer*, because for example, it quoted facts or alleged facts: *De Beers*. In *De Beers*, Walton J held that the test to apply was whether a reasonable person would take the defendants' statement as a serious statement. This is the present case if Henry merely said 'my components are better than George's' that would be mere puff; if Henry said 'my components are better then George's because' then this statement would probably not be treated by the court as a mere puff.

George must also show that Henry's statement was made maliciously, but where the defendant makes the statement knowing it is false, then he is acting maliciously: *Greers v Pearman & Corder* (1927). As we are told that Henry knows that his statement is untrue, there is no problem regarding malice. Finally, Henry must show that he has suffered damage as a result of George's statement. As he has lost the contract with Gamma this is enough, but by s 3(1)(b) Defamation Act 1952, where the words are calculated to cause pecuniary damage to the plaintiff insofar as any trade or business carried on by him, he need not prove special damage.

Thus, depending on the exact words used by Henry, George will be able to sue Henry in malicious falsehood.

Question 46

'If a person intentionally interferes with anothers business that will constitute a tort, but not if such intent is missing.'

Discuss whether the above statement is an accurate summary of the current legal position.

Answer plan

This question calls for a discussion of the role of intent in what are commonly called the economic torts. In answering this question students should not only cover those torts generally grouped in the test books under the heading of the economic torts, but also the torts of deceit, malicious falsehood and passing off.

The following areas need to be discussed:

- conspiracy by unlawful acts and lawful means
- inducing breach of contract
- intimidation
- interference with trade by unlawful means
- deceit
- malicious falsehood
- passing off

Answer

Although we shall attempt to show that the statement under discussion does represent accurately the legal position, it should not be thought that any act which is done with the intent of damaging the business of another is automatically a tort. Such a proposition was expressly rejected by Hoffman J in *Associated Newspaper Group v Insert Media Ltd* (1988), ie English law does not recognise a tort of unfair trading.

We shall first examine the statement as it might apply to the tort of conspiracy. A conspiracy has been defined as consisting 'not merely in the intention of two or more, but in the agreement of two or more to do an unlawful act, or to do a lawful act by unlawful means' per Wiles J in *Mulcahy v R* (1868). Taking the first type of conspiracy, it can be seen from the definition that an unlawful act is required. So in *Mogul Steamship v McGregor, Gow* (1892), where the defendants attempted to obtain a monopoly in the tea trade by reducing their prices to drive the plaintiffs out of business, it was held that the plaintiffs could not sue the defendants in conspiracy, as the defendants had committed no unlawful act against the plaintiffs. Similarly in *Allen v Flood* (1898) the plaintiffs failed as they could not show an unlawful act on the part of the defendants. The fact that in *Allen* the defendants had acted out of spite or malice was irrelevant because such considerations could not turn a lawful act into an unlawful act. The question that obviously arises now is what constitutes an unlawful act, and this includes a crime, a tort, and probably a breach of contract. The House of Lords has recently considered the necessary intent for this tort, and in *Lonrho v Fayed* (1991) held that where unlawful acts or means are used that it is not necessary to show that the defendants had as their predominant purpose an intent to injure the plaintiff, an intent to injure coupled with unlawful means is sufficient, per Lord Bridge. Turning next to the second type of conspiracy, the lawful act conspiracy, this anomalous tort has its origins in the decision of the House of Lords in *Quinn v Leatham* (1901) where it was held that where persons conspired to inflict unjustified harm on another that a cause of action arose. This tort is recognised as anomalous, for it means that two or more persons acting together can turn an act which is lawful into one which is unlawful, and the House of Lords held in *Lonrho v Shell Petroleum* (1982) that it was anomalous and was not to be extended. The necessary intent for this tort was considered by the House of Lords in *Crofter Hand Woven Harris Tweed v Veitch* (1942) where it was held that no action would lie unless the predominant purpose for the defendants' actions was to injure the plaintiffs. As in *Crofter* the main purpose of the defendants' actions was to protect the interests of their members, the plaintiffs failed. In this tort that the pursuit of self-interest is a defence: *Crofter*, and it has been held that a justified purpose may also be a valid defence: *Scala Ballroom v Ratcliffe* (1958). Thus, it can be seen that for this anomalous form of the tort of conspiracy, that intent to injure is an essential ingredient but that it needs to be the predominant intent. If the intent to injure is present but it is not the main intent that is insufficient intent to constitute the tort.

Another way in which a person may interfere with anothers business is via the tort of inducing a breach of contract. This tort has its origins in *Lumley v Gye* (1853), and in *Thomson v Deakin* (1952) it was stated that the tort could take one of three forms, namely direct persuasion or a contracting party to break his contract; where the defendant prevents performance of the contract by some direct and wrongful means; and, finally, where A induces a third party to break his contract with B so that B is unable to perform his contract with the plaintiff. In practice it can be difficult to distinguish between these various forms - see *Stratford v Lindley* (1965). In any event it must be shown that the defendant had the required intent - it is necessary to show that the defendant had both knowledge of the contract and the intent of procuring a breach of that contract. The courts seem ready to infer that the defendant knew that his actions would lead to a breach of contract: *Merkur Island Shipping v Laughton* (1983), and the intent to procure a breach of contract can be shown by proving that the defendant was reckless as to whether a contract was breached or not: *Emerald Construction v Lowthian* (1966). Thus, intent is a necessary ingredient of this tort, and its presence seems reasonably easy to demonstrate in appropriate circumstances. However, even where this intent is present, does not mean that liability will automatically arise. As with lawful means of conspiracy various defences are available to the defendant. These defences were discussed by the Court of Appeal in *Edwin Hill v First National Finance Corp* (1989) and are, firstly, where the contract interfered with is inconsistent with a previous contract with the interferer: *Smithies v National Association of Operative Plasterers* (1909) and, secondly, where there is a moral duty to intervene: *Brimelow v Casson* (1924). Thus, again intent to damage another is a necessary but not necessarily sufficient condition for liability.

Another route by which a person may interfere with the business of another is through the tort of intimidation. This tort was analysed by the House of Lords in *Rookes v Barnard* (1964) and the ingredients are the threat of some unlawful act to a third party to which he submits causing damage to the plaintiff. It seems difficult to imagine this tort taking place without intent on the part of the person making the threat, so again intent is required. In the present state of the law it is an undecided point whether a defence of justification exists to this tort; while it would seem not possible to justify an unlawful act which is an essential element of this tort, Lord Denning has suggested that this defence could be available in appropriate circumstances: *Morgan v Fry* (1968); *Cory Lighterage v TGWU* (1973), so again it may be that intent is a necessary but not necessarily sufficient element to establish liability.

Interference with anothers business may also occur via the recently recognised tort of interference with trade by unlawful means. This activity was recognised as a tort in its own right by the House of Lords in *Merkur Island Shipping v Laughton* (1983). In *Lonrho v Fayed* (1990) the Court of Appeal held that it was not necessary to prove that the predominant purpose of the defendant was to injure the plaintiff, it was enough to show that the unlawful act of the defendant was directed against the plaintiff or was intended to harm him. This tort is still at an early stage of its development by the courts, but it seems that an intent to injure the plaintiff is an essential element, although the scope of the defences to this tort are still rather obscure.

In addition to the standard economic torts that we have considered above, a person may interfere with the business of another in several ways which can give rise to certain well-established torts which we shall now consider. Thus, a person may wilfully or recklessly make a false statement to another with the intent that the other shall act in reliance on it, and if that other relies on it and suffers damage thereby, the person making the statement is liable in the tort of deceit. A necessary ingredient of the tort of deceit is an intent on the part of the defendant that the statement be acted upon, and without such an intent the tort is not constituted. To this extent the statement under discussion reflects accurately the law.

A person may also make a false statement to someone other than the plaintiff as a result of which the plaintiff suffers damage. This constitutes the tort of malicious falsehood, and in *Ratcliffe v Evans* (1892) it was said that liability would arise where the false statement was (inter alia) 'calculated to produce ... actual damage'. Thus, it can be seen that an essential element of this tort is an intent to injure the plaintiff.

Finally, a person may pass off his goods as being those of someone else. In *Erven Warnick v Townend* (1970) Lord Diplock stated that an essential element of this tort was an intent to injure the business or goodwill of another.

Overall, therefore, it can be seen that the statement under discussion is an accurate summary of the current legal position in that the intent in question is always required. In some cases a very particular intent is required, eg in conspiracy to injure by lawful means, and in a number of situations the mere existence of the required intent is insufficient to ground liability, but in all cases the intent to interfere must be present.

Remedies

Introduction

The most important remedy in tort is damages and questions involving damages for personal injury or death are often set by examiners. Such questions may take the form of a general essay or a problem question in which details are given of the plaintiff's salary and family responsibilities. In the later type of question candidates are not expected to produce detailed calculations of damages, but rather to indicate and discuss the particular head of damage which are recoverable and how they would be calculated.

Checklist

Students should have a reasonable grasp of the following areas:
- Types of damages - nominal, contemptuous, general, special damages, special damage, aggravated and exemplary
- Damages for personal injury - pecuniary and non-pecuniary loss
- Damages for death
- Limitation Act 1980, ss 2,11,33

Question 47

James is crossing the road when he is injured due to the negligent driving of Ken. As a result of this accident James, who is married with two young children, will be confined to a wheelchair for the rest of his life. Explain how a court would assess what damages James should receive from Ken.

If James were to die one year after the accident, and before the trial, how would the damages then be assessed?

Answer plan

Although this is written in the form of a problem, it is, in fact, a directed essay on the calculation of damages for personal injury and death. It requires a consideration of the various heads of damage under which James could recover but not actual estimates of the amount recoverable.

The answer should cover the following topics:
- object of damages
- damages for Plaintiff: the various head of pecuniary loss and deductions
- the various heads of non-pecuniary loss
- damages for death

Answer

The object of awarding damages in tort is to put the plaintiff as far as money can do so in the position as if the tort had not happened. Thus, as a general rule, if, as a result of the accident, James has lost money or will have to spend money he otherwise would not have had to spend, he can recover in respect of these sums.

If we apply this general principle to the pecuniary loss that James has suffered, we can see that the first thing James has lost is wages as he is now confined to a wheelchair (assuming for the present that James ceases to be paid any salary by his employer from the date of the accident). James will have lost a certain amount of wages up to the date of trial and this is calculated using his net wages as a basis as James has only lost his take-home pay not his gross pay. For further loss, the problem is more difficult, due to uncertainties of future income, life expectancy, etc. The court will calculate James' net annual loss, the multiplicand and multiply that by a figure based on the number of years the loss is likely to last, the multiplier. The multiplier is not simply the duration of the disability, but a lower figure with a maximum value of around 18 to take account of the fact that James has received the money as a lump sum rather than over a period of years and the 'general vicissitudes of life'. It should also be noted that any award will be final and should James' condition worsen, he will not normally be able to go back to court to claim any added sums: *Fitter v Veal* (1701). Thus, it is essential to wait until James' medical condition stabilises before any trial. Section 32A Supreme Court Act 1981 does allow a provisional award to be made with the right to additional compensation should the condition worsen, but s 32A has been given a somewhat restrictive interpretation by the High Court in *Willson v Ministry of Defence* (1991).

An obvious problem for James is the effect of future inflation. No especial protection is given in respect of this: *Lim Poh Choo v Camden Health Authority* (1980), but recently courts have begun to approve 'structured settlements' in which part of the sum payable to the plaintiff is invested by the defendants in an annuity which can provide an index-linked annual sum for the rest of the plaintiff's life: *Kelley v Dawes* (1990).

It may be, that as a result of the accident, James has a reduced expectation of life. If so, James can recover the earnings he would have received during the lost years: *Pickett v British Rail Engineering* (1980), although following the general principle of damages in tort, James living expenses must be deducted: *Harris v Empress Motors* (1983).

James will also be compensated for any loss of pension rights that accompanies his loss of salary.

James can claim in respect of any future expenses he will be put to as a result of the accident. Thus, James can recover for nursing care and this may be obtained privately even if it is available under the NHS s 2(4) Law Reform (Personal Injuries) Act 1948: for any changes necessary to his accommodation eg provision of ramps; additional costs of lighting or heating and future costs of gardener, tradesmen etc, if James did these jobs himself and now cannot do so; see eg *Willson v Ministry of Defence*.

It may well be the case that James receives compensation from a person other than the tortfeasor and deduction from the previous amounts may have to be made to prevent double recovery.

Under s 82 Social Security Administration Act 1992, no payment for personal injuries can be made unless the compensator obtains a certificate from the Secretary of State detailing the benefits paid or likely to be paid within five years from the accident. The compensator deducts this sum from the overall damages and gives the victim a certificate of deduction. The compensator then pays this deducted amount to the Secretary of State, reimbursing the State.

For other benefits, the general rule is that a benefit received by the Plaintiff is only deducted where it truly reduces the loss suffered: *Parry v Cleaver* (1970). Hence, sick pay or wages paid during the period following the accident are deducted, but not any insurance sums that James receives: *Bradburn v Great Western Railway* (1874) or charitable donations, ill-health awards or higher pension benefits: *Smoker v London Fire and Civil Defence Authority* (1991).

James will, of course, also suffer non-pecuniary loss. Firstly, there will be the pain and suffering that James has endured and will suffer in the future and if as a result of the accident James has suffered a loss of expectation of life and is aware of this, then by s 1(1)(b) Administration of Justice Act 1982, the court is required to take this into account when assessing damages. Next James will be compensated for any loss of amenity, ie his capacity to engage in pre-accident activities, and this award may be made even if James is in a coma: *West v Shepherd* (1964): *Lim Poh Choo v Camden & Islington AHA* (1980). James will also be compensated for the injury itself and to obtain some consistency in this respect, a listing of awards is made in Kemp & Kemp 'The Quantum of Damages'.

Finally, James will be awarded interest on his damages in respect of losses up to date of trial under s 35A Supreme Court Act 1981. For pecuniarily loss the interest rate is one half the short term interest rate from date of accident to date of trial: *Jefford v Gee* (1970): *Cookson v Knowles* (1979). For non-pecuniary loss, the rate is 2% from the date of service of the writ to the date of trial: *Wright v British Railways Board* (1983).

If James dies before trial as a result of the accident, then two courses of action arise. Firstly, under s 1 Law Reform (Miscellaneous Provisions) Act 1934, all courses of action vesting in the deceased survive for the benefit of his estate. The damages which the estate can claim are assessed in a similar way to those in a personal injuries claim, except that a claim for lost earnings in the lost years can only be brought by a living plaintiff s 4(2) Administration of Justice Act 1948. Secondly, an action may be brought under the Fatal Accidents Act 1976 by James' dependents. The dependents can claim a fixed sum of £7,500 for bereavement by a spouse for loss of a spouse or by parents for loss of a child, funeral expenses (if not paid by the estate) and actual and future pecuniary loss. This is calculated by assessing the dependency of the deceased which is normally found by taking the deceases net earnings and deducting a sum for his personal and living expenses and multiplying this sum by the duration of the dependency (which is calculated on a similar basis to the multiplier in personal injury cases). In assessing dependency and duration, any chance of a widow remarrying is to be ignored: s 3(3) Fatal Accidents Act 1976 and by s 4 of the 1976 Act any benefits accruing as the result of the death are to be disregarded. Thus, for example, any widows pension paid by James' employers to his widow is to be disregarded: *Pidduck v Eastern Scottish Omnibus* (1990).

Question 48

It is a general rule of law that damages are awarded to compensate the plaintiff, rather than to punish the defendant. Are there any situation where a plaintiff could make a profit out of the damages awarded to him?

Answer plan

This question calls for a discussion of the following aspects of the law of damages:

- aggravated damages
- exemplary damages
- non-deduction of insurance sums
- possible double compensation under the Fatal Accidents Act 1976
- damages in defamation

Answer

The general principle governing an award of damages in tort is to put the plaintiff in the position he would have been in had the tort not occurred, as far as this can be done by an award of money. In some cases, eg damages for negligent misrepresentation, the loss may be purely financial and it may be possible to calculate this loss precisely. However, in many situation this will not be possible, eg in personal injury cases the loss of wages suffered by the plaintiff can be calculated exactly, but such a calculation is impossible as regards the broken thigh that caused the absence from work. Similarly, precise calculations of damages in (say) nuisance or trespass will generally not be possible. A plaintiff must expressly plead any special damage that he has suffered, eg medical expenses, loss of wages, and will, in addition, be awarded general damages which are not quantified in the statement of claim but are assessed by the court. These general damages attempt to compensate the plaintiff for the non-financial consequences that have flowed from the tort, and represent an estimate by the court, in money terms, of the plaintiff's loss. By definition, therefore, these general plus special damages, together with any interest awarded, should match the loss suffered by the plaintiff.

However, in certain circumstances, the court may make an award of aggravated damages. These damages are still regarded as compensatory damages in that they are awarded to compensate the plaintiff for loss that he has suffered rather than to punish the defendant. Aggravated damages may be awarded where the defendant's conduct caused injury to the feelings or pride of the plaintiff. In *Archer v Brown* (1985) it was stated that sums awarded in respect of aggravated damages should be moderate (see also *W v Meah* (1986)). A recent example of circumstances that might justify an award of aggravated damages can be seen in *Marks v Chief Constable of Greater Manchester* (1992) where the Court of Appeal held that a chief constable's conduct in persisting in a denial of liability in a civil action, despite comments which had been made by a recorder in criminal proceedings against the plaintiff as to conflicting police evidence, was capable of aggravating the plaintiff's damages should she be successful in her civil case, and might be grounds for an award of exemplary damages. It should be noted that in *Kralj v McGrath* (1986) it was held that medical negligence cases were not appropriate for an award of aggravated damages, but that rather the general damages should be increased to take into account the fact that the actions of the defendant had delayed the plaintiff's recovery. This approach ties in with the general principle that the function of damages is to compensate the plaintiff rather than to punish the defendant.

It can be seen from the discussion on general and special damages and aggravated damages that both these types of damages are compensatory in nature, and that a plaintiff will not make a profit out of them. Although greater sums may be awarded in the case of aggravated damages, these increased sums only reflect the increased loss or suffering to which the defendant has subjected the plaintiff. Where truly moderate sums are awarded for aggravated damages this rationale is unexceptionable, but where much larger sums are awarded it may be difficult to distinguish between aggravated damages and exemplary damages, as Lord Wilberforce pointed out in *Cassell v Broome* (1972). The distinction is important because the function of exemplary damages is to punish the defendant, and it is in such situations that one might suggest that the plaintiff is making a profit out of the damages awarded.

In *Rookes v Barnard* (1964) the House of Lords described those circumstances in which exemplary damages could be recovered in tort. Lord Devlin held such damages could only be awarded where authorised by statute, eg the Reserve and Auxiliary Forces (Protection of Civil Interests) Act 1951, s 13(2), in the case of oppressive, arbitrary or unconstitutional acts by a government servant, or where the defendant has calculated that he will make a profit out of the tort, even if normal compensatory damages are awarded.

These categories have been strictly adhered to; thus, in *Cassell v Broome* Lord Reid stated that the oppressive, arbitrary or unconstitutional category did not extent to oppressive action by a company. However, in *Holden v Chief Constable of Lancashire* (1987) it was held that exemplary damages could be awarded for unlawful arrest even if there was no oppressive behaviour by the arresting officer, since the category contemplated that the action be oppressive, arbitrary or unconstitutional and not oppressive, arbitrary and unconstitutional. The last category is illustrated by the facts of *Cassell* where the defendants published a book containing defamatory statements about the plaintiff. The defendants were aware that the plaintiff intended to sue if the book was published with these statements, but they calculated that this was a risk work running as they estimated that the profits that they would make on the sales of the book would outweigh such ordinary compensatory damages. It was held that in such circumstances an award of exemplary damages was appropriate.

In *Cassell* it was held that exemplary damages are only available in those categories described in *Rookes*, and this whole area has recently been considered in *Gibbons v South West Water Services Ltd* (1992). This case involved alleged oppressive and arbitrary actions by the defendant water company, who contended that Lord Devlin's statement of principle in *Rookes*, and its subsequent review in *Cassell* had the effect of restricting exemplary damages to those type of cases where such damages had been awarded prior to 1964. The Court of Appeal reviewed the post-1964 authorities and upheld this submission.

Thus, it can be seen that the situations in which a plaintiff can profit from exemplary damages are limited.

Another way in which a plaintiff may profit from an award of damages is where he sues in respect of a consequence of the defendant's conduct for which he is already insured. In such situations the rule is that insurance benefits are ignored for the purpose of assessing damages: *Bradburn v Great Western Railway* (1874), and a similar rule applies to charitable donations: *Parry v Cleaver* (1970). Thus, a person whose house or car is destroyed by a runaway lorry may well make a profit on the damages he received. Applying the rule in *Bradburn*, the House of Lords held in *Hussain v New Taplow Paper Mills* (1988) that where an employer funded his sick pay scheme via an insurance company that payments so received by an employee should be taken into account in assessing the damages payable in respect of loss of earnings. In contrast, the Court of Appeal in *McCamley v Cammel Laird Shipbuilders* (1990) held that insurance benefits received by an employee did not fall to be taken into account as the payments in that particular case were in the nature of true insurance benefits. The difference between *Hussain and McCanley* depends on whether the court decides, on the facts of the case, that the payments in question are truly sick pay, when they will be deducted, or whether they are true insurance benefits, when they will be ignored. Prior to the coming into effect of what is now s 82 Social Security Administration Act 1992 partial double recovery was allowed in respect of state benefits received by persons who lost wages and sued a tortfeasor claiming for such loss. By s 2 Law Reform (Personal Injuries) Act 1948 only one-half of state benefits received for a five-year period from the date of the accident were deducted. Any benefits received after this time were ignored in assessing any damages payable. The effect of s 82 is to deduct these benefits, but again this deduction ceases after a five-year period, and also s 82 does not apply to damages below £2,500 which are still governed by s 2 of the 1948 Act. Thus, it is still possible for double recovery to exist in respect of state benefits.

Another area where double recovery is allowed by statute is in the award of damages under the Fatal Accidents Act 1976. By s 4 of the 1976 Act any benefits that accrue to the dependents as a result of the death of the deceased are to be disregarded. Thus, in *Pidduck v Eastern Scottish Omnibus* (1990) a widow's pension that was paid to a widow following the death of her husband was held to be non-deductible. The 1976 Act also provides, in s 3(3), that in assessing damages for a fatal accident the chances of the widow remarrying are to be disregarded. So a widow who remarried after being awarded damages for loss of dependency, could make a profit out of those damages, as could a plaintiff whose medical condition dramatically improved after an award of damages, either through an unforeseeable medical improvement, or because of an advance in medical science made after the award, as the original award will dispose of the case: *Fitter v Veal* (1701).

It could also be argued that as by s 1(1) of the Administration of Justice Act 1982 a sum of £7,500 is paid for loss of a spouse or child, that if this sum is paid following the death of a small child that this represents a profit.

Finally, one might consider the position of successful plaintiffs in defamation actions. Where the defendant is a newspaper, juries do seem to forget the principle that the object of awarding damages in tort is to compensate the plaintiff and not to punish the defendant, and the very large damages that are sometimes awarded against newspapers especially do seem to contain an element of punishment. While the man in the street may well find this quite acceptable it does represent legally incorrect principles, and plaintiffs who are awarded sums for damages which are in the six and seven figure range are surely making a profit out of their damages.

Chapter 15

General Defences

Introduction

The general defences to tort are invariably tested by examiners. This may take the form of a specific question, on say *volenti*, or may form part of another question. Thus, contributory negligence is regularly tested in questions involving a variety of aspects of the tort of negligence. Where contributory negligence is tested, apart from the seat belt guidelines in *Froom v Butcher*, candidates would not be required to estimate figures for any reduction in damages.

Checklist

Candidates must be aware of the following defences:

- Necessity
- Statutory authority
- *Volenti*
- Illegality
- Contributory negligence

Question 49

Norman and Mark went out for a social evening using Mark's car. They called at a public house where they both consumed a large amount of drink. Mark then drove Norman home and due to his intoxicated state crashed the car against a lamp-post. Norman, who was not wearing a seat belt, was thrown through the car windscreen and severely injured. Rita, who witnessed the accident, went to help Norman and cut her hands badly in so doing.

Advise Norman and Rita of any rights they might have against Mark. Would you advice differ if, rather than going out together, Norman had met Mark in the public house when Norman had had little to drink but Mark was already intoxicated, and Norman had then accepted a lift from Mark?

Answer plan

The following points should be considered:

- liability of Mark to Norman
- defences available to Mark
    volenti - consideration of case law and statute law
    ex turpi causa
    contributory negligence in accepting lift
  contributory negligence in not wearing seat belt
- liability of Mark to Rita
- defences available to Mark
    volenti
    contributory negligence
- effects of Mark's existing intoxication on any defences available to him

Answer

We must first decide whether Norman could sue Mark, and if so whether Mark has any defences available to him.

Norman must first show that Mark owes him a duty of care. In those situations where a duty of care has previously been found to exist, there is no need to apply the modern formulation of the test for the existence of a duty of care preferred by the House of Lords in *Caparo v Dickman* (1990) or *Murphy v Brentwood District Council* (1990). We could note here the statement of Potts J at first instance in *B v Islington Health Authority* (1991) where he stated that in personal injury cases the duty of care remains as it was pre-*Caparo*, namely the foresight of a reasonable man as in *Donoghue v Stevenson* (1932), a finding that does not appear to have been disturbed on appeal (1992). In fact, a duty of care has been found to exist in a number of cases involving drivers and their passengers: eg *Nettleship v Weston* (1971), but even without knowledge of such cases we could deduce the existence of a duty of care as it is reasonably foreseeable that by driving carelessly a passenger may suffer injury.

Next Norman must show that Mark was in breach of this duty, ie that a reasonable person, or rather a reasonably competent driver, in David's position would not have acted in this way: *Blyth v Birmingham Waterworks* (1856); *Nettleship v Weston*. It seems clear that a reasonable driver would not run into a lamp-post, and so Mark is in breach of his duty. Norma will also have to show that this breach caused his injuries, and the 'but for' test in *Cork v Kirby MacLean* (1952) proves the required causal connection. Finally, Norman will have to prove that the damage that he has suffered was not be too remote, ie it must be reasonably foreseeable: *The Wagon Mound* (1961). This should give rise to no problem as all that Norman will have to show is that some personal injury was foreseeable. He will not have to show that the extent was foreseeable, nor the exact manner in which the injury was caused: *Smith v Leach, Brain* (1962); *Hughes v Lord Advocate* (1963).

Thus, having decided that Mark has been negligent in his conduct towards Norman, we next need to see if any defences are available to Mark. The first possible defence is that of *volenti* on Norman's part, ie that Norman voluntarily submitted or consented to the risk of injury. To establish that Norman was *volens*, Mark will have to show that Norman was able to choose freely whether to run the risk or not, and that there were no constraints acting on his freedom of choice, such as fear of loss of his employment: *Bowater v Rowley Regis Corp* (1944). In the instant case no such restraints were acting on Norman. The next point that we must consider is whether there was any agreement between Mark and Norman whereby Norman agreed to accept the risk of injury. If there was an express agreement that Mark would not be liable to Norman in respect of his negligence then, subject to the provisions of the Unfair Contract Terms Act 1977, that agreement would prevail. There is no evidence on the facts that we are given to suggest such an agreement, so we need to consider whether there was an implied agreement. In cases involving persons who have accepted lifts from persons whom they know to be intoxicated, the courts are usually unwilling to find that the person accepting the lift has impliedly agreed to waive his right to sue the intoxicated driver: *Dann v Hamilton* (1939). Although an implied agreement was found in *ICI v Shatwell* (1965), that case involved such an obviously dangerous act that it was not difficult for the court to imply an agreement that the two defendants had accepted the risk of any injury following from this most dangerous practice. Given then that there is no agreement, express or implied, between the parties, we next have to consider whether the *volenti* defence could be valid in those circumstances where there is no agreement between the parties. In *Nettleship v Weston* (1971) Lord Denning stated that nothing short of an express or implied agreement would suffice to found a defence of *volenti*. However, this view has not been universally accepted, and in *Dann v Hamilton* the court held that *volenti* could apply to those situations where the plaintiff comes to a situation where a danger has been created by the defendant's negligence (though on the facts of *Dann* it was held that *volenti* had not been made out), and in *Pitts v Hunt* (1990) and *Morris v Murray* (1990) it was held that the defence could apply in appropriate circumstances to passengers who accepted lifts from drivers who were obviously highly intoxicated. Thus, it would seem that despite *Nettleship* Mark could raise the defence of *volenti* if he was obviously extremely drunk but, unfortunately for Mark, s 149(3) of the Road Traffic Act 1988 rules out *volenti* in road traffic situations - see *Pitts v Hunt* and compare *Morris v Murray* which was not a road traffic situation.

Thus, Mark cannot rely on the *volenti* defence, but he may attempt to raise the defence of *ex turpi causa non oritur actio*, in that both he and Norman were jointly participating in an illegal activity, namely driving a motor vehicle whilst under the influence of excess alcohol, contrary to s 6 of the Road Traffic Act 1972. This defence was upheld in *National Coal Board v England* (1954) and *Ashton v Turner* (1981), but there must be a causal connection between the crime and the damage which the plaintiff has suffered: *National Coal Board*. In *Euro-Diam v Bathurst* (1988) Kerr LJ stated that the defence would apply where it would be an 'affront to the public conscience' to allow the plaintiff to succeed, and this test was also used by Beldam LJ in *Pitts v Hunt* but Dillion and Balcombe LJ preferred to determine whether the plaintiff's damage was incidental to the unlawful conduct. It is submitted that the defence would fail because there is not the required causal connection between the damage and the crime, as in *National Coal Board* and *Ashton*. In addition, it does not seem to be an affront to the public conscience to allow Norman to recover, and it seems that Norman's damage is incidental to Mark's illegal activity. Certainly in a number of cases passengers have been allowed to recover in similar situations, eg *Dann v Hamilton* (1).

Although the above two defences, which would provide a complete defence to Mark, are not applicable, Mark may be able to raise the defence of contributory negligence to reduce the damages which he will have to pay Norman: s 1(1) Law Reform (Contributory Negligence) Act 1945. By s 1(1) where a person suffers damage as the result partly of his own fault and partly of the fault of any other person his damages will be reduced to such an extent as the court thinks just and equitable having regard to the first person's share in the responsibility for the damage. To raise this defence Mark will have to show that Norman was careless for his own safety: *Davies v Swan Motor Co* (1949). In *Jones v Livox Quarries Ltd* (1952) Lord Denning said that 'a person is guilty of contributory negligence if he ought reasonably to have foreseen that, if he did not act as a reasonable prudent man, he might hurt himself; and in his reckonings he must take into account the possibility of others being careless'. On this basis Norman has been careless in accepting a lift from a driver whom he knows to be intoxicated, see *Dann v Hamilton* and *Pitts v Hunt* at first instance. Thus, any damages Norman receives will be reduced due to this particular act of contributory negligence. In addition, we are told that Norman was not wearing a seat belt at the time of the crash, and as we are told that he was thrown through the windscreen, it is clear that he if had been wearing a seat belt that the extent of his injuries would have been reduced. Although Norman's act in not wearing a seat belt did not contribute to the accident, it has contributed to the extent of the damage he has suffered, and so his damages will be further reduced: *Froom v Butcher* (1975).

Hence, Norman should be advised that he can recover damages from Mark, but these damages will be reduced to take into account his contributory negligence.

Turning now to Rita, she is a rescuer and can sue Mark: *Haynes v Harwood* (1935). Mark will almost certainly be unsuccessful in attempting to raise the defence of *volenti* against Rita: *Haynes*; *Chadwick v British Transport Commission* (1967). The only situation in which a rescuer will be held to be *volens* is where a rescue is attempted in circumstances in which there is no real danger: *Cutler v United Dairies* (1933), which is not the case here. Mark may try to run the defence of contributory negligence against Rita in an attempt to reduce any damages payable to her, but the courts are reluctant to find rescuers guilty of contributory negligence. This has been done where the circumstances warrant it: *Harrison v British Railways Board* (1981). but in judging whether or not the rescuer has been careless for her own safety the courts take into account the fact that by the negligence of the defendant the plaintiff may have been placed in an emergency, and will be sympathetic to a plaintiff who makes a wrong decision in the agony of the moment: *Jones v Boyce* (1816). Thus, on the facts that we are given it seems unlikely that a finding of contributory negligence would be made against Rita, who could recover in full against Mark.

If Norman had met Mark in the public house when Norman had had little to drink but Mark was already intoxicated, then *prima facie* it would be easier for the court to find that Norman was *volens* to the risks of being a passenger in Mark's car. In *Dann v Hamilton* it was said that if the drunkenness of the driver was extreme then the *volenti* defence might apply. However, even if this were to apply to Mark, s 149(3) would still render the defence invalid.

Note

1   In support of this conclusion one might note the recent Scottish case of *Weir v Wyper* (1992) where it was held that the *ex turpi causa* defence could not be raised against a passenger who accepted a lift from a driver who she knew possessed only a provisional driving licence.

Question 50

'In practice, the so-called 'General Defences' in tort are of such limited application that they have little effect on liability.'

Discuss the above statement.

Answer plan

This is a straightforward essay on the general defences in tort, but candidates should not make the error of merely listing and describing the general defences - a discussion of their usefulness and limitations is what the examiner is looking for in this question.

Bearing this in mind, the following points should be considered:

- necessity
- statutory authority
- consent
- illegality
- limitation

Answer

There are a number of 'General Defences' in the law of tort and we shall consider each in turn.

The defence of necessity exists, as for example in the case of *Cope v Sharpe* (1912), but it is not favoured by the courts. Thus, the defence was not allowed by the Court of Appeal in *Southwark Borough Council v Williams* (1971) where Lord Denning said that to allow it 'would be an excuse for all sorts of wrongdoing', and a similar approach was taken in the House of Lords in *Burmah Oil v Lord Advocate* (1965).

It seems, therefore, that the statement under discussion is accurate as regards this general defence.

The defence of statutory authority, although perhaps not a common defence, certainly exists. The rule is that where a statute authorises an act which would otherwise be actionable then no action will lie in respect of that act. Additionally, no action will lie as regards any necessary consequences of that act. By necessary consequences we mean those consequences that cannot be avoided by the exercise of proper car and skill; if any consequences are so avoidable then an action will lie in respect of them. In other words statutory authority is authority to carry out the relevant activities carefully and properly, not authority to carry out the activities carelessly, for that could not have been the intention of Parliament.

The courts nowadays construe statutes liberally rather than strictly, so the House of Lords in *Allen v Gulf Oil Refining* (1981) held that where a statute gave the defendant power to build a refinery it had by implication authorised its operation and so no action would lie in respect of any necessary consequences attaching only to its operation.

Avoidable consequences may arise not only from careless operation of a facility but also from a negligent choice of mode of carrying out the authorised act, as can be seen in the decision of the House of Lords in *Tate & Lyle v Greater London Council* (1985) where their Lordships held that the defendant could be sued in respect of their negligent choice, rather than operation, of a mode of carrying out their statutory powers.

It can, thus, be seen that in the appropriate circumstances the defence of statutory authority is an effective defence, and the statement in question is not accurate when considering this general defence.

The defence of consent, or of *volenti non fit injuria*, is well-established in terms of legal theory, but we need to consider how effective it is as a practical defence. As regards the infliction of intentional harm, consent is a valid defence that causes few problems. A moments reflection will show how it could be a valid defence to an action for trespass to and or trespass to the person. However, when one considers the infliction of accidental harm, a number of problems can arise in practice in establishing this defence.

It must, for example, be shown that the plaintiff voluntarily submitted to the risk of injury: *Bowater v Rowley Regis Corp* (1944), and there were no constraints operating on the plaintiff such as the fear of losing his job. If no such constraints operate and an employee chooses to adopt a dangerous method of working which causes him damage, the courts may find that he was *volens* to the injury: *ICI v Shatwell* (1965), although in practice especially with employees, the courts are reluctant to make a finding if *volenti* and prefer instead to make a finding of contributory negligence. In particular, a finding of *volenti* is rarely made against rescuers: *Chadwick v British Transport Commission* (1967), or persons who are of unsound mind: *Kirkham v Chief Constable of Greater Manchester* (1990), although intoxication does not necessarily rule out a finding of *volenti*: *Morris v Murray* (1990) (1).

Another problem that may arise in raising this defence is that if there was an express agreement between the parties that the plaintiff will run the risk of any injury (1), then that agreement may be caught by the Unfair Contract Terms Act 1977. In particular s 2(1) provides that a person cannot exclude or restrict his liability for death or personal injury resulting from negligence, and by s 2(2) any restriction for other loss or damage must satisfy the requirement of reasonableness. Another very important restriction on the *volenti* defence s that imposed by s 149 Road Traffic Act 1988 which renders void any agreement or notice purporting to exclude liability in situations where insurance is compulsory.

Thus, *volenti* will never be a valid defence in road traffic situations: *Pitts v Hunt* (1990), but it can be raised in cases of non-road transport, eg aircraft as in *Morris v Murray* (1991).

Illegality is a general defence, and is sometimes described as the '*ex turpi causa non oritur actio*' defence. Its most obvious application is where the parties have been participating in a joint criminal activity: *National Coal Board v England* (1954); *Ashton v Turner* (1981). It is, however, not confined to criminal activities but is of much wider scope: *Euro-Diam Ltd v Bathurst* (1988). The precise criterion which activates the defence seems to be a little uncertain - in *Euro-Diam* the affront to the public conscience to grant the plaintiff relief as it would appear to assist his illegal conduct - see also *Thackwell v Barclays Bank* (1986); *Saunders v Edwards* (1987). This test was also adopted by Beldam LJ in *Pitts v Hunt* (1990), while Dillon LJ and Balcombe LJ preferred to base their decisions on whether the plaintiff's claim was based directly on his illegal conduct or whether the illegal conduct was merely incidental.

A final general defence is that afforded by the Limitation Act 1980 and s 2 provides that an action in tort cannot be brought more than six years after the cause of action accrued, or three years in the case of personal injury. Although these time periods will often provide a certain defence, they are subject to some exceptions, and in particular for personal injury actions the court has, under s 33, a wide discretion to allow such an action to proceed out of time.

Returning now to the original statement it can be seen that each of the general defences is subject to a number of limitations which narrow the scope of each defence, but it is submitted that to state that they are of little practical use is inaccurate and misleading, as it can be seen from the above discussion that there are a variety of situations in which they are capable of providing valid defences.

Note

1   One might point out, also, that there is a certain amount of
     confusion in the authorities as to whether agreement is an
     essential element of *volenti*. In *Nettleship v Weston* (1972)
     Lord Denning stated that either express or implied
     agreement was an essential ingredient of *volenti*, but in
     Dann v Hamilton (1939) it was held not to be essential. *Dann*
     has been subject to a certain amount of criticism (see, for
     example, *Pitts v Hunt* at first instance (1989)), but the
     majority view seems to be that agreement is not necessary.
     Should this view be incorrect it would limit even further the
     volenti defence.

Index